# ADVERTISING COPYWRITING
## Techniques for Improving Your Writing Skills

JAMES L. MARRA

*Department of Journalism*
*School of Communications and Theatre*
*The Intellectual Heritage Program*
*Temple University*

Prentice Hall, Englewood Cliffs, New Jersey 07632

**Library of Congress Cataloging-in-Publication Data**

Marra, James L. (date-)
  Advertising copywriting : techniques for improving your writing skills /
James L. Marra.
    p.   cm.
  Includes index.
  ISBN 0-13-007774-7
  1.  Advertising copy.    I.  Title.
HF5825.M323    1993
659.13'2—dc20                                     92-42830
                                                    CIP

Editorial/production supervision, interior design,
  and page makeup: *June Sanns*
Acquisitions editor: *Steve Dalphin*
Copy editor: *Jim Tully*
Cover design: *Joe DiDomenico*
Prepress buyer: *Kelly Behr*
Manufacturing buyer: *Mary Ann Gloriande*
Editorial assistant: *Caffie Risher*

 © 1993 by Prentice-Hall, Inc.
A Simon & Schuster Company
Englewood Cliffs, New Jersey 07632

Printed in the United States of America

10  9  8  7  6  5  4  3  2  1

ISBN 0-13-007774-7

PRENTICE-HALL INTERNATIONAL (UK) LIMITED, *London*
PRENTICE-HALL OF AUSTRALIA PTY. LIMITED, *Sydney*
PRENTICE-HALL CANADA INC., *Toronto*
PRENTICE-HALL HISPANOAMERICANA, S.A., *Mexico*
PRENTICE-HALL OF INDIA PRIVATE LIMITED, *New Delhi*
PRENTICE-HALL OF JAPAN, INC., *Tokyo*
SIMON & SCHUSTER ASIA PTE. LTD., *Singapore*
EDITORA PRENTICE-HALL DO BRASIL, LTDA., *Rio de Janeiro*

# Contents

## Suggested Readings and Assorted Tips                                            **261**

## Index                                                                              **267**

# Preface

My goal in writing this book was to fill what I perceive to be a glaring and wide gap in advertising copywriting education. To understand that gap let's agree on the major areas already filled, because frankly, I didn't set out to add more filling.

First, advertising creative strategy has been filled and then some. There are many excellent books on creative strategy. Even those books claiming to be copywriting books are, in my mind, strategy books for the most part. Their devotion to the writing process and to the act of writing is scant at best. But their devotion to the act of preplanning for writing and matching ad ideas and content to strategy is unquestionably extraordinary.

Second, advertising layout and design has been filled. Again, there are many excellent books on ad layout and design, including the process and procedures for creating thumbnails, roughs, and comps.

Third, formatting ad copy for the various media has been filled. One can turn to a variety of books to learn what format to follow when writing a print ad, a radio script, or television storyboard. In this respect there is an abundance of advice on formatting, often included within the books on strategy and design.

And fourth, advertising creativity has been filled. As with formatting, and exclusive of a few books on the creative process and the generation of ideas, most of the advice on creativity can be found in existing texts on strategy and design.

Overall, available copywriting texts offer broad strokes, including strategy, design, formatting, and creativity within their covers. The nature of each book provides an emphasis on one or more of these concerns.

In my view this leaves a noticeable gap in advertising copywriting education. The gap is writing. The actual putting of pen to paper or fingertips to keyboard. Rarely do you find advice for young people on how to write. And even more rarely do you find advice for young people on how to develop a writing lifestyle, indeed, a way of living for the writer. For example, those who write know all too well that you need to be able to read first. You need to know how the language works and why it works the way it does. This leads to having command of our language, whether command of vocabulary or syntax.

To be skillful in manipulating the language you need a foundation upon which to build. To be able to read and to know the workings of the language seem central to me as prerequisite means for building that foundation. Yet, there's little that students can turn to within our field for guidance in this respect.

A major premise guiding this book is that copywriters are writers first. I doubt that many students have always wanted to be advertising copywriters. Isn't it more that those of you who think you might like to be copywriters have always liked to write? Now at the age when you must decide what to do with your lives, you think you might like to write for a living. And ad copywriting fills that slot.

Things change, and this includes one's goals for actualizing the self. A large part of the value of higher education, it seems to me, is getting in touch with what you like and don't like: what you can see yourself doing and not doing for the rest of your working days and nights, what you dream of doing and not doing as a way of actualizing yourself. If your dream means writing, then I believe this book can help. At the same time, even if your dream doesn't mean writing, then I believe this book can broaden your understanding and insight of what it means to be a writer, especially an advertising copywriter.

Think of this book as lowercase copy and uppercase WRITING. It seeks to provide you with insights to the writing mind, techniques for actualizing your writing life, a program for living and working as a writer, and a means for reading and seeing more deeply into words. In many ways this is the essence of the book's first part, its first three chapters.

Within the book's second part, its next three chapters, the writer's most available resource is closely examined. That resource is words: what they mean, how they interact with each other, and why they behave the way they do.

Within the book's third part, its final three chapters, the exclusive focus is on advertising copywriting, beginning with advertising creative strategy and moving to considerations of ad content and style.

Some of the choice ads in the book get carried from chapter to chapter. I never could understand why many texts seem satisfied to show an ad once, as if it exemplifies just one key concern being discussed at the time. Here, though, we'll carry some of the ads with us, relating them to the various topics of discussion along the way.

You'll also come in contact with writing beyond advertising. So be ready. For example, the writings of Dr. Seuss, Judy Blume, and even Karl Marx and Fridrich Engels are discussed. And since writers should be visually literate as well, you'll be looking not only at ads but also at paintings by John Steuart Curry and Andrew Wyeth.

In many ways I believe the book speaks personally to the need for you to widen your scope of what it means to be a writer. It asks you to be a renaissance thinker, verbally and visually literate. It asks you to be thoughtful and insightful when it comes to words, to bring to words more than a naive framework of understanding. And it asks you to probe beneath the surface of words, to actualize an analytical view of words and how they achieve certain effects, either individually or in context with other words. This is what I mean by widening the scope of what it means to be a writer.

My major fear with the book, however, is that it will suck the playful juices from your pen and keyboard. Then again, I'm convinced that the rules of the game must be understood first before anyone presumes to play the game with any degree of real satisfaction and success.

Still, my advice is for you to take what the book gives, hang it on your writing belt, internalize it over time so that you don't have to spend time thinking about such matters as parts of speech, and go write. Use what works for you from the book. And write. When you're done, write some more. There's no other way to get good at it. And if you read and write deeply, with a thoughtful and perceptive mind at work, you'll become a better writer.

Finally, try to remember this. Don't lose your vigor and verve. Don't lose your playfulness with words. Amplitude, friendliness, playfulness, and a positive view of filling needs and solving problems have a great deal to do with ad copy. If you want to write ad copy for a living, then your writing should reflect this kind of fullness, vigor, friendliness, playfulness, and optimism. And it should reflect your dedicated allegiance to the art and craft of working and living with words.

## ✍ ACKNOWLEDGMENTS ✍

My thanks to Mary Ella for being who she is and encouraging me to be who I am, which meant a great deal to getting so many words down on paper.

My thanks to the kind and conscientious folks at Prentice Hall, namely Steve Dalphin for his faith and encouragement, and especially June Sanns and Jim Tully for their superb production and editing work.

Thanks also to Deborah Morrison of the University of Texas at Austin and Bob Carrell, formerly of the University of Oklahoma, for their perceptive and insightful reviews of the original manuscript. Their comments have prompted key changes in the text. I only wish I had more time to pay closer heed to their suggestions.

Thanks, of course, to the advertising students at Temple University for their vigor and freshness, and to colleagues across the country for their challenges and friendships.

Additional thanks to Temple's Department of Journalism office staff, especially Cheryl Mack and Yvonne Fairfax for their generous and personable assistance.

Thanks to Mike Thaler and Beth Garis who, as graduate students, helped launch the research for the text's first three chapters.

Thanks also to the many individuals within companies whose ads you will see between the covers of this text. These individuals responded to my needs with professional courtesy and diligence.

And finally, thanks to the writing spirit pulsing inside, the one that pushes pen to paper and fingertip to keyboard. Without it I'm certain my life would be less full and complete, no doubt significantly so.

James L. Marra

# Chapter 1

# Writing: Mind and Process

Reflect back to when you purchased this book. Perhaps you were bubbling with anticipation. Perhaps not. But there you were buying something that promised to help you actualize your writing talents. It would help you weave your way successfully through assignments or work. In effect, you placed your faith in it to help you, especially to help you write ads. And what was your view, your expectation or predisposition about writing ads? For example, maybe you thought writing ads couldn't be all that hard. After all, the writing always looks so darn easy. Part of the promise, then, might be that the book wouldn't be all that hard either.

Let's be straight with each other here. Chances are you bought this book and will read it for at least one or more of three possible reasons. One, someone is making you do it. Two, you believe it will help you as a copywriter. And three, you and/or that someone believe you need to read it to help round out your knowledge of how advertising works, in this case on the copywriting creative side. All of the reasons are tied to your view of advertising. You need to meet the demands of someone else, so you buy and read the book. Or, you believe certain truths about yourself in relationship to advertising copywriting, so you buy and read the book. Or, you need to gain a rounded perspective of advertising, including its copywriting creative side, so you buy and read the book. Chances are one or more of those reasons spurred you on to buy and begin reading.

So, you started reading. As you started you carried with you an expectation of what copywriting and even advertising were all about. Shaped by prior experiences and reading, that expectation will probably bump against some of what you'll read here. Somehow things will get difficult. Based on how simple and easy many ads seem, surely the art of writing copy can't be all that hard. Surely, the art of writing anything can't be all that hard either. I mean, everyone writes. Everyone. And the writing in ads seems so downright simple sometimes. Certainly not beyond you and what you are capable of writing.

So you'll read on. Gradually you'll come to notice that we aren't talking exclusively about advertising writing. In fact, we aren't talking exclusively about writing. Before you're through a third of the book we'll be talking more about reading and listening and seeing. We'll be talking about how those acts happen, what goes into them, what controls them. And all of a sudden it might occur to you that you're into some deep waters here. And, goodness gracious, but writing can't be all that difficult. Maybe you'll even say to yourself, "Get to it. I want to write."

Learning to do something, anything, is often difficult. And one of the things that makes it so is the expectation of how simple it is. Often, learning to do something looks so easy to the untrained eye and the unlearned mind. But once you're into it, really immersed in it so that just about everything you experience is viewed through the lens of what you're trying to learn, then you understand that it's not as easy or simple as it looks.

How many times, for instance, have you watched a professional at his or her chosen craft and said to yourself, "With a little practice, I could do that"? Or maybe you've said, "That doesn't look very hard, Michael Jordan excluded, of course." With that in mind, remember this. Good artists make their art look easy and natural. That's what good art is. The difficulty in learning how to do it, and eventually doing it, never show up in the art. It all looks so simple. And it looks simple because the artist behind it makes it look that way.

With the best advertising copy this is especially true. The writing seems so simple, so clear and unmistakable; surely, it can't be that difficult. Well, the fact of the matter is it's not, that is if you're a practiced and polished writer. And the point of our beginning chapters is to lay the groundwork for what it takes to be a practiced and polished writer.

This doesn't mean that a practiced and polished writer goes around analyzing everything the way we will in these chapters. The writer doesn't need to do that, mainly because the writer did it years ago. Over time the writer embeds the analysis and learning into the art and craft of writing. The writer internalizes all that's learned, so that conscious thought becomes more automatic through repeated practice and experience. But for those just beginning, those who haven't had the time or experience to pay homage to the art and craft of writing, the principles of good writing—indeed, the principles of how to think and behave like a writer—need to be hung on the belt. They need to be readily available. And the aspiring writer needs to practice and apply them. In the same way, the aspiring writer needs to practice and apply the dynamics of the writer's mind as it works its way through the writing process.

Let's round out the preface to this chapter by realizing that advertising copywriters are writers first and advertising copywriters second. This means that they think and see like writers, like many kinds of writers. On the other hand, it also means that how they think and see may be unique to them as practicing, paid writers. Not everyone thinks or sees that way, regardless of the fact that everyone writes. Truth be told, some of those who write, write better than others. And the reason is that they're writers in the truest sense of what the title means. They've already paid homage, dues if you will, to the writing God. Now as copywriters, they lift the writing mind, its temperament and practices, over to the field of advertising. Unlike sharpening the ability to read, listen, or see, all of which are steps of preparation for developing the writer's mind, the writer calls upon a unique and individual system of temperament and practices to get the words down on paper. This is what is meant by the writer's mind.

## ✍ THE WRITER'S COMPULSION ✍

A writer writes. And having written writes some more. Why is that so?

Writers often have opinions about why, and many times those opinions focus on compulsion. For example, according to Ernest Hemingway, "Once writing has become your major vice and greatest pleasure only death can stop it." Certainly Hemingway's self-willed death stopped his writing, but these are strong words from one of America's masters. And the words themselves say a great deal about the writer's mind. That mind is driven, regardless of whether one considers the writing act to be a curse or a blessing. In fact, it's driven all the way to death. Death is the only thing that can stop it. Strong words, indeed. And words with a certain ominous tone about them, echoed to a large extent when William Faulkner said that "an artist is driven by demons."

### Ego and Therapy

Whether demons or angels, there seems to be a common influence to those who write, especially prolific writers. Something drives them. Something unknown, mysterious, but there all the same. According to William Zinsser in his important little book, *On Writing Well,* "Writing is an act of ego and you might as well admit it." Think about that, particularly if you consider yourself a compulsive writer. Is it possible that writers are so presumptuous as to assume others are interested to read what the writers write? Or, if the writing is for the self, are writers so presumptuous as to assume that what needs to be written is worth the effort and eventual permanence of putting words down on paper?

Why would someone do that, if not out of need or compulsion, perhaps a desperate one at that? For writers worth the title there is an unstoppable need to write. And if ego is at the core of that compulsion, then what does it say about writers? Are they so filled with themselves? Are they insecure? Perhaps so. Perhaps their view of the world and of themselves within that world demands an outlet. Perhaps they are driven by the need to qualify and define that world and themselves, a need to give meaning to what they experience. Everyone needs an outlet. Some people jog. Others yell and scream. Writers write. In this respect writing can be very therapeutic. It can act as a healer, with the subconscious driving the writer to write to protect and heal the self.

If you consider yourself a writer, do you fit that description? No doubt you've written things other than ads. We all have. Perhaps there was a time you wrote a poem, a story, or a letter. Perhaps you write letters often to friends or relatives. Why? Why did you compose that poem? That story? Those letters? What was driving you? Was it something that bothered you, and you wanted to ease the pain somehow? Was there a burden you wanted lifted, and so you wrote? Often that's the case behind the writing act. And for you to be in touch with such possibilities deepens your understanding of what it means to be a writer.

### Finding and Giving Meaning

Still another driving force for writers is their need to find and give meaning, whether to others or themselves. Obviously, such a purpose, unconscious or not, relates to ego and therapy. In his pioneer book on the writing process, *Writing With Power,* Peter Elbow notes that writing is "useful as a way to work out your thoughts and feelings for yourself alone." As a strong believer in writing first and judging later, Elbow organizes an entire system for easing the pressures blocking writing. He also believes that the "act of *giving*" is at the heart of the writing act. For those of you who consider yourselves writers, you may find it easy to agree with Elbow.

Often, the act of writing serves as a means for helping us find meaning. On a daily basis we confront many realities. Sometimes they're confusing, maybe even depressing. So we may write about them as a means for sorting through their specifics to arrive at a deep meaning. That meaning may be very personal and private. In fact, what we write about those realities may be personal and private as well, acting as viewfinders for our own self-discovery. The writer Georges Simenon, for instance, believed that the urge to be an artist of any kind was nothing more than a fulfillment of a need to find the self.

On the other hand, we may find ourselves writing to friends or even a mysterious and unknown reader. And all the while we're doing it we have every intention of uncovering meaning in what we're writing about. It's just that when we write for a public, regardless of whether that public is one or many, we feel a need to make the meaning or importance of the meaning known. In some ways, perhaps, we treat that public as a confidante.

The history of literature is overflowing with writers who wrote their way to meaning. Their act of writing served as a vehicle for arriving at meaning. Several of the poems of William Wordsworth, for example, accomplished just such a goal. His famous "Ode: Intimations of Immortality from Recollections of Early Childhood" took him over three years to write and, according to many literary critics, serves as a prime example of how a writer can find meaning simply by writing. The same holds true for Wordsworth's "The Prelude," only here we're talking about a lifetime of writing. In this respect, writing through one's thoughts helps to clarify, to bring order to what may seem to be disorder.

Writing isn't mere stenography. Obviously, as we write we think. In thinking and writing at the same time our mental engines churn at full throttle. We burn up the miles of thought, so to speak. Sometimes we may even be out of control, but always our mental engines churn. They must, especially if we're sorting through highly personal thoughts. And even if we're not, the writing act involving something far less personal such as advertising continues to be a mental and emotional challenge. That challenge concerns meaning. It concerns our experiences and the difficulty of sweeping them together into a tight little ball of meaning. For some, this represents the consummate goal and desire of the writer.

## Actualizing the Self

It was Abraham Maslow who considered the actualization of self as a prime directive for a higher order of living. By actualization he meant that one's efforts in life answer an inner call: a kind of "be all that you can be" philosophy. All of us, for instance, have witnessed those whose efforts are out of sync with what they believe they should be doing. They have not matched their efforts with their inner call. As a result they fail to actualize themselves. Still others never hear the inner call. They're deaf to that call, choosing instead to hear others calling. So they go through life in piecemeal fashion, perhaps flitting from one effort to another and rarely, if ever, bending their ear to the voice of the inner self. Not that the inner call is so easy to hear, mind you. Often it isn't.

Every day each of us comes face to face with those influences muffling our inner call. Those influences can take many forms. Friends, loved ones, teachers, even a part of ourselves deluding us from what's most true to ourselves. For the true artist, however, writer included, those influences never hold sway for very long. Somehow the writer always manages to write, regardless of the distractions. Remember, writing is a compulsion. It cannot be stopped, except by death. Try as the influences may, they are doomed to failure.

This overcoming of influences or distractions in order to write is a matter of actualizing the self. Though answers to the question of why writers write can be as varied and numerous as the writers themselves, the fact of the matter is that nothing gets in the way of the writing. Coming from deep within, writing actualizes the individual. It lifts that individual to a higher plane, to a synergistic world where one's efforts mirror an inner truth. All of this sounds grandiose, of course. But there's truth to it. And the point of even bringing it up in the context of this book is to have you make a personal assessment of where you stand in relationship to your writing life.

Having taught now for some time, I make it a habit of asking copywriting students a pointed question on the first day of class. The question is, Who in this class wants to be a copywriter? Invariably a number of hands pop up, some quicker and more eager than others. Then I ask this question, How many of you write letters on a regular basis? And invariably only a few of those hands pop up again. This leads me to a third question which is, What makes those of you who don't write letters think you want to be copywriters?

After many classes with the same questions asked and answered, I'm convinced that there are more students who think they want to be writers than there are students who are writers. There are very good reasons for this, of course. But the point is, if you're not a writer in the deepest reaches of your soul, then face that fact now. Meanwhile, if you are a writer in soul, then by all means carry on.

What I'm driving at here has to do with compulsion and actualization of the self. No one should be a copywriter who isn't a writer first. No one should be a copywriter because it seems, as Jerry Della Femina once wrote of advertising, that it's the most fun you can have with your clothes on. No one should be a copywriter because it's a way to make money. And certainly no one should be a copywriter unless writing is central to that person's life. If it isn't central, chances are excellent that the person won't even get a first job, let alone be very good at the art and craft of writing.

What could be worse than logging fifty-plus hours a week doing something that doesn't match your inner self and that doesn't make you content and fulfilled as a result? Part of the grand purpose in life is to find that which does match your inner self, that which does make you content and fulfilled. With this in mind, don't wait to make an assessment about whether you should be a copywriter or not. Make the assessment now, and make it on the basis of yourself as a writer first and a copywriter second. If you love words, if you write anyway, regardless of who's looking or who's telling you otherwise, if you find reading enriching and enjoyable, and if you experience the writer's compulsion on a regular basis, then copywriting may be for you. Certainly writing is. And whether copywriting is, we'll find out further on.

Now, if you find yourself taking to the words and ideas on these past few pages you may have what it takes to be a writer. If you find yourself writing letters as a matter of routine, then you may have what it takes to be a writer. If you find yourself reading as a way of leisure, then you may have what it takes to be a writer. And when you see ads, if you find yourself reading or listening to the copy, then you may have what it takes to be a copywriter.

Years ago I had the pleasure of listening to Buckminster Fuller speak to a group of students. Buckminster Fuller was one of America's and the world's foremost original thinkers. When he was finished speaking, a student asked him a question. It went something like this, How do you know what your life's work should be?

Fuller thought about that for some time and then answered by saying that you should tap into whatever you've done when the pressure wasn't on. Whenever you had free time, what did you do? When people weren't telling you to do certain things, what did you do? As far back as you can remember, what is it you've always liked to do? "Whatever that is," he said, "that's what your work should be."

I believe this sounds like savvy, solid advice for everyone. In fact, whether economic times are good or bad, think of it this way. Imagine there are recruiters waiting outside your door for any job you want. Any job at all that you truly want. Well, what is that job? What will you be doing in this job, which is any job you want? If you have any job you want, you'll probably be good at it. And when you're good at it, more often than not you'll be rewarded. In short, if you're devoted to what you're doing, success (a relative term, to be sure) will come.

This has everything to do with answering your inner call. If writing is it, do it. No doubt, whether I or anyone else tells you to do it will be meaningless anyway. Since it's your call, you'll do it, regardless. Nothing—not grades, not opinions, not job reviews—will stop you from answering the call, even if you have to answer it at night alone in a dark room after you've spent the day working to make ends meet. In the words of Sanford Kaye, in his book *Writing Under Pressure,* "Writers need to build in their own rewards, and not get caught up in longing or perfecting themselves for acceptance, gratitude or honor." In other words, you write because something inside speaks to you only, and it speaks but one word, "Write." As a personal and often heightened experience not meant for everyone, this is what is meant by actualizing the self.

## ✍ THE WRITER'S DRIVE, FROM MIND TO PAPER ✍

Since we come in contact with many forms of writing each day, on the surface it may seem easy to conclude that writing is simple. Sure, maybe good writing isn't simple, but writing is, especially if you're a compulsive writer. Then you just sit down and write. Of course, anyone who has written seriously knows this isn't true. There are times when the blank page intimidates, when it strikes absolute fear in the heart. Then the compulsion to write surrenders to just about anything.

Haven't we all had occasion to enjoy the washing of dishes so thoroughly and completely that it boggles the mind? Haven't we all had occasion to long for a distraction, any distraction, rather than to sit in anguish over a silent keyboard or unmoving pen? In a way, writing becomes like a monkey on the back. You toss and turn to get rid of it. Even if it means washing dishes.

"Let's face it," noted novelist William Styron once said. "Writing is hell." He was an example of a bleeder, one who suffers through the writing. And haven't we all been bleeders at one time or another? As a reality of the writing act, this difficult drive of having a thought or idea travel the many difficult miles from mind to paper cannot be avoided at all times. But its load can be lessened if we work on our minds and hearts and try to establish an internal code of mental conduct that allows us to win the head game against our fierce competitor, the blank page.

### Fear and Courage

Sometimes, to write is like deciding whether to go on a vacation. There are so many reasons not to. With writing, one of those big reasons is fear. Fear of what someone might say. Fear of what our critical self might say. Fear of confronting that unskilled and unworthy self we call the writer. Fear prevents us from acting. It prevents us from actualizing ourselves. As writers, then, we need to remember that fear gets in our way. It plays tricks on us, so we need to work on eliminating it.

Famed story writer Katherine Anne Porter once said that courage was the first essential for a writer. It makes sense. Without courage, barely a word will find its way to paper. With this in mind, the advice is simple. Be courageous. In fact, be courageous to a fault. Enter the battle against the blank page with your arms flailing and in full view of the enemy. In short, when the page takes aim, fire off a few of your own rounds. In other words, write anything. Then pat yourself on the back and award yourself a medal. Remember, a great deal of overcoming the dreaded writer's block is a head game. So whatever you can do psychologically and emotionally to write, do it. Even it if means applying guerrilla tactics against your enemy, the blank page.

### Internal Locus of Evaluation

As it is with creative people overall, writers don't care so much for the judgment or criticism of others, but a sense of balance is needed here. On one hand we pick and choose our spots of what others say, and then we apply it in a meaningful and beneficial way to our work. On the other hand, however, we also manage to maintain an aloofness from the judgment or criticism of others. In essence, our own judgment outweighs the judgment of others. This is called the *internal locus of evaluation*. It acts as a guiding light for our work. And it is always more important than the dark evaluation of others.

Of course, to actualize an internal locus of evaluation may appear easier to say than to do, especially when you consider the hard and fast realities. For example, others pay us for our work, either by grades or greenbacks, so we must bend an attentive ear to their evaluations. At the same time, however, remember that something drives the writer. To write is a compulsive behavior. This means it is immune to outside influences. It also means that we control it, at least to a degree. We create it. We guard it. We bring it to life, or we bring it to death. First and last, it begins and ends with us, and not with someone else. This is an important point to bear in mind since so many others will appear to rise up against the compulsion. But as long as we know that, we can be ready for it. And the psychological way to be ready for it is to rely on your own judgment. This takes courage, perhaps to a fault. But it's the only way.

### Believing in the Relativity of All Things

David Ogilvy didn't believe in the promise or workability of the Merrill Lynch bull campaign. As unbelievable as that sounds, it serves as testimony for something important to remember. Often, truth is relative. Often, good and bad are relative. This means truthfulness, goodness, and badness don't exist in and of themselves. They exist in contexts that shape how we assess and evaluate them. We'll spend a great deal of time throughout this book fleshing out this idea of contexts and meanings, which slip and slide all over the place. For example, viewed from one angle or by one person a word or image takes on a certain meaning. And that meaning changes when another angle or person comes into play.

As a psychological means for winning the head game against the blank page, your belief in relativity means your view is important. It can be the truth and the good, even when compared to those who are supposed to know better. Who would know better than David Ogilvy if a campaign idea were promising and workable? Even he can be wrong. And if he can be wrong, then certainly none of us should be afraid to be wrong.

Think of it like this. If you believe there's only one way, one truth, or one goodness as a means for writing what you intend to write about, then you'll spend most of your time and energy trying to track down that way, truth, and goodness. Chances are you won't succeed. Instead, you'll end up with a blank page and a massive headache.

For many years now you've been taught that you know very little. Early on in your life your parents had a mission, to teach you to walk and talk. And once you reached school age the mission from your teachers seemed to change. Then it was to teach you to sit down and shut up. So, each year you sat and listened to others who were supposed to know what was true and what was good about this or that subject. You were expected to absorb and be quiet. You were expected to listen and learn. And today? Still you sit with others in rows and try to get the right answers on tests or crank out the kind of copy so and so will like. To be wrong means you're in hell. And rarely do you give yourself the pleasure of knowing you're right. You're too busy listening to others like myself jabbering at you about your wrongness.

Well, when it comes to getting the writing monkey off your back, believe in many ways to right, truth, and goodness. Believe that there are many ways to say what you want to say and still be right. Because rightness and wrongness are relative. Give the words you write to others and you'll see what I mean. Some will like them. Some won't. Indeed, maybe the same person who didn't like them today will like them tomorrow. If that's the case, then what's right? It's relative, not absolute. And since absolute means there's only one way to hit the nail on the head, then it's sure to keep you from picking up the hammer in the first place.

## Coping with Feelings of Inadequacy

You're young and a student. You're bound to feel inadequate. Maybe your entire education seems pointed in that direction. Subjective grades. Intimidating lectures. Uncertainties all around. But if the feeling of inadequacy persists, then it will surely interfere with your writing. First of all, you won't write. You'll feel too inadequate. Second, you won't have anything to write about. Your thoughts and ideas won't be worthy. And third, you won't actualize yourself. Your self won't be worth the actualization.

Naturally, it's easy to sit back and casually observe how inadequate young people feel and then tell them that they shouldn't feel that way at all. The problem, though, is in how to overcome such feelings. For now, though, keep yourself tuned into relativity. This will help you avoid the blackness of having your work viewed negatively by others or by yourself.

### On Being Alone

Assume that you do all the things suggested here and then sit down to write. What do you notice about your writing environment that makes it different from other environments? There may be several things, but surely one of those is your aloneness. Not loneliness, but aloneness. Writing, according to Phillip Lopate, is a "private, solitary act." He suggests that young, aspiring writers "learn to be alone."

You can't write by committee. You must write alone, even if there are others around you. By constructing your writing world, you block out others. Only you and perhaps your characters live in that world. And when you begin to write, it's you and the blank screen or page. That's it. You can rely on no one else but yourself, the sole you, alone in your time, place, and habits.

Many people hate being alone. But if you intend to be a writer, get used to it. There's no other way that writing happens. So make it a habit of being alone at times. To keep from being lonely, surround yourself with ideas, words, and the materials for getting those words down on paper.

### Sincerely Yours, the Writer

If you don't know it and believe it, don't write about it. Of course, for more personal forms of writing such as poetry or fiction, this is easy. Then, you're committed personally to what you're writing. You believe in it. Presumably, you know what it is you're writing about, and this, combined with your commitment to and belief in the topic, means you're sincere about it. But with something far less personal such as ad copy, the problem of sincerity can plague you as a writer. Worse, it can spill over into your writing.

Within the creative circles of advertising there's a legendary tale of the copywriter with the great American novel throbbing between the pages hidden in the top desk drawer. One gathers from this a picture of a lonely, pathetic soul laboring away on ad copy for a distant product, distant in respect to the degree of commitment the writer feels for that product. All of this writing for the product, of course, serves as a means for putting bread on the writer's table and nothing more. Ah, but when the writer finds the time, the real work begins, the work on the great American novel.

Certainly, in some cases this is true. There is, after all, an assumption that ad copy falls short of fine art, let alone great writing. And those with any degree of artistic sensitivity and consciousness are sure to challenge the commercial thrust of ad copy at one time or another. At the same time, supposedly great writers such as Aldous Huxley, for example, are on record describing ad copy as a most difficult and demanding form of writing.

What all of this comes to in the end, however, reflects an important concern for budding writers, especially budding copywriters. That concern strikes to the core of a writer's compulsion, which is to write. But you just can't write about anything under the sun and expect to produce quality writing. You can't, for instance, expect to write about something you don't know or don't believe in and then have what you've written pulse with the electric charge of commitment, a charge felt and appreciated by a reader or listener. As we will see in Chapter 6, a chapter devoted exclusively to the copy for one ad, the writer of that copy knew the topic. More so, the writer believed in it. You can feel that knowledge and belief as you read. They seem to pulse from between the lines, gradually coming to life as you delve deeper into the copy.

Despite the fact that some copywriters chomp at the bit while waiting to pen the great American novel, many actualize themselves by writing ad copy, a difficult and demanding form of writing. They know how difficult and demanding it can be. And they work within it, improving their skills through the daily discipline of writing within a variety of constraints. Asked to get the job done in a limited amount of space or time, copywriters quickly learn to cut to the chase, as it were, to pare and whittle away the unnecessary. Make no mistake about it, that takes considerable skill.

While working within such a rigorous and unforgiving form of writing, copywriters live the writer's life, paying close and careful attention to individual words, thematic consistencies, and stylistic power, enough so as to move someone to do something that wouldn't ordinarily be done. In the best of cases, their writing projects a sincerity about the product and what it can do for a consumer. And for the writers to achieve this, they had to win the head game against several enemies: the commercialism of advertising; the pandering for a product they might not believe in; the assumption that ad copy falls below some standard or other, however elitist that standard may be.

There are ways to win this head game, however. For instance, if you're concerned about the raw commercialism of ad copy and how it panders to an audience, consider this. Compared to other forms of writings such as news journalism, ad copy is very honest and upfront. After all, you can't leave an ad without knowing that it is just that, an ad. Right away, that tells us exactly what we're facing, a commercial pitch for a product, goods, or service. Is the same true of news? Is it true of other forms of writing as well?

My point here is that although advertising may not be pure, little else is either. Life is like that. Ulterior motives abound. Persuasion and manipulation often control our daily lives, whether on interpersonal levels or media levels. And in writing ad copy, the writer makes a pitch for an advertiser. As a voice for that advertiser, the writer must carry a certain amount of belief in the product. Beyond that, and in doing justice to the consumer, the product and the writer's self, the writer must know all about the product in order to tell the straight scoop from his or her vantage point.

The point overall should be clear. If you can't sign off on your writing with "Sincerely yours," then you should rethink what you've written, who you've written it for, and whether you should be writing it at all. However accomplished writers do it, rationalizations or otherwise, they know and believe in what they're writing.

## ✍ THE WRITER'S RITUALS ✍

Throughout these first few chapters we'll talk about habits. Habits relevant to writers. The habits of reading, listening, and seeing. In many ways such habits help a writer actualize the writing self. They add to the mix of what makes for a good writer. Representing a certain lifestyle, they provide the writer with a starting point for improving the craft.

In this chapter we've plumbed into the writer's mind and soul. We've discussed the writer's temperament and the range of influences and obstacles the writer faces on a daily basis. All of these perspectives provide a means for understanding what goes into the writing self. But they also fall short of understanding how the writing act takes place. To this end we need to look at rituals for stimulating and following through with that act.

### The Rituals of Time and Place

Prime advice here is simple. Whatever works for you, do it. As William Zinsser says, "There are all kinds of writers and all kinds of methods, and any method that helps somebody to say what he wants to say is the right method for him." In this respect, anything goes. And part of your responsibility as a writer is to identify what works for you and then to do it.

There are as many individualized rituals as there are individual writers. In my book, *Advertising Creativity: Techniques for Generating Ideas,* rituals are discussed at length, especially as they relate to time, place, and work habits and production. But as discussed in the idea-generation book, these rituals relate more to creativity and the generation of ideas than they do the execution or writing of those ideas. At the same time, the basic rules of time, place, and work habits or production remain intact, even when it comes to actual writing.

What's important here is to discover or even devise your rituals around time, place, and habits or production. In all likelihood, and especially if you're a practicing writer, the rituals are already in place. As creatures of habit, we ritualize and systematize our work efforts. Repetition of the system guarantees productivity. Once the system falls apart, however, our productivity goes down. Thus, the main goal is to keep the system well oiled through dedicated allegiance to personalized rituals.

Create your own little work world. First consider the time you'll spend in that world. Since evidence suggests that we're more productive early and late in the day, think about writing at those times, though, of course, any time will do. Two famous writers, Gustave Flaubert and Lawrence Durrell, suggested this kind of ritualization. For Durrell the best time was the morning. The act of writing, he believed, was analogous to cutting wood. You get up early, grab your ax, and proceed to chop away. When asked about the importance of inspiration to his own writing, Flaubert responded with, "Inspiration? It means sitting down to one's writing table every day at the same time." Even the composer Stravinsky likened the act of composition to practicing a trade with the diligence and rigor of a shoemaker.

Make this promise to yourself. You'll write something at roughly the same time every day. It doesn't matter what it is. What matters is that it takes place. Same time every day. A promise. Try it for at least a week, or try it until it becomes automatic, sort of like showering at the start or end of a day.

If this kind of rigorous scheduling turns out to be unsuccessful, try another promise. You'll write something every day. No time restriction here. And again, it doesn't matter what you write as long as the writing takes place.

When it comes to such things as ritualized times, places, and habits you need to think of yourself as a Pavlovian dog. At a certain time the bell rings and your pen salivates, meaning it's time to write. The same holds true with place and habits. As Virginia Woolf suggested many years ago, everyone needs a room of one's own, especially if you're a woman. Men count too, however.

In this respect, find your place. Make it yours. Make it your writing place, your working place in the world. A favorite chair. A room tucked away upstairs. A desk. Whatever it is, it's yours and yours alone. Make it complete by adding inspirational touches, whatever they are. Pictures. Quotes. Pieces of your writing within view. Schedules relevant only to yourself.

Once you enter that place, make another promise. The first thing you'll do is write a sentence or phrase, if even in your mind. A purposeful, intentional sentence or phrase. It can sum up the day. It can state a belief. It can do anything. But it must be constructed as a piece of writing, regardless of whether it's only a sentence. If it's longer, or if it leads you on to something longer, stay with it. The goal, after all, is to write something.

### The Rituals of Work Habits

Once you're in your place at the self-appointed time and have written your sentence or phrase, stimulate yourself by working within your personal habits. Drink cups of coffee. Chew a pen tip. Drum on the desktop. Jiggle your knees. Pace. Employ any idiosyncrasies that make you uniquely you and that help to activate your writing. Use them. Again, it doesn't matter what these habits are. What matters is that they exist and that you recognize them as part of your writing self.

### The Ritual of Working Up and Down Your Writing Ladder

So, you're sitting at your appointed place at the designated time and you manage to squeeze out a line or two. Do you know where that line is going? Do you know where it fits in among your writing?

My experience with students, even those who are compulsive writers, tells me this. Often they don't have a system to organize what they write. This doesn't mean they don't write or that they're not working within a system while they're writing a certain piece. It simply means that they haven't established a system of priorities for their writing. They haven't organized things into slots or compartments. Or, as the metaphor of the writing ladder suggests, they haven't organized their writing into rungs on a ladder.

Remember, a writer writes and having written writes some more. Scan library shelves and you'll see the truth of this. It's usually not a case of one piece and done. Nor is it a case of one specific genre or type of writing and done. It's more a case of writing in a variety of genres, just as long as the writing takes place. For example, consider famous fiction writers such as Hemingway or Faulkner and notice that they wrote long and short fiction pieces, nonfiction, journals, and letters, among other things.

As writers, Hemingway and Faulkner wrote. And no doubt like us they faced many a new day with all the best intentions of working on a certain piece. Hemingway, for instance, would stop writing the day before while he still had something to write. This was his method for overcoming the dreaded writer's block of the next morning. Yet surely there were those days when it just wouldn't come. But did that mean writing didn't happen?

Like all compulsive writers, you need to systematize your writing, giving it priorities along the way. Conceive of it as a ladder with different rungs. Let me use a personal example.

The fact of the matter is that I'm not that good a writer, though I believe I'm getting better simply because I work at it. Many of you are, or certainly will be much better than I as a writer. Still, I believe I think and behave like a writer. For instance, with no exception I begin every workday with some form of writing. This can take the form of articles, fiction, poetry, letters, or even memos. I arrive at my office early and immediately sit at the typewriter. I curl a sheet of paper around the carriage and proceed to type. Sometimes this leads me to the word processor and work on various pieces, such as this book, for example. Or sometimes I sit at the typewriter for an hour or more. But what am I writing?

As with everyone I have an assortment of friends and colleagues. It just so happens that these days I'm writing letters to them. Sometimes these letters are personal. Sometimes they're business. Sometimes they're a combination of both. And depending upon who it is I'm writing to and what it is I'm writing about, the style changes. The tone changes. In fact, everything changes. Paragraphs may get shorter or longer. The same with sentences. Word choices and the very syntax of how they're arranged reflect certain things about my view of the other person and the goal or objective of the writing. Moreover, as well as helping me contribute my part to friendships or business happenings, the letters are practice. They're a way of limbering up. A way of working on my swing, so to speak. All the things writers do to improve their performance.

I use this personal example to make an important point. There are many types of writing a writer writes. All of these fit somewhere on the writer's ladder. Without creating a hierarchy of importance for these types, each has its place. Each is a separate rung on the ladder. In my case I'm often able to step from one rung to another simply because I've had my foot on the one preceding or following it.

With this personal example in mind I suggest you organize a range of pieces you work on and write about. Then, depending on your priorities for the day or even your mood at a certain moment you shift your writing attention to a particular type or piece. For instance, maybe you start with a letter to a friend. Then you move to an assignment that's due. Eventually you may move again, perhaps to a more personal piece such as a story or poem.

The point, however, is that you keep yourself writing because you're not locked into one type of writing only. Instead, you're able to span genres, if even as an amateur. Being an amateur doesn't matter so much. What matters much more is that you write, regardless of what type of writing it may be. Besides, writing in one genre is sure to improve your writing in another.

To start your writing day with a personal letter or two also seems like good advice, especially if you're intent on being a copywriter. For example, in his book, *How to Get Your First Copywriting Job,* Dick Wasserman states, "If you can write a decent letter, you can write advertising." Behind Dick Wasserman's advice is the belief that to write a decent letter requires certain skills such as capturing the correct tone and style for the person receiving the letter. For instance, think of when you wrote a personal letter to a friend or even an impersonal business letter to a faceless and unknown reader. Chances are in both instances you crafted your letters according to your reading audience. With a letter to a friend you can picture the person. You can recall your conversations, your common interests, and your friend's likes and dislikes. Such knowledge helps you craft the letter. Even in the case of an impersonal business letter you still must make assessments of your audience and then tailor your prose and style to match that audience.

Writing to an audience poses a real-life advertising copywriting situation where copy is written to a specific target market. At the same time, our familiarity with writing letters poses little threat in helping us begin writing. Letters are comfortable. Letters are personal. All of us write them at one time or another. They're a form of writing that doesn't strike fear in our hearts. To begin one's day with a letter seems in keeping with the entire idea of getting started.

Whatever form of writing you use to start, remember this. It's only one kind of writing, one rung on the ladder of your writing life. And you need to systematize and prioritize those rungs. In short, you need to create your own ladder for those rungs, a hierarchy of where the rungs fit in. Then you need to match those rungs with your overall readiness to write. That readiness includes considerations of time, mood, energy, subject matter, and desire. Presumably, the higher up the ladder you go, the more difficult, time-consuming, and draining the writing experience may be.

### The Ritual of Keeping Track of Thoughts and Ideas

Thoughts and ideas are escape artists. Poof, off they go, and then we spend considerable time and energy trying to track them down. And as we all know, many times we're not successful. That's why you need to develop a means for keeping track of those thoughts and ideas relevant to the various rungs on your writing ladder.

Of course, for centuries writers have logged thoughts and ideas into journals or notebooks. As repositories, these journals or notebooks represent the writer's consciousness when it comes to matters of what to write. In the words of Alan Ziegler, author of the The Writing Workshop, Volume I, a notebook acts as a " 'halfway house' for notes and fragments that can get deposited anytime, anywhere, until they are plucked out and find a permanent home in a piece of writing." In this respect, to keep a journal or notebook allows you to maintain a savings account of thoughts and ideas. Then, as you prepare to write, reference to that account helps you to move the pen or type the first word.

Ideally, this type of consolidation of thoughts and ideas relevant to your writing should monitor the framing and shaping of the pieces you write. It should also act as a catalyst for new pieces or as an editor for old pieces. In effect, it prepares you to write and directs you when you begin. Naturally, however, not everyone is so diligent about keeping a journal or notebook, myself included. But this shouldn't prevent anyone from keeping track. Emily Dickinson, for instance, stuffed a dresser drawer with bits and pieces of poems. That dresser drawer is analogous to your notebook or journal. It may even be analogous to your computer disks or files.

So whether it's a dresser drawer, shoeboxes stuffed with notecards, or the more dignified and less cumbersome approach of a notebook or journal, the point overall is to keep track, however you choose to do it.

## The Ritual of Saving Everything

Has this ever happened to you? You finish a piece of writing, read it over, and as far as you're concerned it's about the best thing ever to find its way from pen to paper. Then, you set it aside for the night, proud of your unparalleled accomplishment. When you wake up in the morning you read it again. And low and behold, it's hard to believe you once thought the piece masterful. It grins at you, and since you hate being grinned at, you crumple it up, toss it into the circular file and lose it forever.

That scenario is not uncommon among writers. Once we immerse ourselves in our writing, we feel hot with the fever of it all. We push and shove the words ahead, wrestle them down when they don't obey and hoist them on to the page. It's all very draining and, at times, exasperating. But when we're done, we experience a sense of gratifying relief, like having our hands raised in victorious salute by a referee. And then we immediately pat ourselves on the back and revel in our achievement.

With the morning after, however, comes a more objective and distant analysis of what we wrote. When measured against the celebration of the night before, that analysis darkens the achievement. Finally, in the end, rather than cope with it all, we toss everything out and start fresh with something new. This process is quite natural to many kinds of creative activity, writing included.

By not gloating over our achievements we unconsciously push ourselves to the next task at hand. The danger, however, lies in our losing potentially valuable material. What appears the next morning as pure dung may, in fact, turn out to be pure fertilizer later on, whether later on means a week or years. That's why you should save as much as you can of what you write. There's just no telling when or where it may come in handy. Trends change. Priorities change. And with time you may find that an old story line or piece of ad copy proves to be promising and workable.

Another value to saving your writing is more important in a sentimental way. There is a special kind of joy in finding your work years later when it has long since been forgotten. To rummage through old pages and manuscripts reminds one of days gone by and generally soothes the fragile ego by suggesting how far the writer has come since those earlier days. This may or may not be a matter of distance in professional achievement. And it may well be a matter of distance in respect to writing skill, especially if the writer has sharpened the skills through the years.

### The Ritual of Modeling

As a young writer, chances are you haven't found your style yet (known as your *voice* in literary circles). You're either about to search for it or are in the process of searching for it. But you probably haven't found it, not yet anyway. Still, it will come, especially with time. As you log more and more hours of writing, you'll get closer and closer to your voice. This means you'll get closer to the real you, the real writing you. It will probably take years, perhaps many years. But that should be okay for those of you committed since you have years to give and a soul bent exclusively toward writing.

While you're working away trying to find your voice, experiment. Part of a writer's ritual is to pay close and careful attention to how others write. We'll get into this in our next chapter. But for now, bear in mind that as a budding writer you should have favorites, favorite writers, that is. Just like an aspiring basketball player tries all the Michael Jordan moves on the schoolyard court, you should practice the moves of your favorite writers, whoever they may be. In this respect you need to experiment with your writing. And to experiment means you should apply to your writing what others have done to theirs. In short, the advice here is to get yourself models and then practice writing like them.

Not one model, though. Get several: advertising copywriters or bits of ad copy that turn you on. In fact, if you come across a particularly enticing piece of ad copy, call the agency that produced it and ask to speak to the writer. Or send a letter to the writer. What's the worst thing that could happen? You may get the brush-off. So what. It won't be the first or last time, that's for sure. Remember, there are times you need to have courage to a fault. This may be one of those times.

Go beyond ad copywriters for models. Seek out an editorial journalist, a novelist, a poet. Whoever. What's important is that you begin to find writers you admire and like, and that you use them to improve yourself as a writer.

## ✍ THE WRITER'S PROCESS ✍

Think about all we bring to the writing process. We bring a storehouse of information and perspectives gleaned from what we've read, heard, and seen. We also bring our idiosyncrasies to bear, ranging from our motivations to our need for self-actualization. Combined with our backgrounds and experiences, our knowledge, likes and dislikes, each of us represents a unique nucleus of someone about to write. Obviously, this nucleus controls how we work our way through the process.

Almost like a chemical reaction, the elements in the nucleus influence each other, directing and redirecting the writing act. At the same time, that act is a process. And as much as it is individualized for each of us, it still contains certain steps and procedures. Researchers, in fact, have studied it extensively so that it can be segmented into those steps and procedures. For example, in Figure 1–1, you'll see a list of the various steps as proposed by researchers of the writing process.

Notice how the steps in the list imply a shifting of mental activity. Initially we give thought to what we're about to write. In thinking about it we organize, usually by priorities of general and specific topics or information. Having conceptualized a rough plan of those priorities, especially as they relate to our intended audience, we then proceed to write. But even the writing itself contains shifts reflecting the mental activity guiding it. For instance, we may write quickly at one point and slowly at another, particularly as we get deeper and deeper into the content. At that point we enter a developmental writing stage where the shaping of content becomes important. And when we're done we may revise or rewrite, a kind of polishing to rid the writing of its rough edges.

From Ronald Kellogg, "Attentional Overload and Writing Performances: Effects of Rough Draft and Outline Strategies," *Journal of Experimental Psychology: Learning, Memory, and Cognition, 14*(2), 1988, pp. 355–365.

Collecting Information—Planning Ideas—Translating Ideas into Text

From Lester Faigley, Roger D. Cherry, David A. Jollife, and Anna M. Skinner, *Assessing Writers' Knowledge and Processes of Composing.* Ablex Publishing, Norwood, NJ, 1985.

Prewriting—Writing—Rewriting

From John R. Hayes and Linda S. Flower, "Identifying the Organization of Writing Processes," in *Cognitive Processes in Writing*, eds. Lee W. Gregg and Erwin R. Steinberg. Lawrence Erlbaum Associates, Hillsdale, NJ, 1980, pp. 3–30.

Planning—Translating—Reviewing

Note: Despite the apparent simplicity of these three steps, each step includes multiple levels of thinking such as collecting, planning, generating, organizing, goal-setting, revising, and editing.

**FIGURE 1–1   The Writing Process.**

Of course, any guess at a generalized writing process that applies to all people avoids the important consideration that writing is an individual matter. While some writers may spend most of their time prewriting, others may spend most of their time rewriting. Depending on what works for the individual writer, an individualized process grabs hold and guides the writer through the writing act. So, too, depending on the type of writing taking place, the process may change. One part of it may be lengthened while another part may be shortened.

Still, make no mistake about it, there is a process, as individualized as that may be. What's important is for you to gain insight into the process, particularly your own so that you know what works for you. This may include realizing that you undergo so much frustration while writing simply because you haven't outlined or thought your subject through well enough. Or, it may include your understanding that it's only when the words find their way onto the page that a mysterious and organic sense and meaning begin to unfold. In short, you think while you're writing. In this case you may have to spend more time in the rewriting stage so that coherence and organization are assured.

Whatever your process, know it and stick with it. But don't be afraid to experiment with alterations along the way. This is especially true if you get stuck or notice that you're bogged down in the familiar writer's block. When this happens (it happens to all writers), you can apply Peter Elbow's "freewriting" technique to unblock.

Throughout history there have been pioneer works that change the dominant thinking regarding certain topics or types of creative activity. For instance, James Joyce's *Ulysses* changed the way fiction writers approached their craft. Mike Nichols's movie *The Graduate* changed the way filmmakers and society viewed heroes. And in advertising as well, ads from agencies such as Doyle Dane Bernbach for Volkswagen, or Ogilvy & Mather for Rolls-Royce, changed the way advertising's creative gurus positioned their products' selling message.

As with *Ulysses, The Graduate,* and the ads, Peter Elbow's two books, *Writing Without Teachers* (1973) and *Writing With Power* (1981), are pioneer works suggesting a new way writers should approach their writing. In those books Elbow fleshes out the theory behind the "freewriting" technique. As a means for inspiring a steady flow of writing from one's pen, the technique serves as a workable and practical aid for unblocking ideas. To understand it and then apply it to your own writing, let's spend some time outlining what Elbow proposes for writers.

## ✍ THEORIES AND TECHNIQUES OF PETER ELBOW ✍

In Elbow's first book, *Writing Without Teachers,* one can sense a writer working out his theory, which is then given a tighter and more controlled argument and focus in Elbow's second book, *Writing With Power.* But it is the earlier work that launches the theory and its value for writers.

According to Elbow, writing is an "organic, developmental process" (*Writing Without Teachers,* p. 14). To try to get your writing correct the first time results in failure. Rather, the first time you write you should defer judgment and simply concentrate on getting as much as you can down on paper. This Elbow refers to as "freewriting," or a process of "nonediting" (ibid., p. 5). It is a method for avoiding the more conventional understanding of the writing process, which dictates that you figure out your meaning first and then write. For Elbow, "Meaning is not what you start out with but what you end up with" (ibid., p. 15).

After laying this groundwork for his theory, Elbow then proposes a working format for writing a piece such as an essay, though in all likelihood one could apply the format to virtually any kind of writing. The format includes forty-five minutes of freewriting on any subject, followed by fifteen minutes of reading over what has been written and finding the main point or "incipient center of gravity, in a sentence" (ibid., p. 20). The assumption, of course, is that the writer has written the way to meaning organically and developmentally.

It is at this point that Elbow introduces what will turn out to be a number of metaphors to explain freewriting and the writing process. For example, to write is to cook. Or, to write is to grow. Or, to write is to flow. As Elbow says, "Producing writing, then, is not so much like filling a basin or pool once, but rather getting water to keep flowing *through* till it finally runs clear" (ibid., p. 28).

Elbow goes on to elaborate the metaphors within the context of how writing occurs. Cooking, for instance, involves a "bubbling, percolating" action that results in the "interaction of contrasting or conflicting material" (ibid., pp. 48–49). He urges the writer to concentrate on cooking where words and ideas "interact into a higher, more organized state" (ibid., p. 67). Clearly the cooking metaphor implies a process, one that takes place over time and one that includes the constant attention of the chef.

Though Elbow suggests various techniques such as talking aloud in order to overcome writer's block, it's clear in this first book that he is writing his way to an important theory about the writing process. It's also clear that the theory has yet to be expanded or solidified. But in his second book, *Writing With Power,* the theory expands into a solid whole.

According to Elbow there are two basic skills we use in writing. One is creating. The other is criticizing. These are the two extremes that control our writing. Always they are at cross-purposes to one another, bumping and fighting each other during the writing act. The result is constipation. By judging as we write, we ultimately end up with little or nothing written. This is why freewriting (writing about anything you want) proves so helpful. It helps avoid the wasted time spent worrying. It helps you to think of topics to write about. It helps you to write when you don't feel like it. And overall, it improves your writing (*Writing With Power,* pp. 13–15).

From this point in his book Elbow launches into various techniques as aids for writing. The first variation is the "direct writing process" technique, which involves a rapid burst of writing when you're crunched for time or have plenty to say. With this process you don't digress, such as you might be inclined to do in pure freewriting. Instead, you write down everything pertinent to the topic, all the time without judging. Then when you're done, you go back and revise based on what you've written and what turns out to be the main point or "center of gravity" for the piece (ibid., p. 34).

The second variation is the "open-ended writing process" technique, which is the opposite of the "direct writing process" technique. It invites chaos. Elbow likens it to a sea voyage where you may lose sight of the old land for a while, but in time you will come to new land. With this technique you immerse yourself into freewriting. When you think you've come upon the main point or "center of gravity" you stop. Then you begin a second period of freewriting using the main point as a marker or direction for your writing. Over time you may repeat the process, perhaps finding and refinding the main point as you go. Gradually you will come to the new land when your piece is finished and the main point is clear. "Just start writing," Elbow says. "Keep writing, don't stop writing, except for eating, sleeping, and living, and keep the process going till you have figured out what you are writing" (ibid., p. 56).

The third variation is the "loop writing process" technique. Elbow positions it as the means for avoiding either of the two extremes inherent in the direct writing and open-ended writing processes. He refers to it as an "elliptical orbiting voyage" (ibid., p. 60). Unlike the open-ended technique, here you voyage out, then back. The voyage out may include such clever devices as jotting down first thoughts, creating dialogues about the topic, creating scenes of the topic, varying the audience for the topic, actually lying about the topic, and even varying the time you write about the topic, such as writing as though you're living in the past or future. Then, when you've completed your voyage out your task is to bend "the curve back toward the original goal" and rewrite (ibid., p. 75).

Beyond introducing and explaining these innovative writing techniques, Elbow devotes the remainder of the book to such topics as revising, the importance of feedback, writing and voice, and breathing experience into words. And even though he spends a considerable amount of time doing so, the overall and most pointed message is clear. He believes "everyone can write with power" (ibid., p. 304), especially if everyone uses freewriting along the way. Elbow sees it as a vehicle for taking writers beyond blocks and into their own consciousness where the "center of gravity" regarding any topic can be found. Only by freewriting, whether direct, open-ended or looped, can a writer reach that center. As an organic and developmental method for reaching meaning, freewriting allows the writer to clear away the brush and to see the destination ahead.

We've spent some time examining Elbow's theories for a reason. As a prospective writer you will face the dreaded writer's block. It will rear its ugly head at the most inconvenient times, showing up as the quintessential unwanted guest. But if you're armed with your own weapons, and if you're protected with impenetrable armor, then it won't kill you. To freewrite is a way of arming yourself. And if you can practice the methods expanding from the freewriting process, whether direct-writing, open-ended, or loop, then you're sure to win the battle against the blank page. That's Elbow's belief. And it's a firm one.

### ✍ WHERE DO WE GO FROM HERE? ✍

We've spent some valuable time here rummaging through the writer's mind and ritualistic behaviors. We know that writers often write out of compulsion. There are times when the compulsion is a curse, and there are times, perhaps the most important times, when the compulsion is a blessing. We know that the compulsion is driven by various needs, some of which act as nutrients for the ego. We also know that the compulsion has enemies, with the foremost being the blank page. To vanquish that enemy takes mental and emotional toughness. It takes courage and bravado, perhaps even to a fault. Often it takes a rigid and unwavering belief in the self and disregard for what others may say.

As easy as it is to identify the characteristics of the writing mind, it's not so easy to identify methods or techniques for building one's self into a writer. No doubt, a large part of the techniques depends on whether your writing answers an inner or outer call. As we've discussed, only the inner call is worth paying considerable attention to. And when you hear it, you'll know that through time you've developed your own techniques for writing. In many ways they seem inherent and individualized to your writing self.

Still, regardless of how much of the writer's soul and rituals influence your daily life, there's nothing quite like systematic practice to get better at something. That's where the writing ladder and Elbow's methods come in handy. That's also where we're heading next, to the practice area. But don't be misled. It's not practice where you put pen to paper. It's more like practice where you watch game films. In that way you learn how things get done and what you need to do to actualize your writing self.

### ✍ THINGS TO DO ✍

It's not enough just to read this stuff. You need to put it into practice. So here are some things to do relevant to what we discussed. Take what you will from them. If you feel something works for you, do it again. Or give it your own twist. At the conclusion of each chapter you'll find other things to do.

1.  Build up your courage. Think of someone you either dislike (maybe even hate) or like so much you'd really want to go out with that someone. Write a personal letter where you vent your feelings, either positive or negative. Then imagine reading it aloud to that person. Sure, it's not real. The person's not there unless you choose to have it that way, but the exercise will get you acting on a fear and turning it into something else. At the worst, you'll be writing.

2.   Make an assessment of someone else's critical comments of your written work. List those points of agreement and disagreement that you have. Then, rewrite parts you believe need to be rewritten. Leave those parts where you don't agree alone.

3.   Pick out your best piece of writing. It doesn't matter what it is, just that you think it's your best. Tack it on your wall.

4.   Practice being alone. Develop habits that satisfy you only. Make them private. Make them relevant to your writing life. Do them when you're alone.

5.   Set up a system of priorities for your writing. Create files (paper or disk). Organize them. Then, when you're done, depending on how you feel at the time, open one and write something.

6.   Set up a system for keeping track of your writing and ideas. Try an empty shoebox or file bin. Keep it close to where you work. Then, take out some notecards and quickly jot down bits of writing and ideas on those cards (one per each card). Toss the cards in the shoebox or bin. The next day, read the cards over and see whether anything turns you on to the point of spurring you to write.

7.   Write something you know about and believe in. Then write something you don't know anything about and don't believe in. Read both and feel the difference.

8.   List products, goods, services, or stores you like. Write letters to an anonymous friend explaining what you like about these favorites.

9.   List your favorite writers or favorite bits of writing. Tack the names or bits of writing on your wall. Read more of those favorite writers, but read by way of analyzing their style and how they achieve certain effects and meanings. If those favorite writers are still alive, send them a nice note or letter.

10.   Practice Peter Elbow's technique of freewriting. Sit down and just write. It can be anything. See where it takes you. Then, if you are comfortable doing this, try the variations (direct writing, open-ended, and loop).

# Chapter 2

# Good Writers
# are
# Good Readers

Habits are like a bed. Easy to get into and hard to get out of. Some habits are good. Some are bad. If you're intent on being a writer, then get into the good habits. Like slipping into the bed of reading, for instance. Good writers are good readers. In the words of the poet Wallace Stegner, "If you're not a hungry reader, you're not likely to be a writer. Reading is one way you learn writing. You learn it through the pores, often without knowing you're learning it." So, if you haven't started already, start now. Nestle yourself into the bed of reading, even before you put "black on white" as Guy de Maupassant urged writers to do.

Bear this in mind, too. When we talk about reading we're also talking about listening. Overall, we're talking about the act of receiving words: words both written and spoken; words seen and heard. Good writers have sensitive and perceptive eyes and ears. When they read they see things others don't see. When they listen they hear things others don't hear. Often what they see and hear plays peekaboo between or behind the lines.

Think about the act of receiving words, about what it means and all it includes. It has been part of our lives since day one when loved ones chattered above us. We're so accustomed to it that we take it for granted. But a writer doesn't do that. A writer always relishes the world of words and reveres the process of their interaction and meaning. Words thrill a writer in the same way canvas and paint thrill an artist. The same holds true for any craft or art form. Ever watch a baseball player interact with a glove or bat? With awe and reverence and care. Ever watch a carpenter interact with tools? A gourmet chef interact with vegetables or spices? Or a musician interact with an instrument? With writers it's words. Words are the writer's world, just like hammers, saws, and screwdrivers are the carpenter's world. Knowing that, and understanding the homage that must be paid, writers revere words and the processes associated with them.

So, how do you train yourself to be a writer in the truest sense of the title? By immersing yourself in the world of words. Like a child, you do it by constant discovery of the world around you. You do it by absorption. Immersion. Wonder. You keep yourself open to that discovery, while at the same time gladly surrounding yourself with words, gladly immersing yourself in what words are and do. That's how you start. By dedication. By frame of mind. By labor of love. By a lifestyle of immersion and wonder. And where better to start than in places words exist, such as on the printed pages we see.

## ✍ WELCOME TO READING 101 ✍

On the surface we read words. Generally we read them left to right, one after the other, and in the context of where they're presented to us, such as in a magazine, a book, a poster, or a script. That context widens and shifts when we consider those words as part of something else such as a story, an editorial, a confession, or an ad. As we glide through the words, we carry those contexts with us. We might say, "Oh, this is an ad, so it's trying to sell me something." Or we may internalize a response to an editorial. We may react to it as we read. We may agree or disagree as we read. We may even counterargue as we read. And all the while we're reading we experience a sense that something is going on inside of us. Many times that something is not at all clear. Many times we don't want it to be clear because it seems too difficult to understand. Many times we just want to curl up, drift off and not pay much attention, sort of like watching a Disney movie or cartoon.

That may be how many people read, which means it's important for you to read that way, at least on occasion. But not always. Perhaps not even most of the time. As a writer it's important for you to receive words in many different ways, often ways deeper, thicker, and more active than laziness allows. It's important to understand exactly what is moving inside of you as you receive the words. At the same time, it's important to understand how the writer stimulated that movement in you. In short, when you receive words, it's important to do so like a writer.

Surface and Deep Meanings

One of the first and obvious things to understand about receiving words is that they have meanings. Whether we talk about individual words, sentences, or longer groups of words, they exist not in and of themselves but as meanings. Think of it this way. We listen to the notes or lyrics in a song, and they mean something to us. We look at colors and shapes in a painting, and they coalesce into meaning. And when we look at or listen to words we find meanings as well.

As soon as we ascribe meanings to words we immerse ourselves in the complex world of communication. Consider the word *romance,* for instance. Given the assignment of creating ad copy centered around a romantic appeal for a weekend getaway to a major metropolitan city, students in an advertising copywriting class discovered that romance meant different things to different people. In a roundtable critique of the various pieces of copy, comments such as, "That's not what romance means to me" and "Why is it the men seem to view romance from the bed's point of view?" were standard fare.

Does romance mean a midnight carriage ride up Fifth Avenue in New York City? Does it mean a chilled bottle of champagne beside the silk sheets of a circular bed? Or does it mean something less visual and more abstract such as caring, tingling, swooning, or floating?

The point is that words mean something. And though we can easily run to a dictionary as a bromide for easing the upset of ambiguous and relative meanings, we can't so easily run to a dictionary (or any other book for that matter) and discover how those meanings take on a life of their own once they've entered the minds of their receivers. Often this is because the meanings are *connoted,* or suggested, based on their mediation by things other than the words themselves. Tops on this list of mediators is you, the receiver. In many ways the entire act of creating meaning is your responsibility.

This is not to say that you create any meaning you want from the words you receive. To the contrary, having fixed attention on those words, you are, to some extent at least, bound to those words. What those words yield on one level are *denotative,* or surface meanings. Dictionary-type meanings. The kind that don't require a subjective interpretation from you. Such meanings just are. And they usually are because Webster says so.

As we can see with a word like *romance,* however, surface meanings do little to bring words to life. By their nature, surface meanings avoid interpretation by a receiver. They also avoid intentionality, or purpose, by a sender. And they often avoid the contexts in which words live, such as with other words, as tangents to various social and cultural influences, or within specific environments. This tells us that surface

meanings lack completeness. It also tells us that something else is needed to qualify what words mean. That something else is *deep meanings.*
Once we enter into the dynamics of how one receives and then shapes
the meanings of words, how one sends the words in order to convey
meanings, and how words interact within contexts, we enter into this
other kind of meaning, deep meaning.

Conceptualize surface and deep meanings like this. Surface
meanings provide you with a mechanism, a tool for adjusting your
lens of interpretation. As such they give you a focal or reference point.
But it is only when you adjust your lens of interpretation that the
deep meanings come into full view. These are the meanings tied
directly to you as a receiver, the writer or speaker as the sender, and
the contexts in which the words live. As receiver you have the power
to create those meanings, even to the point of re-creating what the
sender meant. In these respects, meanings live in other places besides
the words themselves.

## Creating Meaning as a Receiver

In a general sense your construction of deep meanings is determined by who you are, especially as you meet certain words. There you
are face-to-face with words. They come to you, and you receive them.
But it is what you give of yourself to the words at the point of reception
that helps create the deep meanings. What happens is that you give
yourself to the words, which means you also give yourself to all of the
contexts inherent to words. These contexts include historical, social, cultural, and environmental influences that have shaped both the surface
and deep meanings over time. Again, the word *romance,* for example,
may convey or stimulate quite different meanings in the 1990s compared to the 1890s. Or, it may convey or stimulate quite different meanings when found in a copy of *Good Housekeeping* compared to a copy of
*Playboy.* And this simply by nature of how different the contexts are
between two centuries or two magazines.

To give yourself to the words suggests a mingling of sorts. On one
hand, words *are.* They exist on the page or in the air. To absorb them or
let them inside requires that you give yourself over to them. When you
do, a transaction occurs, one that finds you acting on the words and the
words acting on you. The essence of that transaction revolves around
who you are at the point of contact. In many ways, then, creating meanings from words depends on how well you know who you are: your
expectations, your knowledge, your likes and dislikes. All the things
that make you who you are. As we shall see further on, creating meanings from the words in ads depends on how well you know the targeted
audience, which in most instances is not you at all but rather some

other person with, perhaps, an entirely different set of expectations, knowledge, and likes and dislikes.

So, the first question for you to answer is, Who are you? Especially, who are you in relationship to the words you meet? What do you expect from the words? What do you already know about the words? What are your likes and dislikes? And since, as Shakespeare suggested, the eye sees not itself but by reflection, what kinds of words surround you? What do you have around you that gives meaning to who you are? What is there in your life that acts as a mirror for discovering who you are?

Of course, this is not a book intent on moralizing about methods of introspection and self-discovery. Still, as skillful readers and listeners, writers know that they give a great deal of themselves to words, whether they read, listen to, or write those words. They know how important it is to be in tune with one's self so as to discover meanings, especially the deep meanings often found between or behind the words. Immersed as they are in the world of words, writers enjoy foraging in that world. They enjoy the hunt. And what they're hunting for are the dynamics and meanings of words.

### Expectations

If the act of receiving words includes a transaction (the words give to you and you give to them), then part of your responsibility as a receiver is to know what you give to that transaction. To define yourself helps the knowing. But beyond that, consider these contributions you make to the transaction. First and foremost, you contribute expectations. You expect certain things when you meet the words. Take this book, for instance. Before you opened it you were primed to expect certain things. The very title, the colors, designs, typography, and words on the front and back jackets predisposed you to expect something of the book. Then such matters as the preface and table of contents refined that expectation in some way. The same holds true for the characteristics of size, page typography, and even the feel of the pages. In short, before you read the first word of the first chapter you were predisposed to expect certain meanings.

This idea of expectations is critical to your understanding of how to read or listen to words. In fact, any act of communication begins with what you are predisposed to expect. That's part of what you give to the words. Expectations. And there is a host of variables and influences shaping those expectations. Your values, for instance. Or your experiences. If, for example, you have read very little about advertising copywriting, yet have a lively interest in it as well as a high regard for books, then immediately you are predisposed to openness for what this book will say. On the other hand, if none of those predispositions are true, then you won't be predisposed to openness. You won't expect to gain much from the reading.

This is why you were asked to answer the question, Who are you? To come to grips with an honest answer will provide you with a backdrop for understanding why you create certain deep meanings from words. It will also allow you to know what expectations you hold when you meet words. At the same time, to ask yourself what those expectations are immediately prior to meeting words is in itself a valuable exercise. For instance, would you bring the same expectations to a piece of advertising copy as you would to a letter you've received from a close friend? Chances are you wouldn't. Well, how are the expectations different? To answer that question goes a long way to understanding how you create meaning.

## Knowledge

Often tied to your expectations, the extent of your knowledge about what you meet in the way of words also goes a long way toward helping you create meaning. For example, once you're finished with this book, advertising copy should never be the same again, at least not in comparison to what it is now in your mind. Presumably some change will occur, a change based on your knowledge of advertising copy. The same will hold true when you read another book on ad copy. The base of your knowledge expands, broadens, and ultimately shapes the meanings you derive from whatever the next book will be. Read still another book and the base expands and broadens again.

In effect, each time you read about advertising copy, you add to your storehouse of knowledge about the subject. In turn, you give more to each piece of reading. Ultimately, your knowledge widens and deepens, invariably shaping the meanings you gain. The result is constant change, often reflected in what you give to your reading.

It is in these respects that what you know determines deep meanings. The more you know, the deeper, rounder, and thicker the meaning gets. With each "new read," the words seem to be saying and meaning more. This is not to imply that the meaning always gets easier to discover or create. In fact, at times it may get more difficult since you end up giving so much more to the words. Still, the extent of your knowledge about a particular subject stimulates such reactions. Mostly they are reactions of the mind. Intellectualizing. Creating meanings evolving from background perspectives and information.

## Likes and Dislikes

As with knowledge, your likes and dislikes also predispose you to the words you meet. In this sense your emotional expectations guide your reactions and even the meanings you gain. On this emotional level your affective responses (likes and dislikes) shape meanings, color them, breathe life into them. This is the other side, the emotional, "heart" side of what you give to words. With knowledge we were dealing with the rational, the "mind" side of what you give. Here, we are dealing with the heart, your responses of liking and disliking.

Think again, for instance, of how you approached this book. You probably internalized certain questions such as, Will I gain anything of value from it? (knowledge) or Will I enjoy it? (likes and dislikes). Again, you glanced at the cover, felt the pages, read the preface, scanned the table of contents, all of the ways we massage the contexts for what we'll read. As a result, your expectations of likes or dislikes were raised or lowered. And depending on how much you like or dislike the book, your emotional expectations will be influenced for the next copywriting book you read. Of course, the entire process repeats itself each time you set out to read something new.

Make no mistake about it, first impressions can be lasting, especially those that deal with likes or dislikes. After initial contact with a word sender and the words sent, we quickly formulate value judgments based on our emotional reactions. Those reactions are often mirror images of what we like or dislike prior to meeting the sender or words. In effect, we carry our likes and dislikes into the words. By way of transaction, they imbue us with a tone and feeling. We then merge or not merge with them, all the while employing our predispositions regarding likes and dislikes as a guide.

## Expectations Met and Unmet

One of the great things about advertising creativity is that it not only allows for the breaking of expectations, it encourages it. "When they start doing all pictures, I'll do all words," advertising Hall of Famer Ed McCabe says. The essence of his words echoes in Hall of Fame art director Bill Taubin's advice for young copywriters that "as creative people, we need to remember that, if everyone is moving in one direction, we ought to be thinking about the other direction." Now, how does such advice fit in here as we discuss the act of receiving words?

To be a good sender (writer or speaker) you must be a good receiver (reader or listener). That premise is guiding this chapter. When it comes to expectations, your awareness of what you give to words turns a light on deep meaning. Before you turn a page or zero in on a sentence, you're armed with certain knowledge and certain likes and dislikes. You carry this arsenal into the words, then confront them according to what you knew before and what you like or dislike. Finally, you transform their surface meanings into deep meanings, those meanings that reach and reverberate inside you according to who you are. In many ways, we see what we want to see, at least to a limited degree.

When it comes to advertising's creative side, bold attempts are made to counter this arsenal of expectations. The reason is simple. Often, advertising is neither wanted nor liked by those on the receiving ends of words. Those watching television want programming. Those reading newspapers want news. Creative advertising gurus know this and thus seek to gain attention. Another advertising Hall of Famer, Carl Ally, put it this way: "At Doyle Dane Bernbach they tend to *goose* the consumer. But this is Carl Ally, Inc., and at Carl Ally, Inc., we punch them in the nose." To punch consumers in the nose means there's no way they can avoid paying attention. In itself, that's an important goal for all advertising ideas.

At the same time, what Ally and others are referring to is the creative idea controlling various copy points. The creative idea—a bull in a china shop, talking margarine, a bunny moving through a bogus commercial—must be different in order to jolt the receiver into paying attention. The ad copy, however, rarely uses the same tact. Instead, it plays to expectations. It talks the language of the receiver. It conveys the correct tone of product and appeal. In short, it brings the wackiness or originality of the creative idea down to the receiver's level in language that receiver can easily understand.

Overall, advertising copywriters know that what they send in the way of words must either align itself with the expectations of receivers or adjust those expectations so as to create a new set of receiver expectations. This is common practice among all writers concerned with communicating to an audience. It is a recognition of what is expected or of what is brought by the receiver to the act of receiving. Assessments of degrees of knowledge, likes, dislikes, and even values and purposes in receiving words give writers a tighter and clearer bead on their targeted audience. This is why you're encouraged to "know thyself" when it comes to developing a richer and fuller appreciation for what words mean. And what you're asked to know about yourself we've categorized as your expectations, including your base of knowledge and your likes and dislikes.

To see how such things as knowing who you are and how expectations can impact on the meanings of words, read the following example of highly successful selling copy.

> The proletarians have nothing to lose but their chains.
> They have a world to win. Workingmen of all countries,
> unite!

Are you angered by these words? Are you sympathetic? Curious? Skeptical? As you read them did you find yourself trying to identify their source? Or trying to recall when, where, and if you've seen them before? What about yourself did you give to the words? And how did that help shape their deep meaning?

Of course, the surface meaning of the words is very clear, isn't it? Someone urges the working classes around the world to group together in order to lose their chains and win a world. Very clear and simple. But, on a deeper level, a level reverberating beyond the denotative or surface level, the meaning of the words may thicken or change. Consider, for example, if your father devoted himself to a workingman's union all his life and that your conscious being were shaped to an extent by that devotion. Or, consider how the meaning changes if your father never believed in unions. In fact, consider the change in light of the possibility that for your father unions represented the death of our great society. Add to that the possibility that your conscious being was shaped by that belief.

On the surface level the words mean exactly what they say. There is no argument, no debate, no ambiguity. But on the deeper level the meaning thickens, perhaps drastically. It's as though we've entered into another realm of meaning, one that's relative to our individual personalities. Moreover, that other realm consists of emotions, reactions, and opinions, each reflecting a program of highly personal and individualized expectations, knowledge, and likes and dislikes. Once you discover what they are, you can then understand how and why certain deep meanings take shape inside you.

For the record, the words you were asked to read came from *The Communist Manifesto* by Karl Marx and Friedrich Engels, a book, like it or not, that rang the emotional register of millions of people around the world and managed to pass one stern copy test after another.

Perhaps you knew that. If you did, then you immediately responded to the words with that little piece of knowledge in mind. No doubt, knowing the source of the words helped shape their deep meaning for you. For example, perhaps you had a predisposition toward the work and the authors. You liked or didn't like them. You trusted or didn't trust them. Whatever that predisposition was, be assured that it helped you create a thicker and deeper meaning.

In effect, because of who you are (in this case, what you knew and liked or trusted) the deep meaning of the words took a certain shape. On the other hand, if you didn't know the source of those words, then the meaning would have been different. Of course, the point overall is that being in touch with your expectations, knowledge, and likes and dislikes helps you to create deep meanings from words.

And while we're in the middle of this somewhat weighty discussion, consider this. What happens if you overlay your expectations, knowledge, and likes and dislikes onto the context in which you read the quote by Marx and Engels? That context is this book. You didn't read the quote straight out of *The Communist Manifesto.* You read it as it was printed in this text. To be an astute reader, you will have to consider that wrinkle.

You've been asked to respond to the Marx and Engels quote. But what happens to the quote and to this book as you consider the question of context? Surely, no one expects to see a quote from Marx and Engels in a text on advertising copywriting. If that's true, how does that help shape your expectations of what the words in this book will mean? Are they changed somehow? Or, how does it help shape your likes and dislikes for the book? If you disliked the quote by Marx and Engels, did you transfer that dislike to this book, and are you now reading these words with dislike? And if that's true, are you predisposed to dislike the rest of the book?

Not to get ourselves too bogged down in such a discussion, but the point overall, especially in this chapter, is that you try to develop and sharpen your skills in receiving words. To do that you need to be a lively and active reader or listener. You need to be aware of the many influences inherent to words, including contexts and, of course, yourself as an influence.

Here's an important lesson. As you give yourself over to words, know what it is you're giving. Since you are at least partially responsible for creating meaning, then to "know thyself" is to come closer to that meaning.

Let's say, for instance, that you're given an ad to read. You read it and gain some meaning from it. Why does that ad mean what it does to you? If you were someone else, would it mean the same thing? Suppose you had no interest in advertising whatsoever, would you give the ad the same meaning? Presumably you have an interest in advertising. The danger in that is simple. You read ads differently from the way most people do. Ads mean something different to you from what they mean to most other people. And make no mistake about it, forget that little tidbit of information and your days as a copywriting genius are numbered.

So, back to the question of who you are. What do you give to the words you meet? Be sensitive to that question. It's not the last time you'll see it. In fact, you'll see it often in one form or another, so better now that you get used to it. The difference later on is that you won't always be asked to receive words with a pure you guarding the gate. Rather, you'll be asked to receive words with varieties or versions of you at the gate. In short, you'll be asked to become others so that you create meaning from many different points of view.

Of course, you've been asked a difficult question, Who are you? As if that's easy to answer. We all know it's not. But even in pressing yourself for answers to many of the other questions asked, you've been forced to dig inside. Chances are insights flashed in your mind along the way. Perhaps your assessments of meaning in the quote by Marx and Engels seemed clearer or more appropriate to something inside you. Or perhaps the meanings of those words seemed to deepen and thicken. That's part of establishing yourself as a writer. The beginning stages, to be sure. But vital nonetheless.

## Re-creating the Meanings of a Sender

It's certainly true that without a receiver (you) there is no communication, regardless of what's sent. It's also true that without a sender there are no words, let alone communication. That's why the sender (writer or speaker) is so important as a mediator of meaning. It's almost as if a sender winds up and delivers a pitch, knowing from the beginning what that pitch will be. It's your job as receiver to figure out the pitch before it crosses the plate.

With most communication, however, the situation is a little different. There is a twist. Here, the sender wants you to know what the pitch is. The sender wants you to hit it. In fact, the sender wants you to hit a home run. Unfortunately, the sender isn't always in control of the pitch. In actuality, there are times when the sender is completely out of control. There are times when a straight ball is meant, but a curveball crosses the plate. And there are other times when the pitch never comes close to the plate but you're expected to hit it anyway.

Let's assume, though, that the sender has fairly good control of the pitch. When the pitch is released the arm that threw it knows where the ball is going. Call that intentionality. It's another type of deep meaning. Your job as receiver is to understand the intention. And you can do that by practicing reading or listening like a writer or speaker. In other words, you read or listen with the persona of that writer or speaker. You try to dig into that mind. You forage about in the world of that mind's words until you discover what was intended. After all, words don't appear out of nowhere. They have a source. If written, they come from a pen attached to a hand acting upon the advice of a mind. Take the minds of Karl Marx and Friedrich Engels, for example.

Marx and Engels were nineteenth-century European revolutionaries. They were intent on the overthrow of the capitalist system, believing it was constructed and vested for the good of the few and not the many. The few they termed *bourgeoisie*. The many they termed *proletarians*. Their intent in writing *The Communist Manifesto* was to incite revolt among the proletarians (workers) against the bourgeoisie (owners).

With these perspectives in mind, the words of Marx and Engels should take on a slightly new meaning, perhaps a bit deeper than it was before. Perhaps a bit darker as well. We know, for instance, of a dark intent on their part, especially as we understand it in light of our being

Americans and, presumably, willing members of our own capitalist system. But notice how the authors' words echo their intent. Notice how the words contrast losing something with winning something else. Here are those words again.

> The proletarians have nothing to lose but their chains.
> They have a world to win. Workingmen of all countries,
> unite!

There is a bold, unadulterated promise in the words. Proletarians will lose their chains and win the world. What a prize! What a benefit! The receivers of the words are promised the loss of nothing of value, only something detestable. With that rather pleasurable loss comes the gain of something extraordinary, the world, followed by the selection of the reading audience ("workingmen of all countries") and the call to action ("unite!"). Notice, too, the use of an exclamation point to drive home the call to action with emotional intensity. In these respects this passage summarizes some sound rules of advertising copywriting, even though Marx and Engels would surely toss and turn in their graves at the very thought.

Now remember what we're doing here. We're not reading to discover deep meaning from ourselves, such as we did previously. We're reading to discover that meaning from the authors. We're reading to discover their intention, which in turn will open up a new level of deep meaning for us to consider. Remembering this, why is it that Marx and Engels selected the words and punctuation that they did? Why didn't they simply write, "The proletarians have nothing to lose and everything to win. Workingmen, unite"? The answer may be this.

Believing there was considerable power in numbers, Marx and Engels relied on proletarians everywhere to overthrow capitalism. Bound to their goal, the two revolutionaries sought to expand the reach and quantity of those numbers. Further, they simplified the promise and reduced it to the essence of what had been read during the entire text of the *Communist Manifesto*. Quite simply, that essence centered on how proletarians (workers) as a class were shackled by the bourgeoisie. What better way, then, to express and summarize the shackling than by the image of chains? Think, for instance, of all that word and its consequent image suggest as a deep meaning for the millions of proletarians laboring away in mines and factories around the world.

Finally, for Marx and Engels the only way for revolution to succeed was if all proletarians united (power in numbers), regardless of whether they labored in mines or factories. The goal was to convince the proletarians that though they were all toiling away in different boats, in a larger sense they were all living in the same boat together, that of oppression and despair. The way to safety was simple: Band together to keep from capsizing.

Given this background of information, it's certainly easier to understand why Marx and Engels chose the words and sentence arrangements they did. But even without such background information there are clues leading the perceptive reader to the same conclusions. For example, plurals are given to proletarians and workingmen. This suggests many factions of people. In addition, the appeal of the promise ("a world to win") appears more enticing when contrasted with what is lost in the process ("chains"). The old maxim of emphasizing one thing by contrasting it with another is at work here. If you want black to look very black, place it against something white, for instance.

Consider, too, the placement of the lone action verb, *unite,* at the end of the sentence. This, along with the exclamation point, should seem intentional to you. After all, the authors could have arranged the words and punctuation differently, but they didn't. They opted instead for an action verb as a final word. Finally, consider the directness and crispness of the quote. Both the words and sentences are sparse, terse, to the point. Certainly this aligns itself well with the directness and terseness of the message. The authors were not talking about something namby-pamby or inconsequential here. They were talking about vast numbers of human beings and the entire world, leading them no doubt to a hard-hitting and direct form of expression.

The fact that Marx and Engels were revolutionaries intent on the overthrow of the capitalist system serves as a backdrop for understanding their intentions in writing what they wrote and how they wrote it. It also serves as a catalyst for constructing deep meaning in mob psychology, the power of rhetoric, and rhetorical and persuasive communication.

By understanding a writer's motives behind the words we read, we're better able to deepen the meaning. We're also better able to exercise more insightful and flexible assessments of that meaning. In many ways these assessments of the sender's meaning demand that we activate a mechanism in our minds. That mechanism is a switch. And that switch catapults us quickly and skillfully from our minds as receivers to the minds of the senders. In an important sense we lose ourselves and become the writer or speaker. We interpret words, not from the receiver's point of view, but from the point of view of the sender.

With this in mind, consider the following copy line taken from a direct mail piece from a bank: "Complete every question on form that pertains to applicant using same color ink." Clearly the denotative or surface meaning is unmistakable. The receiver is to complete every question on the form that pertains to him or her using the same color ink.

As it stands, I actually received this direct mail piece and read it through. Based on the surface meaning of the line you read, I made an assumption that I should answer the questions only if I use the same colored ink, presumably the same colored ink used on the mailing. And if I didn't use the same colored ink, well then, there must be another applicant the bank had in mind. Now, this may sound ridiculous, but given the words as they are placed within the message, that's precisely what they say and mean on the surface level.

The writer's error in that message is known as a *misplaced modifier*. As I think back on my first reading of it, however, I reacted according to the words as they were presented. I read them left to right, gathering surface meaning as I progressed along from word to word. One word influenced the meaning of the next and so on, so that by the time I finished the message I had gathered up a tight little ball of truth known as surface meaning. Unfortunately, that little ball of truth was suspect. Or, to resurrect an analogy from pages ago, it seemed to me that the writer may have thrown me a very wild curve ball.

The result of this curve ball was that I retraced my steps and attempted to piece together a new meaning, perhaps a deep meaning based on the writer's intention. That meaning went something like this: As applicant I am asked to use the same colored ink in writing answers to the questions. Thus, I shouldn't switch pens in the process. That new interpretation of meaning, however, was really a matter of re-creating the writer's intention. I took it upon myself to create that meaning since the surface meaning appeared to lack sense.

Of course, this entire discussion points to a central process in the act of receiving words. As receivers we react to those words presented to us according to certain sets of expectations. We expect to read or hear words in sequence, one word following another and so on. This is the way we gather up the truths of what the words mean. In effect, we accumulate meaning. As we read or listen we transform those words into cumulative meanings. As a result, our response to the second word is really a product of our response to the first word.

From the writer's point of view, the succession of words directs the reader to the meaning the writer would like to convey. But if something grinds against the gears of normal reading (or listening), the intended meaning gets lost or shifted. This is what happened with the message from the bank. What the writer intended or meant isn't what came across from the words as they were successively positioned in the message. The responsibility, then, was left to me to reconstruct what the writer really meant. The goal is to reconstruct a writer or speaker's meaning, especially using our arsenal of expectations. To do that let's use my mind since I was the one who was sent the message from the bank.

For me to reconstruct the writer's meaning, I had to make certain assumptions about the message and the writer. Those assumptions were based on my knowledge that the message was from a bank and that writers, being human, were prone to writing errors. Actually, I would have liked to grant latitude and assume that the writer knew what he or she was doing. But then there was the problem of the bank.

Banks, I assumed, were serious business enterprises. Normally they don't joke around, perhaps fearful that they will be perceived as jokesters with their customers' money. Obviously, this assumption, transformed to an expectation, helped shape my view of the message. Overall, it led me to believe there was an unintentional error made and that the writer simply didn't know or had overlooked what he or she was writing on the surface level. In turn, this led to a new surface meaning for the message. And though it didn't really thicken or deepen the meaning of the message overall, it did color my critical view of the writer and the bank. Because I believed there was another intention of meaning in the written words, I became critical of the writer for the error in meeting that intention and critical of the bank for allowing the error to slip through the cracks.

By bringing our expectations to bear on the words we meet, we transform meanings, often so that they can fit within our own pre-scribed values or codes. This means they fit with who we are, and who we are includes all of what we give to those words. We've termed what's given *expectations*—expectations fleshed out by our knowledge and likes and dislikes.

At the same time, it should be clear that all of what we have dis-cussed depends on something larger and more involved than even our-selves as receivers or writers and speakers as senders. This largeness of something is called *context*. In fact, when we discussed receivers and senders as givers of meaning we were also discussing the importance of context. For example, my own frame of knowledge about banks and writers provided a context for my assessment of meaning about the bank's message. Likewise, your likes or dislikes for Marx and Engels provided a context for your assessment of meaning from their quote. By way of a large leap, then, what we are left with is this: No words exist apart from their contexts.

## Re-creating Meaning from Contexts

Derived from the Latin *contextus,* context means to join together, at least on the surface level, in this case the level of Webster's dictionary. The dictionary, or surface, meaning also states that context is "parts of a sentence, paragraph, discourse, etc., immediately next to or surrounding a specified word or passage and determining its exact meaning." In this respect, context includes all those words surrounding a word.

Context also includes other influences such as punctuation or syn-tax (the structural arrangement of words in a sentence). If we can assume for the moment that context is critical to understanding meanings of words, then we are advised to look around the words to enlighten ourselves about their meanings. This, of course, goes back to our discussion of how the meaning of one word is shaped by the words preceding and following it. Beyond looking at the word whose meaning we're after, therefore, we must also look at the words around it. This will deepen the meaning.

Webster's goes on to say that context also means "the whole situation, background, or environment relevant to a particular event, personality, creation, etc." Clearly this takes us beyond the surrounding words, punctuation, or syntax and into other areas such as ourselves, the writer, or the medium and environment in which the word is found.

Conceptualize this matter of context like this: At the center you have a word. It doesn't matter what the word is. It can be any word you want it to be. However, you're so close to it that you can't tell what its deep meaning is, sort of like not being able to see the forest for the trees. Moreover, the very meaning of the word itself seems shaped and colored by all of the shadows and light cast upon it by other sources. Your job is to look away from the word, to fix your analytical eye on all the sources that give shape and color to the word's meaning. First, you look at those words surrounding it, then the punctuation and syntax. You then understand some of the sources of shadow and light.

But that's not enough, so you look further away to those influences beyond the immediate context. You look to social, cultural, and historical influences. You look to yourself and your expectations, to the writer's apparent intention, and to the medium or environment in which the word is found. This rounds out your discovery of context and allows you to see the word's meaning more fully and completely than if you were to see it on a single plane of meaning existing in and of itself.

### The Importance of Words around Words

Let's take Webster's dictionary at its word and begin to dig the meaning from words by looking first at those words around them, including their punctuation and syntax. And since we have done some of this before in previous discussions, we'll simply skim over those redundant parts. With this in mind, let's return to the familiar Marx and Engels quote. Here it is again.

> The proletarians have nothing to lose but their chains.
> They have a world to win. Workingmen of all countries,
> unite!

Of course, you read one word after another, left to right, line by line. But notice how the meanings of the words thickened and deepened as you proceeded through each line. For example, in line two you met a simple pronoun, *they.* That pronoun had no meaning whatsoever until you attached it to something else, in this case *proletarians,* the antecedent. Then the meaning was clear. The same holds true for all of the other words, again referring back to the idea that words don't mean anything apart from their contexts.

As you read the passage word by word and left to right, notice how the meaning of each new word takes shape from the words around it. For instance, in the first sentence the subject, *proletarians,* would be relatively sterile in meaning if it weren't qualified by the promise of losing their chains. This promise shapes the meaning of proletarians. Now you can envision what the life of proletarians must be, at least as seen by the authors. And as we discussed previously, the use of a word such as *chains* is loaded with all sorts of negative connotations, probably meant to incite the anger of proletarians. As you proceed word by word notice how the same dynamic of creating meaning holds true for each word you meet.

Beyond how meanings of individual words accrue as we read, notice little things as well that create meaning for you. For example, the quote contains three verbs, two *haves* and one *unite.* Have is a bland verb, simply there to suggest ownership. But again as we have discussed, the verb *unite* is an action verb. It calls for action on the part of the proletarians. Juxtaposed with the bland or "quiet" *haves, unite* takes on more significance since no other verb upstages it. In effect, it's allowed to rule the roost of impact and even meaning in the quote. Nothing distracts the reader from it.

At the same time, notice how the subjects of the sentences are plural. Each subject amounts to the same thing despite the three different names of *proletarians, they,* and *workingmen.* Overall, expressed as plurals the subjects reinforce the meaning of group effort. In this regard recall our discussion of the authors' intent on clumping all working people together to achieve power through numbers.

Another point to be considered is how the world to be won in sentence two is *a* world, not *the* world. The difference suggests that the world to be won is one of many possible worlds. It is a world open to interpretation. It may be a private world, a complete world of people, or an abstract world of ideals depending on how one chooses to interpret it.

Further, what is to happen with that world? It is to be won. This choice of the infinitive "to win" carries with it a certain meaning. To win implies a form of competition yielding winners and losers. In other words, winning a world will mean a fight of sorts, perhaps even a revolution. Now consider how effective an alternative word such as *gain* or *procure* or *achieve* would have been compared to *win.*

No doubt, the deeper you dig into the quote the more meaning you derive. That's precisely the point about contexts. To look around the individual words yields thicker and deeper meanings. In recalling the importance of a consolidated and unified group effort to Marx and Engels, you can continue to deepen the case for that effort simply by referring to their use of the plurals in the sentence subjects and their use of one action verb, complete with its exclamation point. But you couldn't do that if you weren't in tune with the contexts around the key words. In short, knowing these contexts allows you to yoke together a deep meaning for the quote.

As Americans we can easily take moral objection to such an appeal on the part of Marx and Engels, for they leave little or no room for individuality and individual choice in the matter. They have clumped everyone together as one. They have trumpeted their own cattle call. To many of us that may be objectionable or offensive, no doubt for good reason. At the same time, their words literally incited millions of people. We can assume, then, that they knew their audience. They knew which buttons to press to incite that audience to action. And they were practiced and accomplished writers of persuasive rhetoric. Obviously, there is something to be learned from them as a result.

## The Importance of Theme, Media, Time and Place, and Form of Expression

As well as looking closely for words around words, looking for other contexts beyond words themselves can deepen meaning. As we know, words don't exist in a vacuum. They exist as part of contextual relationships. Earlier we discussed two of those relationships, namely yourself as receiver and the writer or speaker as sender. In the preceding paragraphs we discussed still other relationships, namely words around words complete with matters of punctuation and syntax. Of course, all of these relationships shape meaning, at times to a considerable degree. The same holds true as we look beyond the words themselves. Here, we can look to vital contexts such as theme, media, time and place, and form of expression.

*Theme.*   A *theme* refers to what the words are about, the essence of meaning, in effect, or as Peter Elbow called it, the "incipient center of gravity." What's written or spoken about as a theme lends meaning to words. For example, with the Marx and Engels quote the theme is revolution. Our knowing this colors the meanings of the words. In a sense, because the theme is what it is, we expect certain types of words or word arrangements.

As receivers we expect that the words and those arrangements will match with the theme, or at least our expectations of what should match with the theme. The same holds true for the writer or speaker.

In many ways the theme dictates the choices of words and their arrangements. If you recall, the bank mailing I received contained an inappropriate message, one in which the meaning didn't make sense. Importantly, though, I determined that it didn't make sense based on certain assumptions about the theme, in this case the bank or the request for completion of a form.

In advertising, the theme, the "incipient center," is usually one of two things. It can be a feature or selling point of a product, goods, or service advertised. Or, it can be the benefit received from the product, goods, or services. Put simply, the benefit answers the question, What will this product, goods, or service do for me? Perhaps it will save you time. That's a benefit. And if it controls or dominates the ad, then it is also the theme. Once you've identified it as the theme, you have also identified an important context for discovering the deep meaning in the ad. As we will see further on, the theme tends to dictate and control the copy in an ad.

*Media.* Even though it's old hat by now, Marshall McLuhan's dictum that the "medium is the message" still holds true. Often the medium lends meaning to the words. For example, the words that come from our television sets may be interpreted very differently by us compared to the words that come from our newspapers or magazines.

Beyond the media vehicle, the environments within the media and which surround the words also color meaning. An ad surrounded by news, for instance, may convey a "newsy" meaning, one suggesting accuracy, truth, or believability.

As a context the medium merges with our expectations in much the same way the theme did. Our code of expectations is primed based on the medium carrying the words. Newspapers give us news. News shows give us news. To those media we grant certain allowances such as truth and believability. We expect them to be truthful and believable. However, when it comes to advertising, such is not always the case. In fact, it's often not the case. With advertising we expect salesmanship. As its own form of expression between a sender (the product) and receiver (the consumer), advertising is suspect. It seems vested for the purposes of the advertiser. And though there is plenty of evidence to suggest that consumers generally believe advertising is needed and beneficial for society at large, there is also plenty of evidence to suggest that advertising is suspect in terms of truthfulness and believability.

As it pertains to meaning, the bottom line of media is that it merges with our expectations and uses its own capabilities such as sight or sound to shape or color the meanings of words. As astute receivers of words, we need to be sensitive to the medium delivering the message. We need to know that because the medium is what it is, it carries with it certain meanings that attach themselves to the words. There is this carryover effect of the media coloring the meaning. Recall, for instance, our earlier discussion of how you relate to a book, itself a medium, and how this relationship colors your own interpretation of meaning and even your liking for a book.

*Time and Place.* When we talk of time and place we're actually talking about when and where the words are seen or heard. This can be as broad as a period in history or as narrow as a time and place within a day. For example, Marx and Engels wrote their manifesto during a time in which exploitation was rampant. It was exploitation of the worst kind, the kind that would abuse young and old alike. Writing during the Industrial Revolution, Marx and Engels witnessed this exploitation. Whether their book could be written now and be considered reasonable is questionable. But for then, namely the middle of the nineteenth century, there was more reason for it. The same holds true for the place in which their words were read by many, generally a stifling and demoralizing home and workplace.

Now as we bring things more up to date and begin to center our discussion on advertising, consider the importance of when or where you see or hear certain words. For example, to hear the words "Where's the beef?" in a TV commercial yields a quite different meaning than if you were to hear those words spoken on Muscle Beach in California. Notice what's changed. A part of the theme has changed, in this case a hamburger as opposed to a person. The medium has changed, in this case a voice from television as opposed to a voice on a beach. And the place has changed, again the beach.

Of course, both time and place overlap with the consideration of a medium. But take time and place beyond the medium. Take them to the actual meeting with words, once again mediated by you as the receiver. The point in time and place when you meet words will color their meaning. For instance, the fact that you read the Marx and Engels quote at this time, particularly this time in history, colors the meaning for you.

Or, think of reading this book at this time and place, whenever and wherever that happens to be. Your impressions and interpretations of the book and particularly its meanings may be colored differently by late night as opposed to early morning reading. Or, they may be colored differently if you read it in a hammock versus at a desk. So, time and place are significant contexts for deepening your interpretation of meaning, not only the time and place in which words are shown or said, but also the time and place you meet them.

*Form of Expression.* Still another context is that of the form of expression for the words, including those images that surround them as well as environments such as typography more closely aligned with the words themselves. Obviously, images deepen meanings in words. To read the word *excitement* in an ad for a sports car conveys a certain meaning. But that meaning is deepened and brought to life if the image accompanying the word is one of a roller coaster.

Naturally, it's virtually impossible to discuss anything about advertising copywriting without due consideration given to images. In and of themselves images speak volumes of words. We'll address this important context in more detail in the next chapter. But clearly their consideration as a context for gaining meanings from words is critical to the advertising copywriter, especially if one considers that words themselves are very often builders of images.

Beyond images that surround words, there are those forms of expression more closely tied to words. The typeface and size, for instance, color meaning. In this respect, examine jewelry ads and notice how often elegant and seraphed typefaces are used, no doubt to convey and enrich meanings associated with high quality, luxuriousness, or elegance. There are even more subtle forms of expression to consider such as the tone of expression, often conveyed through actual word and word arrangement choices. With form of expression, how the words are presented is most critical. Here, you're not considering what the words are. You're considering how they are presented, graphically in print and orally in speech.

## Break Time

We've certainly been into some thick and weighty stuff here. Perhaps you're thinking that reading or listening never seemed so difficult or complex before. Perhaps you're longing for those halcyon days thirty or so pages ago when to read or listen meant something simpler and easier. At the same time, you haven't been promised a rose garden when it comes to becoming a writer in the truest sense of the word. So take solace in the following: Anything worth doing well demands dedicated time and effort. And the dedication begins by honing your skills at receiving words. Over time you become an astute reader or listener. Over time you nurture that part of you, the writer part of you, that pays close, careful, and insightful attention to how and why words mean.

What has been laid out thus far should be considered a starting point for writing. Close and careful scrutiny of words and their contexts yields deep meanings, the kind that reach deep inside each of us and the kind that reverberate when they do. They seem fuller, thicker, more developed and perhaps more precise. That's what you're after when you meet words. And the way to achieve that goal is to give due consideration to yourself as a receiver, the writer or speaker as a sender, and the many contexts coloring the meanings of words. Once you do that by way of practice and repetition, you'll be paying homage and dues to the art of writing, and you will be sharpening your own skills as a writer.

Think of it all like this. Imagine how much a gourmet chef, professional carpenter, and baseball player know of the intricacies and subtleties of their chosen craft. With dedication to the craft, one's skill and learning improve. One gets better and better at it. One begins to understand things not understood or perhaps even seen by others. One becomes a connoisseur, a master craftsman, a skilled ballplayer. It never happens overnight. And it only sometimes happens over a lifetime. Still, if you're dedicated, if you commit yourself to its happening, you take plenty of comfort in that fact alone. Even if you never arrive at the top, you will have experienced the journey of the craft. You will have experienced the means, even if you don't achieve the ends. And there are many who would argue that the means are always more important and more valuable than those ends.

## Gusto

End of break time and of musings. Now let's apply what's been discussed to an actual piece of advertising, in this case magazine ad copy for a beer. Without seeing the actual ad and only reading the ad's words and using what we've discussed to this point you should be able to create deep meanings. Here are the words.

> You only go around once in life. So grab for all the gusto
> you can. Even in the beer you drink. Why settle for less?
> When you're out of Schlitz, you're out of beer.

Right away, in knowing that you're reading words from an ad you are able to place them in a number of different contexts, each of which helps you create meaning. On the surface level, for example, you know that someone (the writer or sender) is inducing someone else (the receiver) to believe something. This something has to do with enjoyment of life and, ultimately, Schlitz beer. That's all well and good as surface meaning, but it certainly falls short of what the ad means on a deeper level.

If you're a woman, you probably react to the words differently than if you're a man. After all, there are words in this ad that seem to be more manly than womanly. The word "gusto," for instance. Immediately this should tell you that there is a certain reader the writer had in mind. Who is this reader? Or, in the language of ad writers, who is the target audience or target market? Is it you? Or is it someone else?

If the audience is you, then the words will take on a particular meaning specific to what's important to you. But is it possible that the audience for these words is not you? Again, if you're a woman there's a definite question as to whether the words are meant for you. Even if you're a man, the words might not be meant for you, depending on what type of man you are. Look at the words again.

> You only go around once in life. So grab for all the gusto
> you can. Even in the beer you drink. Why settle for less?
> When you're out of Schlitz, you're out of beer.

Are you an adventurer? A risk-taker? A pleasure-seeker? A macho man? Do you drink beer? If and when you do, do you want that beer to be full, rich, lagered, strong? If so, you might be that audience. If not, you might not be.

Notice the choice of words on the part of the writer. The first word, "You," is personalized, as if it's addressed to a specific individual, in this case you as you read. To "go around once in life" carries with it an attitude or belief in *carpe diem,* in living for today, in letting everything all hang out while pleasure reigns. Or, as a follow-up to the line, you're to "grab for all the gusto you can." Naturally, this includes "the beer you drink." No reason to "settle for less." No reason to settle for less than Schlitz. And remember this, of course, "When you're out of Schlitz, you're out of beer."

Clearly, the writer of the ad had a specific reader or target audience in mind when composing the copy. You can discover who that target audience is if you think like the writer. As with all ads, the writer writes on behalf of the advertiser, in this case Schlitz beer. The purpose of the writing is to bring Schlitz and the audience together, to persuade the audience that there is something about Schlitz that will fill a personal want or need. The writer knows this and strives to make it happen. For that to occur, however, the writer writes with the audience in mind, tapping into that audience's wants, needs, and lifestyle.

Now, what is there about the words that helps you draw a mental picture of the audience? If you go back several paragraphs, you'll notice descriptions such as adventurer, risk-taker, and pleasure-seeker. These are prospective descriptions of the audience, a means for creating a mental picture of that audience. And they are derived from an analysis of the ad's words.

As the copy reads, "You only go around once in life. So grab for all the gusto you can." Do you think you would be reading the same words in an ad targeted toward women? Senior citizens? Or young children? Probably not. The words tell you who the audience is. They are chosen intentionally by the writer to bring the product and audience together. As much as they may be the writer's words, they are also the audience's words. They are the words relevant to that audience. And the writer writes them with the audience front and center in the mind. That's how the writer creates the common ground between advertiser and audience.

Two key words in the first two sentences of the copy are "grab" and "gusto." These are action words, strong words, virile words, vigorous words. They are the words of a particular type of man. Chisel-jawed. Muscular. Angular. A hair-on-the-chest type of man, one who knows what he's about and isn't willing to settle for something less than what he wants. A man with a strong grip on life, especially its adventurous and physical side. A gutsy man. Maybe a sky diver. A rafter on the Amazon. He likes his steak charbroiled. He has occasion to wash with Lava soap. He's that type of man.

We're probably not too far wrong in our description of the target audience for this ad. And it was the words, especially "grab" and "gusto," which gave it away. To *grab* is a strong action similar to clutch or grip. *Gusto* contains the sound of gut. It's a visceral word, a bodily word. A word you're not likely to find in a perfume or lingerie ad. And a word that acts as the core for the creative concept of the ad. Both the product and the audience are united around that word. It drives the ad, giving it verbal power and meaning for product and audience. In many ways it acts as the ad's theme, the "incipient center" of meaning for the ad.

Beyond grab and gusto, however, we meet other words. But notice how they ring true to the grab and gusto kind of feeling. For example, the writer leads the reader from grab and gusto, which can be applied to many things, to beer. This rules out many things except, of course, beer. The writer follows with, "Why settle for less?" This is an especially telling question since the reader has already been showered with complimentary descriptions of his lifestyle. It's almost as if the reader has been urged to respond, "Yes, yes. That's me. A gusto kind of guy." Then, given that he is a gusto kind of guy, he is asked to come up with reasons why he shouldn't prefer gusto in his beer, which, of course, would be against his lifestyle.

Naturally, because of who the targeted reader is he'll prefer gusto, not only in his beer but probably in everything else. Moreover, because of who he is he's not about to settle for anything else. To settle is not in his vocabulary. Not this man. Remember, he knows what he's about. He selects. He doesn't settle. And finally, the last line, "When you're out of Schlitz, you're out of beer," cements the appeal with the mortar of the product name.

We've dissected this brief piece of ad copy, mostly from the point of view of the writer and the prospective or targeted reader. To follow the dissection, you've had to role-play a bit. You've had to become that writer and that reader. For a brief moment you've had to leave your own skin and enter into someone else's. That is precisely what copywriters (and perhaps *all* writers) do, at least on occasion. They leave themselves behind—their values, opinions, attitudes—in favor of someone else, the reader or audience. And in picking up on these frames of reference, you've gained insight into why the words are as they are. You've broadened your view of the meaning, which is exactly the purpose of astute and pointed reading.

No doubt, as we've dissected our way through the words in the Schlitz copy, you have also applied our discussion of contexts in your analysis. Recall, for instance, how the first word of the ad, "You," personalizes the message. It pulls the reader in because of the personalization. But as you move through the rest of the ad copy, notice how each word and sentence builds on what has been said previously.

Because "You only go around once in life" you might as well "grab for all the gusto you can." One sentence necessarily follows the other. It picks up on the notion that life is short, that it's to be lived to its fullest while we're still around to live it. The next line, "Even in the beer you drink," sweeps us to the message center, gusto in beer. It's a transition, leading the reader from a pointed and accurate statement of what's important in his life to an overlay of that importance onto beer. The line following, "Why settle for less?," affirms the reader's lifestyle, especially as it pertains to beer. And the final line, "When you're out of Schlitz, you're out of beer," ties the product to the gusto in the reader's life.

In short, each word and each sentence builds upon the other, giving the copy its deeper meaning, which happens to be tied directly to the reader's life. If you recall, this is what is meant regarding the importance of words around words.

The other contexts, theme, media, time and place, and form of expression also deepen meaning for the reader. For example, we have identified "gusto" as a one-word theme for the ad's copy. It controls the copy, breathing life into it and connecting it to the reader's likes and dislikes as far as his own life is concerned. No wonder, then, that the copy revolves around that word. Its reason for being is announced in the first line where "You only go around once in life." Because you do, then you're to "grab for all the gusto you can." That gusto is transferred to the beer you drink, which should be Schlitz.

Because the copy is in a magazine, the reader is liable to spend some time with it. He's liable to read it since he's accustomed to reading within that medium. That's why the copy is so vital to the ad. And depending on when and where he reads the copy, the meaning will change somewhat. For example, if he's reading the copy at midday, a hot and steamy midday, it may stimulate his desire for a cold beer. Or, if he's feeling particularly gusto-like while swinging in a hammock, it may do the same. The point is that all of the contexts come into play in determining meaning, the same way they did when we examined the Marx and Engels quote. Even the form of expression is important, though you've been cheated a bit in this respect. You haven't read the copy in the context it was meant to be read, as part of an ad, complete with a visual. So, let's look at the complete ad as shown in Figure 2–1.

**FIGURE 2–1**   Advertisement courtesy of The Stroh Brewery Company.
Reprinted with permission of The Stroh Brewery Company,
Detroit, MI.

Notice how the image of the man looking out to the sea confirms all
that we've discussed. He's a strong man, a virile-looking man. He looks like
he has a grip on life. He looks like he's in the middle of life, not on its fringe.
The ruggedness of the ship and the vastness of the sea lend themselves to

his adventurous nature. They become a part of him and the adventurous life. In the eye of life's storm is where you will find this man. He is not about to take shortcuts or to bypass the vigor and adventure of life.

At the same time, in thinking like he would think, let's imagine seeing this ad in a magazine. Perhaps you don't quite look like him. But then again, maybe you want to. Maybe, in some highly personal and private ways, you believe you're like him. There's a similarity there, a kind of kinship or blood brotherhood linking you with him, if even in your dreams or aspirations. Moreover, you like him. You like what he's doing, and you like what he stands for. Now it's simply a matter of transferring that liking to Schlitz beer. You know the man. You like him. And since he apparently drinks Schlitz, then you should, too, especially if you want gusto in your life. In many ways both of you are gusto personified.

By bringing these contexts and expectations to bear as you see and read the ad, you create the ad's deep meaning. You bring it to life in much the same way the writer intended. By putting together all of the aspects of how to receive words, you establish yourself as a writer. This isn't the same as writing, mind you. But it is the same as thinking like a writer, especially an advertising copywriter.

Think of our discussion about contexts, expectations, and the need to read like a writer this way. You need tools to write. They help you do your job. They provide you with frames of reference for writing with intent, with purpose. Considering all of them will help shape your writing decisions from the theme needed all the way to the individual word used to convey the theme and give it power.

Yes, to this point it has been a matter of viewing others and how they write. In a sense, it's like being an observer where you watch and listen to others to discover some tips or clues for how to get good at your craft. From Marx and Engels to an emissary for Schlitz beer, the message is the same. Writers are on top of their craft. They know the ins and outs. So, if you're intent on being a writer, then it's wise to be intent on learning how writing achieves what it does. What are its effects? How do we receive words? How do we react to them in certain ways? And how does the writer manipulate the language to achieve responsive results? That has been the essence of our discussion.

## ✍ WRAP-UP ✍

Here's something to remember. *Who* receives *what* from *whom* and in what *contexts*? This leads to deep meaning. You can be the receiver, the *who*. Chances are, though, that in advertising copy you're not. This means you need to think like whoever is targeted by the ad. To do that you can rely on what the person's expectations are. In other words, what does the person bring to the ad in the way of knowledge and likes and dislikes? This can mean knowledge and likes and dislikes about the product, the words, the medium, or anything else that influences what the reader reads.

When it comes to the words and theme, the *what* of what's written or said, you need to link it to the receiver, the sender, and the contexts. You need to determine why the words are what they are, and, of course, this means you must surround all of the influences on those words.

In respect to the sender, the *whom* in our single-sentence description, you need to try to uncover the intention. What's the purpose of the words from the sender's point of view? What is the sender's intent? Again, you need to immerse yourself in the words and their contexts to discover this part of the meaning.

And finally, the *contexts,* those surrounding influences of the deep meaning, help you to add breadth and depth to the words. As shapers of meaning, they cannot be taken lightly. Often, they are essential tools on the writer's belt. They tell the writer what to be careful of and what can or cannot be done under certain circumstances. Beyond this, they reflect back to the writer's intention and to the reader's expectations. Overall, they exert influence on every aspect of the reading or receiving act.

It all sounds so easy, doesn't it? Yet, as any writer worth his or her salt will tell you, it's not. Not in the least. In fact, we have complicated the situation, haven't we? Before this chapter, writing may have seemed like a simple act. But it isn't. Not if it's done well, that is. It's an act of culmination. It's a product and result of other things, of time and influences and temperament and mind-set.

Being an astute receiver of words is the beginning of the writing act. If you can't get into that, then you should probably challenge any desire you have to be a writer. Because a writer loves words, words are the means by which a writer actualizes the self and the craft. Writers know this. That's why they pay close and careful attention to how words *mean.* They know that it's a matter of interaction—one word bouncing off another and heading straight for a particular reader from the mind of a particular writer, and in the context of a specific theme, medium, time, place, and form of expression—all of this giving *deep meaning* to what's written.

You want to improve your writing skills? Then be a skillful and insightful receiver of words. Skillful and insightful regardless of what you receive, the words of Marx and Engels included.

### ✍ THINGS TO DO ✍

1.   Select a passage from a book, article, or ad. Then read it from different perspectives. First read it as you would ordinarily read it.

Then read it as if you were someone else, presumably the person who would ordinarily be on the receiving end of the passage. Finally, read it as if you were someone who would totally disagree with the passage. Jot down your perspectives from each reading.

2.   Select one copy line from an ad you admire. Write down the surface meaning of the line. Then write down what you believe to be the deep meaning. Describe that deep meaning according to you as a receiver, the copywriter's intention, and the contexts around the line.

3.   Take a piece of your own copy, something you've written before reading this chapter. Pick out an important word in the copy. Jot down how that word's meaning is shaped by the contexts, including the words around it.

4.   Practice the "one-word theory" of ad copy. Assume that each ad has one word acting as its core theme or the "incipient center of gravity" for the ad. Select two or three ads where this is true. In one word each, identify the theme or center of those ads. Then select an ad in which the theme or center is absent. Compare the differences between the two types of ads.

5.   Take the copy for a magazine ad and imagine it as a radio or television script. Does it work? Why or why not? Imagine it as part of a script for a play or movie. Does it work? Why or why not?

6.   Select ad copy that you admire and describe what the audience looks like. Remember, this audience is one person, a typical member of a target audience. Then describe what that person's life may be like day to day. Finally, describe the copywriter. Is it a man or a woman? Young or old? And what can you imagine about the lifestyle of that writer?

# Chapter 3

# Good
# Writers
# Can See

In the words of the famous American architect Louis Sullivan,

> You cannot express unless you have a system of
> expression; and you cannot have a system of
> expression unless you have a prior system of thinking
> and feeling; and you cannot have a system of thinking
> and feeling unless you have a basic system of living.

Sullivan's words are at the root of our first three chapters. In a large sense the three chapters suggest methods for actualizing a writing lifestyle, a frame of mind, and coordinated methods or habits for serving the writing master and eventually earning the title of writer.

If you look inside Sullivan's words you'll see a theory of creative expression, writing or otherwise. It's a theory based on a hierarchy beginning at the bottom with a mode of living, and ending at the top with the writing act. Bridging the gap between the two are the acts of thinking and feeling. But notice how those acts follow on the heels of a mode of living or a lifestyle. One necessarily precedes the others. Or, as the German philosopher Schopenhauer said regarding reasoning, "It can give only after it has received."

In developing the ability to read or listen to words as we practiced in Chapter 2, you're beginning to flesh out that lifestyle. It's as if you should expect yourself never again to live in the world of words quite the same way. Since words represent a great deal of your life's involvement, your changed view of them, your reactions and the like, should alter your life in some way. In addition to reading or listening, however, there is another habit or lifestyle you need to get into. It involves seeing. It's the habit of being a good viewer, of being able to understand and derive surface and deep meaning from what you see.

The act of seeing, like the act of reading, is critical to understanding what it means and what it will take to be a good writer. Think about it. Many times what else are words but builders of images? Think back, for example, to our discussion of the word "romance" in Chapter 2. There we discussed how individuals conceived of different meanings for the word. And if you recall, those meanings were rooted in visual images.

Of course, much has been written about how writers as creative people think in images. In fact, many great ideas (those "things" that copywriters are responsible for creating) begin with images. The invention of pyramids, rockets, poems, novels, and, of course, many ads typically began with images.

Beyond the importance of images to words themselves or to the generation of "big ideas," we also have the pervasive and mammoth importance of images to successful advertising, even if that advertising contains words. For example, the so-called big idea in advertising is one that creates an appealing and overriding sense of unity between the words and the images. Or, if there are no images per se in an ad and it relies strictly on words to convey its message, what are we to make of how the words are shown, the typography? Obviously, use of typeface and size are themselves visual matters suggesting meaning. The point of all this discussion, then, is to impress upon you the importance of images to the art of writing, let alone to the art of creating successful advertising.

What needs to be understood in this respect, however, is that you don't have to be an artist to be visually literate. You don't even have to be an artist to deepen your understanding of how a viewer creates meaning through visual images. At the same time, however, you should be visually literate. And you should embed such literacy into your lifestyle, which means you should be conscious of the ways meaning gets created through visual images. Not to fret though. You'll find that it's not too unlike the way meaning gets created with words.

## ✍ MEANINGS IN IMAGES ✍

If you recall from Chapter 2 we divided meanings in words into two general kinds, surface and deep. On the surface level, meaning consisted of more denotative or "dictionary-type" definitions of terms. On the deep level, however, meaning changed to include the kind of reverberative effects experienced when we begin to look between or behind the words. Recall, for example, the job of the astute reader to discover the writer, especially the writer's intention. Or, recall how meaning might expand and deepen once we consider our own personal reactions to words, reactions based on who we are or choose to be. Once that happens we move to a new level, the deep level of meaning.

In respect to visual images the same type of phenomenon exists. In many ways we receive those images using much the same abilities we use when we receive words. In fact, the characteristics of words themselves, words as verbs, nouns, plurals, and singulars (recall again Chapter 2), are not unlike the characteristics of visual images. To a fairly large extent, however, the names of the visual characteristics do change, although the end result is often the same. What we need to do, then, is to walk through the terminology as it applies to those characteristics or traits common to visual images.

## VISUAL ELEMENTS

Assume you have a blank page in front of you. That is your ground. Assume you touch a pen to the page. That is a dot and your first figure. Then you move the pen along the page and you have a line, a new figure. Once you turn left or right with the pen you begin to have a shape. Close the line, and the shape is completed, a newer figure yet. From here you may add other dots, lines, shapes, and perhaps even color, all of which exist as figures on your ground. Though we won't put pen to paper in photography, the same rules apply.

This certainly sounds simple enough, but how does it relate to meaning? The answer is it relates to meaning in much the same way one word and then other surrounding words relate to meaning. On one level you have a surface meaning, that "dictionary-type" meaning which suggests little about the deep meaning. For example, look at the image in Figure 3–1 and try to determine what it means in respect to surface meaning.

Of course, we all recognize the image as the backside of our dollar bill. Very familiar. With us much of the time, even in our sleep on occasion. Not a day passes by that we don't touch one. But of importance to us here are the visual images on this backside of the bill, images that we probably haven't paid much attention to over time.

### Frame

On the surface level, notice in Figure 3–1 that the various images are framed by a white border and then, within the green ground, the images are framed again by the number and word "one" repeated four

FIGURE 3–1    The back of the United States of America dollar bill (not legal tender).

times in each corner. On the top horizontal plane the United States of America is identified. On the bottom horizontal plane the bill itself is identified. In both instances, the words help to complete the frame.

The importance of a frame for deriving meaning from visual images cannot be undervalued. The frame draws the eye into the visual images. It fixes the eye on whatever the artist, designer, or photographer wants to be seen. As famed art theorist Rudolf Arnheim observed, a frame "defines [the] reality status of a work of art." It also "implies that the matter seen in a picture is not to be taken as a part of the world's inventory but as a carrier of symbolic meaning."

In the case of our dollar bill, the eye is fixed on those images within the frame, primarily on the large, shadowed "One" and the familiar motto "In God We Trust." But notice how the images flanking that large "One" and the motto create a sense of compositional balance to the bill.

On the left side of the bill we see the images of a pyramid and eye, the Great Seal of the United States. These images are framed by a circle outlined with graphic flourishes. Within the circle we see other frames with the Latin expressions *Annuit Coeptis* on the top and *Novus Ordo Seclorum* on the bottom. On the right side of the bill we see an identical circular frame and flourishes for the dominant image of the eagle. The number of original American colonies is represented by the thirteen stars in the circle above the eagle's head as well as the thirteen leaves on the olive branch in one claw and the thirteen arrows in the other claw. A representation of the American flag on a shield completes the image.

All of this discussion and description centers on the denotative or surface meaning of the various images on the backside of our dollar bill. In fact, a translation of the Latin phrases is also denotative. From the left side of the bill, the phrase *Annuit Coeptis* means "He

[God] favored the beginning." The phrase *Novus Ordo Seclorum* refers to Virgil's prophecy of return to a Golden Age. From the right side of the bill, the phrase *E Pluribus Unum* means "from many comes one." This translation of the phrases completes the surface meaning of the images on the dollar bill. But as we know, all of the foregoing discussion does little to provide us with the deep meaning of the images we see. And as we also know, it is the deep meaning that concerns us the most, for it is here that we discover the power behind messages, whether visual or verbal.

### Lines and Shapes

Because visual images contain lines and shapes, it stands to reason that surface meaning can be derived from those lines and shapes. For example, in the case of our dollar bill, we can describe the surface meaning of the various lines expressed as simply a governing horizontal line format containing sweeping or circular diversions and contrasts with that format. We also have the verticality of line as seen in the pyramid and uprightness of the eagle and flag. Regarding shape, we see the circular frames for the two dominant images. Again, all of this is surface meaning. But what, by way of interpretation, do these lines and shapes mean on a deeper level?

Understand that lines, like words, suggest meanings apart from the fact that the lines are horizontal, vertical, or diagonal. For example, a horizontal line suggests rest or peacefulness. A vertical line suggests formality and dignity. A diagonal line suggests action. Of course, the validity of such generalizations depends to a large extent on the context of those lines, the environments in which they're seen, and how they play off of other lines or images. But the general rule of thumb is that horizontal, vertical, and diagonal lines suggest those deeper meanings.

With our dollar bill we have all of the lines represented and thus a hybrid of meaning. But notice how the lines in the three separate images of Figure 3–2 suggest the meanings we discussed. In the first image the dominant horizontal lines are at rest, suggesting tranquility

**FIGURE 3–2**   **Lines and Directions Suggest Meanings: Horizontal lines suggest rest and tranquility. Vertical lines suggest dignity and formality. Diagonal lines suggest action and excitement. Art by Brad Grier, Lebanon, PA. Reprinted by permission of Brad Grier.**

 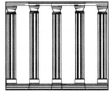 

and peace. In the second image the dominant vertical lines suggest formality and dignity. In the third image the dominant diagonal lines suggest action and excitement.

In much the same way that lines suggest deeper meanings, shapes also suggest deeper meanings. For example, a circle suggests harmony and unity. A triangle suggests strength and will. And a square suggests dullness. Think, for example, of all the symbolic, deeper meanings of such common expressions as a family circle or a circle of friends.

Similarly, notice how often you see a triangle or an abstraction of a triangle as a logo design for companies intent on conveying their strength and solidity. Or, consider the possibilities of a triangle as symbolically suggesting strength. In this respect we have such familiar threesomes as mother, father, and child, or Father, Son, and Holy Ghost. Even on an architectural or structural level the triangle has always been one of the strongest shapes in the universe. For instance, try as we may, we have difficulty crushing a triangle. In fact, the famous geodesic dome in Houston (the Astrodome) is constructed and gains its strength from triangles.

In reference to a square, think of the connotations attached to that word and image. To be square, for instance, is to be out of it or uncool. In addition, variations of these shapes—ovals, diamonds, etc.—would suggest similar meanings, at least to varying degrees.

## Colors

As with lines and shapes, colors also suggest meaning. To name a color or to give it a surface meaning is one thing. But to interpret what that color may mean on a deeper level is quite another. Consider, for instance, the colors of the American flag. Denotatively they are red, white, and blue. But as aesthetic theoretician Monroe Beardsley suggests, those colors also convey deep meanings. For example, as a color symbol for blood, red can mean the devotion and sacrifice of our forefathers. White can mean the purity of our country. And blue can mean the "overarching justice of the sky."

Of course, Beardsley's interpretation of the colors in the American flag is very subjective. But certainly that interpretation can be judged reasonable given the events of American history and the generalizations we can apply to the American people and our country at large. The point, though, is that colors, like lines and shapes, mean something. Red typically means action. It is an impassioned color. White typically means purity. Consider the traditional whiteness of the wedding dress, for example. Blue, the color of aristocracy, typically means authority and rightness. And if we revert back to our dollar bill, think of all the meanings associated with the color green.

## The Represented Image

Once you put together lines, shapes, and colors, you create an image. This image can be a representation or an abstraction of a particular reality. In current visual communication theory, terms such as sign, icon, index, and symbol have been used to dissect visual images and explain how they convey meaning. Without laboring over the complexities of these terms, bear in mind that visual images represent signs.

If images are iconic signs, there is a great deal of resemblance between the images and the realities they are supposed to depict. Realistic photographs, for instance, would fit in well here. With realistic photographs we have a closeness of resemblance between what is produced and what served as the images for the production.

If images are indexical signs, there is more of a cause-and-effect relationship between what we see and what served as the images for the production. For example, an image of smoke coming from a house suggests a fire. In this respect there is a logical, causal connection between one image and the other.

If images are symbolic signs, there is an association made by the viewer, one that might not necessarily be a matter of cause and effect. For example, an image of a cross suggests all sorts of associations such as Christianity, sacrifice, brotherhood, sin, and punishment. In this regard a cross stands as a symbol for something else, usually something abstract and more ideological than real and physical.

It is often difficult at times to distinguish the differences in deep meaning based on the actual images or the viewer's perception of the images. Where does one end and the other begin? But as we will see further on and similar to our discussion of words in Chapter 2, deep meaning is often a combination of both.

For now, understand that once lines, shapes, and colors are put together, images result. These images can be close to or far from their representations in reality. These images also carry with them certain conventional meanings that weigh upon the viewer's mind as it thinks about what the images mean. Many of these meanings are products of established codes developed over time, such as those meanings of association that we noted as symbolic meanings for a cross. In effect, images as representations of certain realities can be viewed as resemblances, as suggestions of cause and effect, and as symbols of something other than what they are in everyday reality. Bear in mind, too, that this does not mean one of these alternatives necessarily rules out the others.

## Symbols

As we've just discussed, symbols play a large part in conveying or deriving meaning from images. If we think of symbolism as a kind of universal reality that exists with just about anything we see, we could even argue that any image, regardless of whether it's a mere resemblance of an object or not, carries with it symbolic meanings that expand and deepen beyond a denotative or surface meaning. If symbolism refers to something standing for something else, usually an abstract concept, idea, or belief, then whatever we see has the potential for taking on deep meaning.

We're now beginning to enter into the importance that both viewer and artist have to meaning when we discuss how symbolism expands and deepens meaning. A little later we will delve more completely into that importance.

At this point consider the possibility that all images may be symbols of something other than what those images suggest as everyday representations of certain realities. Again, refer back to the cross as a symbol for a number of abstract concepts such as sacrifice or righteousness. Or, if I asked you to call up the facial image of one you loved dearly, could you ascribe to it deep, symbolic meaning? Similarly, could the book you're now holding actually be a symbol of meaning beyond the ordinary fact and reality that it is a book with certain obvious characteristics such as size and weight?

Consider, too, the backside of our dollar bill. For instance, can the images of the eye and pyramid symbolize, as Beardsley points out, "the material strength and duration and the spiritual welfare that is above the material." And can the thirteen olive leaves and arrows symbolize America's power in peace and war? Or is it conceivable, as noted art theorist E.H. Gombrich suggests, that the eye and pyramid can express "the hopes and aspirations of the New World for the dawn of a new era."

The main point of such theorizing is to suggest the very real possibility that images, regardless of what they represent, convey meaning beyond their depictions or abstractions of certain realities. And this, precisely, is what entry into deep meaning is all about.

## VISUAL COMPOSITION

To appreciate fully how the integration of visual elements leads to meaning requires an understanding of the principles underlying visual composition. As with words, graphic elements such as lines, shapes, and colors combine to act upon one another and create what is often referred to as the *gestalt* of visual meaning. That gestalt, or wholeness of meaning, depends on how the visual elements are composed so as to move or direct the eye to key images, thus generating attention or focus on those images. This attention or focus then dictates the stimuli for meaning.

Think of composition as arrangement. Just like we arrange our living room furniture to create certain effects and accommodate specific needs, so an artist or photographer arranges the visual elements in such a way as to meet his or her requirements for those effects and needs. How those elements relate and fit together in a context, either by placement or size, determines to a large extent what will be conveyed by way of meaning for the viewer.

Much, of course, has been theorized about the basic principles of visual composition. But for our purposes, their essence can be summarized in four terms: balance, emphasis, sequence, and unity.

### Balance

Quite simply, *balance* is the symmetrical or asymmetrical placement of optical weights (mass, shape, etc.) within the field of vision. For example, the visual composition of our dollar bill is very balanced or very symmetrical since the weight of the elements to the left of center approximate the weight of the elements to the right of center.

Now, if you go back to our discussion of how a vertical line tends to suggest formality and dignity, and a horizontal line tends to suggest rest and tranquility, you can see how a balanced picture or photograph may also suggest those meanings, depending upon whether the dominant weight of the entire composition is upright or flat. To achieve balance the artist or photographer can also manipulate such elements as color, shape, or texture.

### Emphasis

The principle of *emphasis* centers on techniques used for highlighting what dominates the eye's attention and focus. Again, just like a living room arrangement, a certain piece of furniture can be positioned to attract considerably more attention than other pieces of furniture. The same is true with any visual field. Inevitably there are highlights, those images that stand out and demand attention.

Emphasis can be achieved by use of techniques such as contrast, direction, proportion, and placement. For example, if an artist wants a chair to stand out, then to show it in contrast to nothing around it or in contrast to anything but a chair would help to emphasize it. Similarly, if an artist wants black to look extremely black, then to juxtapose it with white would again help the emphasis.

With direction, the artist arranges elements in such a way that they point or lead the eye to that image to be emphasized.

With proportion, the artist creates a relationship in size of one visual element compared to another. Here, the familiar golden rule of trying not to divide the visual field into halves applies. Typically, it's better to divide the visual field into fifths so that an unequal distribution of weights allows the eye to focus on whatever images are most important.

And with placement, the artist selects where to place the images in relationship to one another so that those most important stand out.

Naturally, each of these techniques influences the other to an extent. For example, direction can be achieved by placement of images. Or, contrast can be achieved by an unequal distribution of weights such as that noted in the description for proportion. Still, to be aware of such techniques allows you to understand better what you see, how it came to be, and the dynamics at work in conveying meaning.

## Sequence

*Sequence* refers to the eye-flow through a visual field. Typically, the eye begins at the upper left of a contained picture or photograph and moves sequentially through the images to the lower right. What results is a reverse **S** or **Z** pattern of eye movement. Clearly, however, an artist has the power to completely alter that typical eye-flow simply by adding a color, changing a shape or size, or realigning the weights of the visual elements. Still, our tendency is to start at the top left and work our way down in much the same way we're patterned to read left to right and top to bottom.

## Unity

The principle of *unity* refers back to the gestalt of meaning mentioned earlier. It is a principle dependent on the gestalt theory of the "law of grouping." Here, a wholeness or completeness of the visual composition sweeps together in the mind of the viewer. Much of this is due to the continuity, proximity, or repetition shown in the composition. The continuity, proximity, or repetition depends on the interrelationship of all the visual elements including the lines, shapes, colors, or the texture and tone that result from such techniques as lighting. In effect, the composition becomes unified in the mind of the viewer, many times because the variety of elements lose their separateness and appear to belong to the composition as a whole. All of the elements, then, bend to this dominant wholeness. And this, too, is a fundamental precept of Gestalt psychology.

Naturally it's one thing for us to articulate the various terms and concepts vital to understanding visual composition, but it's quite another matter to see something and understand how those terms and concepts work in what we see. In this respect the following four figures in Figure 3–3 a–d highlight the concepts of balance, emphasis, sequence, and unity.

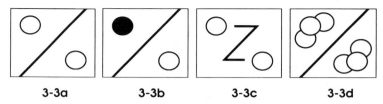

3-3a          3-3b          3-3c          3-3d

FIGURE 3–3    Principles of Composition: Figure 3–3a conveys a sense of bal-
              ance. Figure 3–3b creates emphasis through the blackened
              dot. Figure 3–3c reflects sequence or eye flow, with the eye
              zigzagging through the elements. Figure 3–3d creates unity by
              grouping the elements together. Art by Brad Grier, Lebanon,
              PA. Reprinted by permission of Brad Grier.

## ✍ APPLYING OUR UNDERSTANDING ✍ TO WHAT WE SEE

To follow this thread of how the visual elements and principles of visual
composition help convey meaning, let's consider the reproduction of a
famous American painting as shown in Figure 3–4. The painting, titled
*Baptism in Kansas,* was created by John Steuart Curry in 1928.

On the surface level this painting represents a ritual of baptism,
presumably in a midwestern town. Many people are represented in the
painting, mostly spectators. Chief among the people, however, are the
preacher and woman in the tub of water. They are the baptismal ini-
tiator and initiated, respectively. We can generate certain surface
meanings about the environment in which the baptism is taking place,
namely that it's a flat, plain-like rural area.

But if we also follow our assumption that visual elements and
principles of composition help us to understand better what we see,
what can we derive as meaning based upon how these elements and
principles interact in the painting? For example, do you gain a feeling
of restfulness more than excitement from the painting? In trying to
determine what the most important images are, would you opt for
members of the crowd or for the preacher and woman? No doubt, you
have probably made judgments about these and other issues or questions that may have popped into your mind. What's important is to dissect the images in the painting to understand how these judgments or
assessments came to be.

In regard to line and shape, for example, notice how most of the
images taken in total suggest a restful flatness of line and a harmo-
nious completion of a circle. The sense of restfulness evolves from such
images as the horizon, the similar heights of the spectators, and the flat
and spacious stretch of land.

At the same time, the juxtaposition of vertical lines such as that
conveyed by the windmill, or the fact that the preacher and woman are

FIGURE 3-4   John Steuart Curry. *Baptism in Kansas.* 1928. oil on canvas. 40 ×
50 inches. (101.6cm × 127cm). Collection of Whitney Museum
of American Art. Gift of Gertrude Vanderbilt Whitney 31.159.
Reprinted with permission of the Whitney Museum of American
Art, New York, NY.

higher than the spectators, suggests a certain formality and dignity in
the scene. Notice, too, how the windmill with its diagonal vane points
both up to the sky or heavens and down to the preacher, perhaps acting
as a conduit or vital link among the man, his act, and the holy transfer-
ence of that act to and from the heavens. So what we have, simply by
way of line and shape is the peacefulness of the people and setting juxtaposed and contrasted with the formality, dignity, and perhaps higher
authority attached to a supreme being or power.

In reference to the representation of images and their symbolism,
notice how the images are iconic or closely related to what we can
ascribe to reality. The barn looks like a barn. The cars look like cars of
that period. And the people, dressed as they are, look like people of
that period as well. But as we discussed earlier, such surface meanings
of the images stop short of giving the painting its just due when it
comes to what it can mean. With the people, for instance, notice the

supplicating gesture of the woman about to be baptized. Notice the firmness of the preacher's hold on her. Notice the many downturned heads of the spectators. Finally, notice that many of those spectators are singing or praying. Presumably a hymn or prayer book in one man's hand suggests song or prayer. And rap music it is not.

Taken together as an integrated whole of all of the people in the painting, there appears to be an unmistakable suggestion of reverence for a higher order. And when you consider the graphic link of the wind-mill and vane to the preacher and sky, and the graphic portrayal of that preacher in the middle of the spectators, there is also an unmistakable suggestion of the oneness of this cluster of humanity as it exists in this part of the country and with God. What we receive as viewers is a somber and stark impression of the setting and its people, particularly as they interact around the hub of the baptismal scene.

If we go even further and step into the principles of visual compo-sition, we can see how these possible meanings reveal themselves through the painting. For example, the meaning of dignity and formali-ty is conveyed by the dominance of balanced symmetry in the arrange-ment of images. The preacher and woman approximate the middle of the painting in the same way they approximate the middle of the crowd. The link of humanity to the heavens is also approximated by the divi-sion of land and sky.

With the principle of emphasis, we can see how various focal points exist. Clearly, for example, the contrast of the windmill with the lighter sky, combined with the windmill's ability to attach itself to the land while still relying on the sky for its function, serves to highlight the windmill, perhaps emphasizing its importance even more than if it were not contrasted and linked in such a way. At the same time, the preacher and woman are emphasized by having all bodies turned toward them. Notice, also, that they are emphasized through their physical isolation and separateness from the throng.

By emphasizing the preacher and woman, the artist reshapes the standard eye-flow pattern of the reverse **S** or **Z** and thus alters the sequence of viewing. As we discussed, sequence refers to eye movement through the images. Normally we start at the upper left and work our way in a zigzagging fashion to the lower right. In the painting, however, the emphatic dominance of the preacher and woman forces our eye toward the painting's center.

It's also possible that our eye initially fixes on the windmill because of its contrast with the dominance of horizontal lines and the sky. But even if that were the case, our eye would still be forced down-ward to the preacher and woman. In this instance, the lines of the windmill and the pointing of the birds and vane stimulate that down-ward eye movement. Overall, it seems clear that the repetition of lines and circular shapes, combined with their enclosure and pointing toward the painting's center, directs our most focused attention on the baptismal scene itself.

The result of effective use of balance, emphasis, and sequence can be seen in the painting's unity, arguably the lifeblood of visual composition. With unity all visual elements sweep together into a discernible, dominant, and dynamic whole that becomes both the receptacle and provider of meaning. In our painting, wholeness and not separateness dominates, again by nature of line, shapes, and their weights. For example, the repetition of concentric circles, beginning with the tub and working outward to the roofs of cars above the heads of the people, provides a singularity of effect. We see and thus react to the sense of wholeness, containment, and harmony.

In addition, the proximity of individual people to one another and of nonhuman elements such as the base of the windmill to the cluster of people also serves to unite all of the elements together. Further, the juxtaposition and mingling of lights and darks, and the continuation of lines and shapes, create a sense in the viewer that everything in the painting belongs there. Remove something and you endanger the entire painting. That, in itself, is a valid and major test of unity in any art form, writing included.

What we have done with the Curry painting is to dissect the main elements of visual language and the principles of composition. We took the painting apart piece by piece. But our purpose was not to cut away the pieces simply for the sake of cutting. Rather, our purpose was to cut for the sake of understanding how meaning evolves through the visual language and composition. And to this end, notice how the individual pieces contribute to the whole. As viewers of the painting we should experience an inward spiraling of understanding where everything sweeps to the center of a dominant and singleminded meaning. Surely that meaning may be ours and it may vary to an extent from individual to individual, but given how the pieces contribute to the whole, the prospect for variation seems limited.

This same inward spiraling of understanding can be experienced with another painting shown in Figure 3–5. The painting, *Christina's World,* by Andrew Wyeth, uses iconic images, those resembling reality. We see a young woman leaning on her palsied arm and apparently staring at the buildings on the horizon. As you study the painting, however, dissect it in terms of its visual language and principles of composition. Notice, for instance, how the arc of mowed field and the wheel ruts lead the viewer's eye to the house in the upper right.

Since positioning of images helps determine eye flow, notice how the artist had positioned the young woman in such a way as to lead your eye toward the house and barn. We see the line of her palsied arm

FIGURE 3–5   Andrew Wyeth. *Christina's World.* (1948). Tempera on gessoed plane,
32¼ × 47¾". Collection, The Museum of Modern Art, New York, NY.
Purchase. Reprinted with permission of The Museum of Modern Art.

leading to her shoulder and head, then ultimately carried through with
an implicit line to the house and barn. Indeed, with her head turned,
she appears to be looking in that direction. Also, notice the artist's use
of balance and imbalance to create focal points through contrast. Here,
the woman lies directly below the barn and slightly to the left of the
painting's horizontal center. At the same time, her contrasted position
below and to the left of the house sets her apart. And isn't it the woman
who draws our eye first in the painting? Her white dress contrasts with
the darker field. Her dark hair contrasts with both her dress and the
field, making her the focal point. Yet given her line of view toward the
house, we cannot stay fixed for long on her image. Instead, we experience our eyes moving toward the house and barn.

   Now, coming off of the Curry painting with its abiding sense of
communal reverence and awe, we see in the Wyeth paining the stark
contrast of isolation, perhaps with a hint of yearning or despair. In the
Curry painting the mixture of elements disallows despair as a possible
deep meaning. But in this Wyeth painting the mixture of elements
encourages it. Seen alone in a sweeping vastness of field and sky,
braced on her palsied arm, and faceless to the viewer, the young woman
strikes at the viewer's imagination and empathy, stimulating quite different responses than those experienced with the Curry painting.

In looking closely at both the Curry and Wyeth paintings, we see the impact of lines, shapes and positioning of visual elements on meaning. For example, the repeated circles in the Curry painting convey a sense of harmony and oneness. But, the governing triangular shape in the Wyeth painting (from barn to house to woman to barn) conveys a different sense, one a bit colder and sterile perhaps. Still, for each painting the artist's facility with design and palette directs our individual interpretations. Keeping ourselves open, we merge with the paintings, carrying ourselves into the images while at the same time being directed by the artistic decisions controlling those images.

## Meaning from the Viewer

As implied in our discussion of the Curry and Wyeth paintings, much of the meaning we derive from images is dependent on ourselves. Recall our discussion from Chapter 2 when we read passages and interpreted them from the point of view of us as readers. As with the importance of the reader in gaining meaning from words, the same holds true for the viewer in gaining meaning from images. Naturally, this doesn't mean that we control the entire process as we weave our way to meaning. In many instances we are controlled by precisely what we have discussed in the preceding pages, the artist's manipulation of the elements of visual language and the principles of visual composition. Even still, however, if we assume that visual images, like words, have meaning, then we cannot discount the contribution of the viewer to the meaning.

To understand how we contribute to meaning we need to know who and what we are. Such understanding of ourselves helps us isolate the expectations or predispositions we carry into our visual experience. In fact, one could argue that the very appeal of art relies on some degree of expectation on our part, an expectation that connects us with the images in a meaningful way. In essence, a correspondence takes place between the form and content of the art and us as viewers. The success of that correspondence depends on how effectively the form and content join with what we bring to the art. And what we bring includes our expectations or predispositions. As with Chapter 2, these expectations may be formed from our knowledge or likes and dislikes.

In art criticism and aesthetic theory the relative importance or priority of expectations has been bandied about since Plato. Some more contemporary theorists such as E. H. Gombrich, for instance, believe it is the "power of expectation rather than the power of conceptual knowledge that molds what we see in life no less than in art." In short, we see what we expect to see, given our backgrounds and the context in which we are seeing something. In effect, we do our own meaningful reading into the shapes we see, such as what all of us have experienced when we look at the amorphous shapes of clouds. This is what Gombrich means when he refers to "the beholder's share" in providing meaning to what is seen. As viewers we invariably test the images for meaning based on our predispositions, our expectations, all of which take root in our own knowledge and likes and dislikes.

As we discussed the two paintings by Curry and Wyeth, we often crossed the line from the supposed and apparent meaning in the work of art to the projected meaning from the viewer. No doubt, such a line is easy to cross, so easy, in fact, that it's often difficult to tell where one line begins and the other ends. If we are receptive viewers, then we merge with the images we see. If the images are compiled and composed in such a way as to make it easy for us to merge, then our entrance into them is quick and sure. But if that compilation or composition confounds us, then we may resist. And surely, that resistance may well be linked to the kind of expectations we bring to the work of art.

As you picture the two paintings in your mind, try to recall what you brought to each when you first saw them. For example, did you bring to them a knowledge of visual language and composition that influenced your reading of them? Did you see the paintings the same way as you might have seen them if you hadn't been exposed in the first part of the chapter to the elements of visual language and the principles of visual composition? Did you, in fact, see the Wyeth painting any differently since you were exposed to them after our discussion of the Curry painting?

The hopeful hint in all of these questions is that you brought to the paintings certain knowledge gleaned from the earlier part of the chapter. Perhaps this knowledge shaped your interpretation of the meanings in the paintings. Perhaps it made the paintings larger, richer, fuller, and thicker in terms of what they meant and how the meanings evolved. Yet, even given this recent knowledge, which may have predisposed you to "seeing" certain meanings in the paintings, you probably brought your own personality and expectations, your own "self," to bear in the initial viewing of the art. For example, imagine how much more poignant and meaningful the Curry painting of the baptism might be for someone who has experienced life in that part of the world at that point in time as compared with someone who hasn't.

Now, as you identify your own personality and expectations, your "self," can you understand how that self helped or hindered your meaningful viewing of the painting? Or, with the Wyeth painting, can you imagine how much richer and fuller the meaning is for someone with a palsied arm than it is for someone who has no such trait?

What all of this implies is that the broader our experience and knowledge, the more we bring to the richness and fullness of meaning in what we see. Taken a step further, the broader our experience and knowledge, the more we have to draw upon when we sit down to create and write. But if by chance we lack the breadth of experience and knowledge, we are still able to rely on our ability to empathize in order to create that richness and fullness. In a sense, when we empathize we "surrender" ourselves to the work of art. We "step out of and beyond" ourselves, experiencing an "in-feeling" with the images.

Certainly all of us have experienced this phenomenon of being one with the art, of being involved, perhaps to the point of losing ourselves. It happens to us with characters in films or novels. We end up losing ourselves in the emotions, plights, or situations of others. The same holds true if we enter a work of art and then absorb it into ourselves.

To experience firsthand the richness and fullness of meaning based on how we contribute to it, let's look at a familiar image. It's shown in Figure 3–6.

We have commented extensively on the elements of visual language and the principles of visual composition. But as you did with the two paintings, can you identify what you bring to this image as the potential for meaning? If, for example, your goal is to accrue as much of the dollar bill as possible during your lifetime, then did that fact shape what the image meant to you? And did our initial discussion about the symbols of pyramid, eye, eagle, leaves, and arrows alter that initial predisposition toward meaning? Answers to such questions go a long way toward improving your visual literacy.

### Meaning from the Artist

As with the senders of words, the senders of images, the artists, have intentions. These intentions may be private or public. If private they are more personal, more self-involved, more focused on giving

FIGURE 3–6   The back of the United States of America dollar bill (not legal tender).

meaning to the artist. In some ways they may be therapeutic, almost as if they are salves for the emotional or psychological wounds the artist suffers. If public, however, they are societal, perhaps to effect a change or to communicate a message of some sort.

What's important here, as it is when revealing the meaning in the sender of words, is to recognize that the artist constructs the art in a certain way. As with writers or speakers, the artist always works within the realm of possibilities, given the tools at his or her disposal. The artist can shape, color, or position the elements however he or she wants, depending of course on what the artist expects the total composition to achieve.

The observant, skillful viewer knows that there is purpose and intent to the composition and how the various elements are arranged. The viewer knows that the artist, like the writer, must make decisions about what to include as well as what to exclude. Though some theoreticians and artists argue that these decisions are often unconscious, stemming from some unknown, mysterious, and soulful artistic sensitivity and insight, no doubt conscious decisions are made as well. And they rely on the artist's vision and handling of his or her tools to create certain effects or stimulate certain meanings in the viewer's mind.

Recall, for instance, our discussion of the Curry painting *Baptism in Kansas*. In that painting all of the lines and shapes seem to have a purpose, that of creating a meaning within the bounds of religious reverence and awe. But it is the artist who manages to convey such a meaning by thoughtful arrangement of the elements. Once we dissect those elements and then assemble them meaningfully in the greater whole of the painting overall, we are able to "see" beyond what they mean to us and into what the artist intended.

When it comes to advertising art versus fine art, the intentions of the artist become more visible, clearer, and more oriented toward the public. After all, advertising is a public form of expression. It is anything but private and personal, at least in respect to the advertising writer and artist. When advertising is completed, it must communicate something salient about the product, something that will link the product with the needs or wants of the target audience. In combination with words, the art must help achieve this effect. With that in mind, let's look again at the Schlitz beer ad (this time in Figure 3–7) and then discuss the possibilities of the artist's intention.

In Chapter 2 we managed to wring dry the writer's intentions in using words such as "grab" or "gusto" in the ad. But what can we make of the images while using the same kind of argument we applied to the words? For example, like the words, the images need to be in perfect and precise line with the product. Not only that, the images need to be in perfect and precise line with the words and vice-versa. Put another

You only go around once in life.
So grab for all the gusto you can.
Even in the beer you drink.
Why settle for less?

When you're out of Schlitz,
you're out of beer.

© 1970 Jos. Schlitz Brewing Co., Milwaukee and other cities.

FIGURE 3–7    Advertisement courtesy of The Stroh Brewery Company.
Reprinted with permission of The Stroh Brewery Company,
Detroit, MI.

way, there needs to be a unity of purpose that sweeps the words and
images to a single, dominant center, often called a theme, that "incipient center" of meaning. In Chapter 2 we identified the theme by one
word, "gusto." Gusto in the product and gusto in the target audience.

Look at the man in the ad. You see a man of gusto. Vigorous. Rugged. Alive. You see a man with leathered skin. A chiseled, angular face. And he's dressed in a rugged jacket with the color and texture of the wilderness. In short, everything about him shouts "Gusto," even the lively expression on his face, complete with his strong, white teeth.

Imagine being the artist having to decide who the man in the ad would be. Imagine looking through photographs of male models to make your decision. And imagine that you have an image in mind prior to that decision. The image might not be completely fleshed out. Maybe you don't know exactly what the man will look like. But you have a pretty good idea of what his looks should suggest. Then you match your intention for the purpose of the ad with each of those photographs.

Beyond selecting the man to convey the theme of "gusto," the artist then must arrange the elements in the ad. Naturally the elements are arranged purposefully, with intent. Here, the intent is to link the product with the target audience, particularly the product's primary benefit for that audience, that of "gusto." That's what the product will mean for the audience. That's what the audience will get from the product. And as we discussed in Chapter 2, everything will bend to that benefit or theme.

Notice in the arrangement or composition of elements how the artist positions the Schlitz can. The hands holding it extend beyond the ship. The can breaks the plane of water and sky. In effect, it is emphasized because of its contrasted position relative to the other elements in the photograph. In fact, it also serves as a directional device leading the viewer's eye from the man's face to the copy below.

As an extension of the man, both physically in respect to its being held in his hand and psychologically in respect to its being a symbolic selection of the "gusto" in his lifestyle, the product acts as a hero in the ad. Like our preacher and woman in the Curry painting, the product is at the optical center of the ad. As a result, it helps to balance the ad, top to bottom and side to side.

Even closer in to the man, notice how the artist has arranged the elements. The riggings of a large sailing ship suggest the masculinity and strength of the man and, by way of association, the product. Clearly, this is not a lake-bound sailboat. It is a sailing ship meant for more rugged and adventurous waters such as the open sea where we see it in the picture. Now, imagine replacing the Schlitz can with a bottle of cologne or some other product. In fact, imagine using the same scene for other brands of beer. For Coors. For Miller Lite. For Bud Light. For Heineken. It's not the same, is it?

It seems obvious as we dissect the visual elements that the artist knew the purpose of the ad. All of the elements contribute to the meaning. But it's not a private meaning for the artist. It's a public meaning, and the public is the male beer drinker, slightly older, rugged, adventurous, and a seeker of pleasure and risk.

As with words, to unravel the arrangement of images leads to meaning. It does so by way of several routes. We can throw our own expectations and predispositions into the arrangement, whether that of words or images. We can assume intention on the part of the writer, speaker, or artist and then make assessments of meaning based on the arrangement. Or, we can even consider the arrangement based on its context.

## Meaning from the Contexts

In Chapter 2 we discussed context as a matter of words around words, theme, media, time and place, and form of expression. And we discussed it with the understanding that meaning can be enriched when one considers the surroundings in which words are found. The same holds true for images. For example, consider going into an art gallery and seeing an ad as opposed to seeing that ad in a magazine. Immediately, the environment or context in which the ad is seen changes its meaning.

Without belaboring the importance of context, consider the Schlitz ad and how the various elements—the man, the sailing ship, the Schlitz can, the open sea—blend with one another to create the gestalt of meaning. These are images around images. Take the man out of the ad, and the meaning isn't quite the same. Remove the can, and again the meaning changes. Replace the open sea with a desert and you enter into the surreal. The point is that images around images provide meaning to each other and within the entirety of the framed scene or picture.

A similar situation exists when we consider media, time and place, and form of expression. Again, the Schlitz ad serves as a prime example for each. The medium of photography within a magazine creates the lifelike, iconic picture as an objective representation of reality. Depending on when and where that picture is viewed, the meaning may change. View it in the morning after a full night of beer drinking and perhaps Schlitz may not seem so appealing. Perhaps, then, gusto is something you would rather be without. Likewise, viewing it while swinging in a hammock, sitting at a desk, lounging on a beach, or riding in a cab will change the meaning, if even to a slight degree. And again, as a photograph, the picture depicts reality, leaving little room for abstracted or indeterminate meaning on the part of the viewer. This form of photographic expression, coupled with the fact that the picture is an ad, guides the meaning so that we view the images differently than if we were to be looking at the same basic images drawn by hand and arranged together as a piece of museum art.

✍ **WRAP-UP** ✍

Overall, the controlling premise to the previous discussion of context is that whether we talk about words or images, the rules for determining meaning stay the same. In fact, the rules stay the same even when we consider meaning in the viewer or in the writer, speaker, or artist. Yes, the terminology changes, but the essence stays the same. For the artist, the elements of expression consist of frame, line, shape and color, those graphic elements that are ultimately arranged into a visual composition. Arranging the composition by applying those elements is a matter of knowing how to balance, emphasize, sequence, and unify.

Bear in mind that our discussion of the visual image has been simplified to a great extent. There are complete books that deal with aspects of the subject. To do it justice in a brief chapter is problematic in that you must pick and choose your spots. You must cull, not add. Also, this text makes no pretenses at being an art theory book. Still, there is a guiding purpose to these first three chapters. The purpose is simple. It's based on a premise that to be a writer you must know how and why words and images *mean*. That way you can make them mean what you want them to mean when it comes time for writing. In a nutshell, the purpose is to lay out the beginning steps to being a writer.

Metaphorically, think of our discussions in the past two chapters like this: If you don't know the dynamics behind the meanings of both words and images, you might as well go to home plate without a bat, to your building site without a hammer, and to your kitchen counter without the necessary ingredients for your gourmet dish. To read or listen, and to see, are necessities for the writer. To sharpen those abilities can't help but make you better at your chosen craft.

✍ **THINGS TO DO** ✍

1.   Use a piece of cardboard or simply a piece of paper. Cut out a square or rectangular hole, say 3″ × 5″, so that there's a frame of cardboard or paper around it. Then hold the cardboard or paper in front of your eyes and fix your view on various sights, wherever they may be: Your living room. Your bathroom. Outside to your yard. Along the street. Get your mind's voice chattering away about the elements of visual composition applied to what you see. Move the cardboard or paper slightly to create more or less balance, emphasis, sequence, and unity. Shift the contexts by changing places and thus changing your view.

2.   Take a 5-minute walk and make everything you see a symbol of something else. That tree you see? Can it be striving of nature for

perfection, forever upward, reaching toward the light of universal life? Get it?

3.    Go to an art gallery. Pick out a favorite work of art. Sit down and stare at it. Create meaning for it by having your mind's voice talk to you about the visual elements, visual composition, your expectation, and the artist's intent. Do the same thing with an ad. The magazine, *Communication Arts* is particularly enjoyable and useful here.

4.    Imagine using a piece of fine art for an ad. In fact, for what products would the Curry and Wyeth paintings be especially appropriate or inappropriate? Put a different product in the "Schlitz" man's hand. What would the product be?

5.    During the next movie or television show you see, pay close attention to how the director and cinematographer compose the shots. Imagine being that director or cinematographer. Get behind the camera and follow it along.

# Chapter 4

# The Writer: Words, Words, Words

You've thought about how you write, how you read, how you listen, and how you see. Now think about what you write.

Words. Words as part of our English language. Words grouped together and framed in by such seventh-grade English-language concerns as punctuation, quotation marks, paragraphs. Hundreds or thousands of words. No two alike. No two meaning exactly the same thing. And all of them living within the framework of our English language, including all that language entails. Sentences. Paragraphs. Punctuation. Quotation marks.

Words. That's what you write.

What a fascinating thing, words. Slipping and sliding all over the place. Meaning this or that just because you changed the medium or time of day. Changing here or there just because you put a certain word in front of or behind others. Words. Big words. Little words. Soft words. Hard words. Pretty words. Ugly words. Sweet words. Sour words. Hairy words. Bald words. Words.

Let's get small for a minute and think about the tiny parts of words, the letters of the alphabet. Put the *s* in the word *words* in the front and not the back and you get the word *sword*. One change in the positioning of that letter of the alphabet and everything changes. The word is no longer the same as it was. Now it's sword, not words. Words. Change a little something, give a little tweek here or there, and everything changes. Like fire hose. Or, fire hosé.

What we're about to do in this chapter is to surround words and the English language. We're going to look at them from a distance and from close up. Then we're going to grab them in our hands and work them over. We'll smash them, smooth them, perhaps even make love to them. Words. And they begin with letters of the alphabet.

## ✍ THE ALPHABET ✍

A, B, C, D, E, F, G, H, I, J, K, L, M, N, O, P, Q, R, S, T, U, V, W, X, Y, and Z.

Words are made of letters. And like words, letters *mean*. Just on their own they mean. When combined with other letters they may mean more, of course. Still, on their own they mean. For example, *A* doesn't mean the same thing as *T*. Right away, for instance, it sounds different. And it is different. *A* is a bit softer, isn't it? If you had to give the letter *A* a color, what would it be? Blue? Yellow? Red? If you had to give it a texture, what would it be? Silk? Burlap? Mud? And what about *T*? Doesn't it sound hard? Rough? Tough? Doesn't it feel like steel? A knife's edge?

The point here is that letters suggest meaning on their own. Those meanings may not be of the surface variety, but they do echo in our minds so that we attach certain feelings or emotions or even objects or colors to them. In short, they *mean*.

George Eastman wanted a memorable name for the camera his company produced, so he thought of the hardest-sounding letter in the alphabet, *K*, and put it at the beginning and end of the camera name, Kodak.

Think of products and their names. Let's take pain relievers. Tylenol. Panadol. Nuprin. Advil. Bufferin. The list, of course, could go on. But what do you notice regarding the letters in those names? Tylenol or Panadol, for example? Hard-sounding letters begin the names. Hard sounding for strength and power. And the "ol" sound? Medicinal? Soothing?

Think of shampoos. Tegrin. Silkience. Heavenly Body. Finesse. Suave. Let's take Tegrin, for instance. Just the first letter, *T*, tells you something about the shampoo. In other words, the first letter helps you get the meaning. So, what is the meaning? Is it that you'll get softer hair if you use Tegrin? Shinier hair? Fuller hair? Probably none of these things. What you'll get is some kind of disease control. You'll get some medicine. You'll get something scientific, something straight from the lab, and something that's strong. At least you better or its name shouldn't be Tegrin.

*T* versus *S*. *T* versus *F*. Which is the strong letter, the "gusto" letter? *T*, obviously. Letters begin the movement toward meaning. Sometimes they even mean on their own. Tegrin versus Silkience. Tegrin versus Finesse. Right from the start, from the very first letter, we begin to build the meaning, just as we build the meaning from the first word to the next, to the one after that, and so on.

Right from the start we know *T* is tough. And right from the start we know *S* and *F* aren't usually as tough as *T*. SSSSSSS. FFFFFFF. TTTTTTT.

S? Weary and soft. Airy and moist.
F? Full and lacy. Breathy and breezy.
T? Short and hard. Punchy and solid.
S? A mellow breeze on a summer's day.
F? Maybe the same.
T? A thunderclap.
S? Anita Baker.
F? Gloria Estefan.
T? Guns and Roses.

Letters can mean. Letters help build meaning in words. Words help build meaning in sentences. Sentences help build meaning in paragraphs. And before you know it you're writing.

Letters have gender. *S* is feminine. So is *F*. *T* is masculine. So are *D* and *K* and *P*.

Writing for a woman? Try *S* or *F*. Sheer. Silky. Sensuous. Felicitous. Finesse. Fascinate. Writing for a man? Try *T*. Tough. Taxing. Tattoo.

Primarily because of their sound, letters are one of your first considerations when you write. Bear in mind that when readers read they listen to a voice in their heads, their reading voice. That voice sounds the letters and words. And depending on what is attached to those sounds—images, gender, emotion—the reader gains meaning.

## WORDS

Throw letters of the alphabet together in some acknowledged and understood way and you end up with words. Even if you don't throw them together in some acknowledged and understood way you could still end up with a combination of letters that mean something. That's because letters in combination with each other convey meaning through their sound.

### Words Mean as They Sound and Sound as They Mean

Chances are you won't find many of the so-called words below in a dictionary. They're words from the poem "Jabberwocky," by Lewis Carroll, author of *Through the Looking Glass*. And though you won't find the poem's words in a dictionary, you should notice right off that they direct your mind toward meaning. They stimulate that meaning because of their sound. This poetic device is known as *onomatopoeia*. The sound of a word echoes its meaning. Let's look at the poem to discover how we create meaning from the sounds of words.

> 'Twas brillig and the slithy toves
> Did gyre and gimble in the wabe;
> All mimsy were the borogoves,
> And the mome raths outgrabe.
>
> "Beware the Jabberwock, my son!
> The jaws that bite, the claws that catch!
> Beware the Jubjub bird, and shun
> The frumious Bandersnatch!"
>
> He took his vorpal sword in hand;
> Long time the manxome foe he sought—
> So rested he by the Tumtum tree,
> And stood awhile in thought.
>
> And, as in uffish thought he stood,
> The Jabberwock, with eyes of flame,
> Came whiffling through the tulgey wood,
> And burbled as it came!
>
> One, two! One, two! And through and through
> The vorpal blade went snicker-snack!
> He left it dead and with its head
> He went galumphing back.
>
> "And has thou slain the Jabberwock?
> Come to my arms, my beamish boy!
> O frabjous day! Callooh! Callay!"
> He chortled in his joy.
>
> 'Twas brillig, and the slithy toves
> Did gyre and gimble in the wabe;
> All mimsy were the borogoves,
> And the mome raths outgrabe.

What are we to make of many of the words in this poem? Go to Webster's and you won't find those words. You won't find them anywhere except in this poem. But does that stop them from meaning something? Taken individually and together, they guide us to meaning. And though that meaning is slippery and dependent on the many factors we discussed at length in Chapter 2, the words have the power to direct us toward meaning. As we'll soon see, much of that power resides in the sounds of those words.

In the poem's first line we know it was brillig and there are slithy toves. Well, what is brillig? And what are slithy toves? We answer those questions through associating the sounds of the words to words we know. If you recall from Chapter 2, we carry our expectations and knowledge into what we read. *Brillig* sounds like brilliant. *Slithy* sounds like slippery or slithering or, perhaps, slimy. *Toves* sounds like toads. Perhaps you've made other associations for these words. In doing so you've created meaning for them. You've also begun to establish a scene in your mind.

As the first stanza continues into the second line, we find that the meaning of toves is modified. These toves do something. They gyre and gimble in the wabe. Clearly, they move. But moving doesn't adequately describe what they do. They gyre and gimble in the wabe. That's different, isn't it, than schlumping and rollipoding? It's different from galumphing, which our man or creature with the sword does after he apparently kills the Jabberwock in the fifth stanza. To gyre and gimble suggests quick gyrating, spinning, or flitting action. To do so in the wabe suggests water or wave. Perhaps these toves are little salamander-type creatures.

As we finish the stanza the scene is fleshed out with mimsy borogoves and the mome raths outgrabe. All sorts of associations click in our minds. Flimsy. Mangroves. Foam. Rats. Outgrowth. Outreach. Yet, because of the lack of obvious and direct sound association to other words we may know, certain words such as raths or outgrabe stand more on their own. For example, raths may be rats, but they may also be some form of plant life. The word itself suggests a plant image we can attach to it, perhaps due to the fact that it follows borogoves, which predisposes us to think of plants, or that it precedes outgrabe, which predisposes us to think of something reaching or jutting out. Yet, it may also suggest an animal of some kind peeking or reaching out from something else.

As we finish the first stanza it should be clear that we're in some strange territory here. Weird creatures inhabit this territory. And the territory itself seems alive with plant life, an association we make because of borogoves and groves. Is this territory dense? Probably not, given that it's also brillig there. Is it dry? Again, probably not, given that our weird creatures seem to live in some kind of water.

In the first stanza alone, eleven of the twenty-three words we read grew from Lewis Carroll's imagination. Short of relying on our own sound associations to other words and meanings, we have no reference points for giving meanings to those eleven words. The same holds true with four words in the second stanza, *Jabberwock, Jubjub, frumious,* and *Bandersnatch.* What is a Jabberwock? A Jubjub bird? A Bandersnatch? And a frumious one at that.

We're to beware of all those creatures, presumably creatures that fly. But look at the combinations of letters for those creatures, combinations yielding sounds that in turn yield meanings. The hard sounds in Jabberwock, for instance. To jab. And wock as in knock or sock. Then, common and legitimate words follow in the second line to flesh out the description. This is a creature that bites and claws.

Or the Jubjub bird, perhaps not as vicious as the other two, at least based on the sound of its name. In fact, can't you hear the bird squawking "jubjub, jubjub"? Perhaps the bird was named for the very sound it made. And finally the frumious Bandersnatch. Frumious for furious or fuming? From that description we imagine a vicious creature. And its name does nothing to change our minds. Hard, vigorous sounds again through the use of B, N, D, and TCH.

In the third stanza we experience a shift to a character, presumably a person of sorts, perhaps a knight of long ago. He takes hold of his vorpal sword. Think of that word, *vorpal.* Then imagine or actually grab a handsaw or long strip of metal and wave it back and forth. The sound it makes is vorpal-like. Vorp. Vorp. Vorp.

We know that this person has sought the manxome foe for some time. Think of that word, *manxome.* The hard, crusty sound of $X$. Further down in line three, think of what a Tumtum tree would look like. Is it spindly? Void of leaves or branches? Probably not. In your imagination isn't the tree fuller and thicker than that? Isn't it a bit like a weeping willow, perhaps? Well, if that's true and if that's how you imagine it to be, how do we manage to see the tree that way? Is it because of the roundness and fullness of the UM sound?

In the fourth stanza we find our hero standing in uffish thought. Now, what is *uffish thought*? Is it iffy? Is it slow and plodding, or quick and piercing? Is our hero standing there scratching his head or resting his chin in his palm and saying, "Uh. Uh. Daa, uhh"? Perhaps so.

And then in the middle of his uffish thought comes the Jabberwock. Like a whiffle ball it whiffles. Unlike a sword it doesn't vorp. More so, it whiffles through a tulgey wood. That word, *tulgey.* Is the wood sparse or dense? Is it thin or thick? Doesn't tulgey suggests density and thickness? And why? Is it because of the UL sound? Finally, we hear the Jabberwock. It burbles. To burble is just as it sounds. Can you see the bubbles of spit at the beak? And is burble the same as gag, choke, cough, hack, whinny, scream, yell, or roar?

In the fifth stanza we're back to our hero again, this time in the middle of the action as his vorpal blade goes snicker-snack. Cut, cut, cut. Can you hear his blade cutting bone? Does it trim the bone? Does it snip the bone? No, it cuts the bone. Cut is different from trim or snip. And then with its head, the head of the Jabberwock, our hero goes galumphing back. Does this mean he races back? He skips back? He zips back? Or is it more of a jog or trot or even waddle? A slow and heavy trip back? Not a bounce. Not a sprint. More like da-dum-da-dum-da-dum.

And finally, in the sixth and next to last stanza we meet another person, a narrator who speaks to our hero. Meanwhile, our hero is beaming, apparently proud of his conquest. It's a frabjous day. That is, it's a fabulous day, isn't it? And how does one make that frabjous day known? How does one give justice to how frabjous the day is? By calloohing and callaying, of course. Sort of like yahooing and hooraying. Following the calloohing and callaying this new person or perhaps our hero chortles in his joy. To chortle sounds like something Santa Claus might do.

It's not a giggle. It's not a burble. It's a chortle, a little bit heavier than a giggle or burble perhaps, a little bit fuller and thicker, a kind of bubbling, chuckling, and gurgling sound rising from the gut.

Even with such nonsense words as those from the imagination of Lewis Carroll, we gain meaning. The sounds of those words guide us to that meaning. As we read one letter and one word to the next, we accrue meaning. As we move on through the words and lines, the meaning may be altered or embellished somewhat such as what happened when we read "tulgey wood" or the description of the Jabberwock.

But it was the sounds of the words that did the trick. And the importance of sound is not restricted to those kinds of nonsense words we read in Carroll's poem. The importance of sound exists in many real words as well.

Of course, as we pore over the words we've read the entire discussion should sound familiar. It circles back to our second chapter and the way we read or listen. At the same time, what we're doing here is focusing more attention on specific aspects of words, in this case their sound. With this in mind, what do you give as meaning to the following words?

Luscious. Ineffable. Pre-eminence. Delicious. Excruciating. Hocuspocus. Lummox. Cute. Cuddly. Hippopotamus.

The list, of course, could go on forever. Because of our experiences, our knowledge, and acquaintance with such words over the years, we attach meaning. But that meaning also grows from the sounds of those words. For example, to sound out luscious or delicious involves an experience in what those words mean. The words themselves roll around in our mouths. They're juicy words. Rich and full words. Moist words. Just by their sounds. The same holds true with many other words as well.

Consider hippopotamus, for example. From the Greek for horse (*hippos*) and river (*potamus*), the word originated to describe this particular animal. But over the years and through associations the word has been fleshed out to provide a descriptive meaning, perhaps of anyone who is overweight. At the same time, the sound of the word lets us know that we're not dealing with a thin, spindly, underdeveloped creature here. To roll the letters and sounds around in our minds or mouths suggests in itself the word's meaning. The same also holds true for the other words in our brief list. And yes, a hippopotamus seems to fit with lummox. You don't even need Webster to tell you that's true.

Recall the names of our products from the beginning of the chapter. Names for pain relievers and shampoos. Let's add cereals to the list. Cheerios. Kix. Product 19. Frankenberry. Trix. Lucky Charms. Rice Krispies. Notice how appropriate the names are to the individual brands. Notice how you couldn't very easily lift one name and apply it to another brand. For example, Product 19 just can't be the name for the cereal inside a Lucky Charms box. Nor vice versa. And what would you think if a cereal were named Tegrin or Panadol? Would you eat a cereal named Tegrin or Panadol? Would you take a pain reliever for your excruciating headache if the pain reliever were named Cheerios or Finesse?

The point overall is that the sounds of words generate associations in our minds. These associations then guide us to meanings. Whether we've accumulated those associations over time or through our particular language and culture is really immaterial. The fact of the matter is that they exist, and as writers we need to be aware of their existence. This is true even if we consider the gender in words.

## Words and Gender

Remember *T* and *S* or *F*? One masculine. The other two feminine. Remember "gusto"? A man's word. At least a certain kind of man.

Now, let's not get uptight about the sexes. There are women. And there are men. Women are not men. Men are not women. This has nothing to do with things like gay or lesbian movements. Each to his or her own, I suppose. But it has everything to do with men being men and women being women. It has everything to do with the accrual of womanhood or manhood coursing through time, culture, and our blood, and all this whether we like it or not. Be it good or bad, it has everything to do with pink and blue, Barbie dolls and toy soldiers, Girl Scouts and Boy Scouts, Jockey underwear and lace panties, hair on the face and no hair on the face, and fatherhood and motherhood.

Yes, real men can eat quiche. And real women can eat rare steaks. But when it's all said and done, men are men and women are women. The letters of the alphabet know that. And words know that, too. *T* and *S*. Gusto and silky.

Those words used to describe products for women know that. And those words used to describe products for men know that. Check out the copy in a magazine ad for Luminesse Lipstick from Cover Girl. First, check out the word "Luminesse." Not quite a full-bodied beer, is it?

> Nothing else captures the spirit of satin like Luminesse
> Lipstick. The shimmer of it. The fashion and feel of it.
> Rich, creamy color spun with luminous pearl and
> polished to the softest sheen. So lips look radiant.
> Feel satiny. Hour after hour. Cover Girl®
> Luminesse Lipstick. In a collection of spirited
> shades. Capture it.

Beyond the product name, Luminesse, notice how the writer's selection of words corresponds with the intended reader, a woman. A young, spirited woman. But make no mistake about it, she's a woman. Yes, she's a type of woman. And not all women are that way. But then this product isn't meant for women who aren't that way.

No masculine words here. They're feminine. Spirit of satin. Shimmer. Rich. Creamy. Spun. Luminous. Pearl. Softest. Sheen. Radiant. Satiny. Spirited. Shades.

Notice how the words match the product with the reader. The words mirror the product. They show and tell you what the product is and what it does. The product, too, is feminine, just like the reader. So what you get is a circling inward to the femininity of the overall message.

Notice, too, the *S* sound. Spirit. Satin. Shimmer. Spun. Luminous. Softest. Sheen. Satiny. Spirited. Shades. *S* slips off the tongue. It breezes past the lips. It's light and airy.

Notice how the words sound as they mean. Shimmer moves. It bobs a bit in the ear, especially with the *mmmm* sound that vibrates. Yet, another word, *softest,* stays still. The "off" sound inside the word fluffs and pillows in the ear.

Now imagine these words used for a full-bodied beer or tires or sledgehammers or a bank or a securities firm. No go, right? These words have a gender. They have a gender because the product has a gender and the reader has a gender. Yes, because of that they may contribute to the stereotype we have of the sexes. You wrestle with that dilemma on your own. But the words have a gender that is unmistakable.

The same holds true for the copy lines that follow. All feminine in keeping with the product category, cosmetics, and the targeted readers, women. Hear the sounds. Notice the gender.

> Brush on the blushing softness of colors like Soft Misty Pink or Soft Fresh Peach. Feel the silky softness glide across your cheeks. (These lines for Maybelline Brush/Blush.)

> See your lips in their best light. The glistening light of Moisture Gloss Stick by Maybelline. Whipped with moisturizers and splashed with sheer, dazzling color. Discover the silky shades of Moisture Whip Gloss Stick. For soft, shining, sensuous lips. (These lines for Maybelline Whip Gloss Stick.)

Again, hear the sounds. The "ush" sound. The "iss" sound. The "off" sound. The *S* or *O* sound. The sounds of *ahhhs* and *ooohs*. Rounded sounds. Moist sounds. And notice the gender of the words, a gender matching the feminine nature of the products and the readers.

But what happens if we turn the tables and look at other types of products and readers? Tires and male readers, for example? Are the sounds the same as those we heard in the ads for cosmetics? Are the words the same?

Here is a line of copy for Uniroyal Tiger Paw Plus tires. Hear the sounds. Notice the gender. Of course, first notice the product name. Tiger Paw Plus. Tough.

> An excellent example of high technology protecting you from
> the harsh realities of the real world,
> a formidable barrier against tread punctures.

Now, one could build a case that this line of copy could apply as well to our cosmetic ads, at least in terms of content or subject matter. Imagine, for instance, the copy line in a Maybelline or Revlon ad. High-tech cosmetics protecting you from harsh realities, such as what you look like without cosmetics. Sounds farfetched, doesn't it? But in terms of what the line says, its content, it's not so farfetched. What is far-fetched is the tone, the flavor, the personality, or the atmosphere of the words applied to cosmetics. They just don't seem to work. They're not right. But they are right for tires.

Ordinarily we don't think of tires as feminine. We think of them as masculine. We think that men buy them. We think that men hold exclu-sive sway over who pays attention to tires. There is this kind of associa-tion. With this in mind, look again at the words in the copy for Uniroyal Tiger Paw Plus.

These hard, masculine sounds carry over to the copy. The *X* sound, as in excellent and example. The "ek" sound as in technology and, to a degree, protecting. And the image of harsh or stern. Not very feminine, is it? Also, we have a formidable barrier. Would you use the word *formidable* in writing meant for women? There may be instances, yes. But probably not ordinarily. We also have tread punctures. Hard, masculine sounds. *T, D, P,* and "unct." As with the ads for the cosmetics, the words match the product and reader, in this case the masculine product and reader.

Naturally, not all words have gender. This is the English language, not the French language. At the same time, much of our language evolved through other languages, French included. Other languages often make careful distinctions between pronunciation and meaning based on gender. And though we're not locked into gender with our language, it does play a role, especially as we apply somewhat stereotypical assumptions about men and women.

The point, though, relates to our awareness of how gender associations help create meanings in words. Once identified with a gender, a word carries with it the assumptions we make about the sexes. A man is not considered voluptuous. A woman is. A man may be seen as chiseljawed. A woman isn't. Stereotypes? Yes. And try as we may to avoid them, they do exist. Sometimes they're inaccurate, untruthful, perhaps even bad. But one thing is certain. They carry a large amount of the responsibility for how words mean.

## Words and Age

Consider the following groups of words. They suggest various ages.

Then he slithered and slunk, with a smile most unpleasant,
Around the whole room, and he took every present!
Pop guns! And bicycles! Roller Skates! Drums!
Checkerboards! Tricycles! Popcorn! And Plums!
And he stuffed them in bags. Then the Grinch, very nimbly,
Stuffed all the bags, one by one, up the chimbley.

....

On Wednesday, during an arithmetic review, I heard a bird go peep.
Lots of other kids heard it too and so did Mr. Benedict. I know
because he looked up. I went back to my problems but pretty soon
I heard it again. Peep.

....

No Frizz...No way...No How!

....

There's nothing worse than a bad haircut. You go around
looking like a dork...half apologizing always conscious,
totally out of your groove for about a week.

....

While we all hope we'll never need long-term health care,
the unfortunate fact is that nearly 50% of all people do at
some point in their lives. And while thinking about
long-term care may not be pleasant, not planning for
it can be a whole lot worse.

Of course, we could debate forever how the words in each of these quotes say what they mean based on their personalized address to specific readers. Overall, they say what they mean to distinctly different people. For example, when the last quote talks about long-term health care (the content of that quote) who else could it be speaking to other than an older person? Are teens interested in healtħ care? Of course not. They haven't the foggiest idea about health care. In fact, they don't even care. Often they drive like maniacs. Or live recklessly. What do they care? At this point in life, as far as they're concerned they're going to live forever. So health care is meaningless. But what about older people, the kind that drive as if their lives depend upon it?

The point here is that the content of each quote reflects a particular person. That person has certain demographics. Part of those demographics includes age. Again, the last quote about health care contains words in combination that reflect a certain age. Notice what the words say. First, the words are hopeful. Yes, "we all hope we'll never need long-term health care."

But these words are followed by words that, in essence, tell the reader to get real. This, as the copy points out, is unfortunate, but it's real nonetheless, "the unfortunate fact is that nearly 50 percent of all people do at some point in their lives."

As if to placate the reader, the writer then states that long-term care may be unpleasant to think about but not planning for it is worse. A whole lot worse. And thus the stage is set for the persuasive appeal in this ad for the AARP Group Health Insurance Program.

At the same time, notice the tone of that quote. Notice how the words are put together, suggesting that as much as it's important to say what you mean, it's also important to say it in a way that reflects that meaning. For example, each of the two sentences contains over twenty words. Fine. But what difference does that make?

To answer that question look at the first four quotes taken, respectively, from Dr. Seuss's *How the Grinch Stole Christmas*, Judy Blume's *Are You There, God? It's Me, Margaret?*, an ad for Loreal's Anti-Frizz, and an ad for Reebok. Count up the words in those quotes. Except for the quote from *Are You There, God? It's Me, Margaret*, you won't find any single lines close to the amount of words found in the AARP copy directed at older people. What does this tell you?

For one thing, it might tell you that older people take their time, at least more than younger people. For another thing, it might tell you that older people are into different things than younger people. Remember that the first four quotes are meant for younger people, say those under the age of thirty. You, for instance, as in the case of the Reebok ad. Perhaps even the Loreal ad. Or the younger you, as in the Dr. Seuss and Judy Blume quotes.

Well, what are those older people into? Perhaps we can answer that in single words. Security. Understanding. Compassion. Empathy. And what's more secure, understanding, compassionate, or empathetic than words expressed in a way that tap into the older person's complex mix of concerns, values, attitudes, and lifestyle. Imagine, for instance, being an older person in our country. What are the things that concern and worry you? What are the priorities in your life?

All right, so you want to take your time, simply because if you don't, you rush headlong into something very unappealing. Also, you want to take your time because your entire life has been filled with not taking your time. Thus, you have about had it with not being able to stop and smell the roses all these years. All you want is peace, but the threat of the great unknown disturbs that peace, which, by the way, is acknowledged by the ad writer.

Meanwhile, the writer knows about you. The writer feels as you feel. In effect, the writer says, "O.K., let's take our time here. Let's slow things down a bit." The result is the copy you've read. Key words, those in combination with other words, link with the older reader, with that reader's worries and concerns. Words such as *hope, care,* and *worse.* Placed as they are in longer sentences, they create an ease for this particular reader. They massage the reader in a way the reader likes to be massaged, especially at this point in life.

Don't kid yourself. Age impacts on what's important to you in life, sometimes in surprising ways and with surprising power. If you're older (you'll have to get into this and trust me on this one), then things like health care and long sentences can be soothing. You don't want life to end. Yet, you know—deep down inside you really know—that life is being threatened. Beyond this you know that all you have worked for could go up in smoke. Puff. Gone. There is that haunting reality to life at your stage as you live it.

But what about those who are younger? Imagine, for instance, being very young. Sevenish, let's say. You read Dr. Seuss's *How the Grinch Stole Christmas* and you come upon words such as *slithered* and *slunk* or *nimbly* and *chimbley.* The playfulness in those words matches with the playfulness of your age. They match with the uninhibited delight you might take in words. Words like *chimbley.* Itself a word that tickles and makes you chuckle. Also, notice what the Grinch has taken: Pop guns. Bicycles. Roller skates. Drums. Checkerboards. Tricycles. Popcorn. And plums. Not exactly presents meant for your grandparents.

Even in the quote from Judy Blume's *Are You There, God? It's Me, Margaret,* the very words, their content and arrangement, suggest a certain age. Clearly the scene takes place in school. But it's not college, is it? To hear a bird peep seems young, younger at least than college age. And *kids* isn't exactly the way one would refer to college-aged students.

In the ad copy for Loreal's Anti-Frizz, we move up the age ladder a bit, but just a few years. Use of the word *frizz* gives it away. More so, when juxtaposed together, the three phrases *No Frizz, No Way, No How* capture the rapid clip and rhythm of today's teen language.

And in the ad copy for Reebok we're face to face with the word *dork.* No doubt a word spanning teen and college-aged years. A word carrying all sorts of connotations, mostly negative. And a word with absolutely no direct relevance to the life of the reader for our AARP health-care ad.

There's just no way that each of these quotes can be meant for the same reading audience. The words and their arrangement suggest otherwise. Instead, the writers have tailored the quotes to specific audiences. One of the keys to separating those audiences is age. As we go through life and the years pass by, our age and all that goes with it dictate a certain tone and feel relevant to our years. It all makes wonderful cosmic sense. There is a grand purpose behind it. For our purposes, though, it also makes wonderful sense in the choices we make regarding words and how we express them. Very pointed and tailored, the words and their arrangements—their syntax—help us address a reader on his or her terms. Chosen carefully they help us focus on that reader, and age is an important part of that focus.

### Words and Tone

The writers of our quotes, Dr. Seuss included, select their words to communicate meaning. As we discussed in Chapter 2, that meaning can be of two types, surface or deep. But as we know, that meaning resides in one, two, or all of several places. The reader or listener. The writer. The contexts of expression. And the words themselves as they have come to reverberate with meaning over the course of time. They reverberate with gender. With age. And with levels of knowledge and interest.

Consider, for example, the following quote from an ad for John Nuveen & Company, an investment firm. The ad was placed in *The Chronicle of Higher Education,* a publication primarily serving administrators and faculty in colleges and universities across the country. The headline reads, "You have the wisdom of Socrates. The Knowledge of Einstein. The Vision of Jefferson. Now where do you get the money?" The following phrases are located within the ad's body copy, "hallowed halls of learning and bastion of our nation's brain power," "ensconced in facts," and "sagacious team."

What do you notice about those words, particularly words such as *hallowed, ensconced,* and *sagacious*? They may not be as gender-based as other words. They seem to cross over male and female boundaries. But they do seem somewhat age-based. After all, we can't expect our prototypical reader of Dr. Seuss or Judy Blume to know what those words mean. So, it must be someone older. Yet not everyone in this particular age bracket would necessarily know what the words mean either. There must be something else at work here. And truth be told, there's a certain aloofness, a certain elan or haughty dash, a certain hoity-toityness about the words. A deep-voiced, slightly British accent to the words. Pompous? Maybe. Condescending? Perhaps.

One thing's for sure. They're not the kind of words you'll find in Dr. Seuss or Judy Blume, unless, of course, those authors are playing with them. But they are the kinds of words you'll find in an ad meant to reach those safeguarding higher education. Now, what is there about those safeguarding higher education that separates them from others not involved in higher education?

One of the tangible benefits in getting educated is that you expand your vocabulary. Presumably, when you're finished with your education you'll have more words at your disposal than you had when you began. This will make you sound smart in certain circles. It doesn't necessarily make you smart (other things do that). It simply makes you sound smart. It reflects on your smartness, on your education, on your dedication to improving yourself, at least in terms of your vocabulary.

Words such as hallowed or ensconced or sagacious probably won't work with other audiences, regardless of the contexts in which they're expressed. They're just not that relevant. But on their own or in combination they can work with this specific audience, which has spent much of its time discriminating between words and their meanings. The more discriminate the audience is, the more there is a need to refine the language, to choose the most correct and appealing word.

Think about this in relationship to the writer's word choices in the Nuveen headline and copy phrases. *Wisdom. Knowledge. Vision.* All words that carry a special meaning to the intended reader. Words close to the heart of that audience. Words reflecting the interest and loyalties of that audience. *Hallowed. Ensconced. Sagacious.* The same effects realized through these words as were realized through wisdom, knowledge, and vision.

Yes, instead of "ensconced" the writer could have chosen *buried* or *covered* or *hidden.* Instead of "sagacious" the writer could have selected *wise.* But those words are a bit more (ahem) pedestrian. They're open-collar words. Even blue-collar words. They don't wear horn-rimmed glasses. They don't wear vests and bow ties. They're not corduroy words. But *ensconced* and *sagacious*? Their very natures are more upscale, more aloof perhaps.

To flesh out even more how words reflect a certain quality, feel, or tone, here is the copy from a classic Steinway ad created by those at Young and Rubicam.

> There has been but one supreme piano in the history of music. In the days of Liszt and Wagner, of Rubinstein and Berlioz, the pre-eminence of the Steinway was as unquestioned as it is today. It stood then, as it stands now, the chosen instrument of the masters— the inevitable preference wherever great music is understood and esteemed.

Again, notice the writer's choice of words. *Supreme. Pre-eminence. Masters. Inevitable preference. Esteemed.* These are not exactly words you'll find in the *National Enquirer.* These words are more upscale, more aloof.

The writer could have written that the Steinway has been but one *great* piano in the history of music. Instead, the writer wrote that the Steinway has been but one *supreme* piano. The word *supreme* carries with it all sorts of upscale connotations. And again, the word *great* steps down a notch or two from *supreme.* It's more pedestrian, more common, and less in keeping with the type of person who would be interested in a Steinway piano.

The same holds true for the other words in the copy, words such as *pre-eminence* and *esteemed.* Surely the writer could have written that the Steinway's noteworthiness back then was as unquestioned as it is today. But *noteworthiness,* though it may come close to the meaning of *pre-eminence,* isn't quite the same. The word *pre-eminence* suggests the upscale quality, again the hoity-toity tone of both the reader and the product. Ditto for *esteemed.* The writer could have chosen *respected* instead of *esteemed.* But *respected* doesn't have the same ring to it. It doesn't convey the quality of richness or elegance that's conveyed by the word *esteemed.*

Now contrast the choices of words in either the Steinway or Nuveen ads with these words from an ad in *TV Guide* for VCR Plus, which starts with the headline, "Taping 'Back To The Future III' without VCR Plus+ is a thing of the past."

> Now you can tape "Back To The Future III" faster than
> a time-traveling DeLorean with VCR Plus+, the amazing
> one-step VCR programmer. Here's how it works.
>
> ....
>
> VCR Plus+ is so advanced, you'd think it's from the
> future. But fortunately, you can get it today.

Though you've only read part of the body copy, notice how the words carry with them a certain quality or tone. For example, immediately in the headline you read the word *thing.* As a word, "thing" is very ambiguous. It lacks specificity. It can mean or refer to a spectrum of more specific objects, beliefs, or attitudes. That's not my thing. The thing is.... There's a thing about him.... The thing I'm trying to say is.... The word is nonspecific. It doesn't discriminate. Instead, it incorporates many "things." This is very unlike more specific and pointed words (both in content and tone) such as *sagacious.*

Inside the body copy a similar dynamic takes place. For instance, all of the words in that first body copy paragraph are common and easy to understand. Moreover, the word *amazing* is an hyperbole, an exaggeration, which seeks to describe the product. There is little specificity about the word *amazing*. In fact, we often use it to describe many "things." But as an exaggeration, it plays into the more indiscriminate reading style of those who watch a great deal of television. You can't read and watch television at the same time. You can try. Many college students do. But let's face it, to read as we've described it in Chapter 2 means that you're extremely focused on what you're reading. You're exercising several mental processes at the same time. You're involved. Anything beyond that kind of reading would be a distraction.

This is not to put forward a value judgment on those who read versus those who watch television. It's simply an observation of what may be a reality, an important reality. The placement of this ad in *TV Guide* is no mistake. The ad is for a product with pointed relevance to television. More so, the ad is for a particular reader, one who may skim more than read. One who may choose not to discriminate as much between words, or at least not as much as someone who has been trained to discriminate between words. And as an exaggeration, the word *amazing* plays into that lack of discrimination.

Similarly, the end of the copy, which in fact is the final paragraph of body copy for the ad, uses conversational contractions with *you'd* and *it's*. There is a quality of voice to those words, a kind of lifelike speaking of one person to another. At the same time these words are not those you would associate with coat and tails. It's easier to associate them with rolled-up shirt sleeves and a comfy pair of chinos.

Try comparing the words from the Nuveen and Steinway ads with the words from this VCR Plus+ ad. You'll find that judgments about their essence relates to their tone. Naturally, the tone relates to the product and to the reader. Imagine, for example, using the word *amazing* in the Steinway ad. It just doesn't seem to fit. Yet, the overall message tries to convey the amazing track record and performance of the Steinway piano. But rather than doing so by use of the word *amazing,* the writer selects words more appropriate for the proper tone, words such as *supreme* and *pre-eminence.*

What's important to remember here is that because words are living, breathing, and organic beings, they have a life of their own. It's a very transcendental view of words. They're not stuck on a page somewhere, lifeless and dry. Instead, they pulse and flow beyond the page. And as we discussed in Chapter 2, a great deal of that pulsing and flowing involves us as readers and writers, in addition to the contexts in which the words are presented. At the same time words just *are,* carrying with them the life of gender, age, and tone; in short, meanings accrued over time. Choose one word over another and you change the tone. Right away, the meaning and impact of the word and other words surrounding it change from what they might have been had you selected a different word.

This is very important stuff to remember. It's an important part of what makes one person a writer and another not.

## Words as Parts of Speech

Think of it like this. You're an artist. A painter. A carpenter. A pianist. A dancer. A landscape architect. Whatever. And as an artist you rely on certain indispensable tools or qualities. Always you know where to find those tools or qualities. As a painter, for instance, you know where to find your palette and brushes. More so, once you're with them they become an extension of your painter's self.

Or think of yourself as a carpenter. You wear a belt. You hang your indispensable tools on that belt. You know exactly where to find them. And those that you use the most you keep within easy reach. Over time, you don't even have to look for them on your belt. You simply slip your hand down to the right spots and there they are.

Or think of yourself as a dancer. You're in precise tune with your muscle quality. You feel things that others don't feel. You know what your muscles can and can't do. And you know how they behave under varying degrees of physical stress. So you monitor them as you dance, all the while keeping in symbiotic touch with their performance and capabilities.

When we talk about words as we have up to this point, and now words as parts of speech, we're really talking about how you as a writer will use your palette and brush, the tools on your belt, or the muscles in your mind. For example, some parts of speech are more handy and important to you than others, sort of like the importance of a hammer or ruler versus a plane or drill to a carpenter. First and foremost, when it comes to parts of speech the action verb should be within easy reach on your writing belt.

Here's a question to ask yourself. Do you know what the parts of speech are? If you can answer what they are, then ask yourself another question: Do you know how the parts of speech are used? What they're for?

If you don't know what the parts of speech are or how they're used, don't worry. But learn them now. As formal designations for words, the parts of speech guide you to more effective means of written expression. In a way it's a bit like knowing how the colors on your palette interact with one another once they're placed on a canvas, or what tool on your belt represents the best choice for a particular task. The same holds true for knowing the parts of speech and how they are used.

With all of this mind, here are the parts of speech: noun, pronoun, adjective, verb, adverb, preposition, conjunction, and interjection.

A noun names a person, place, or thing.

A pronoun replaces a noun.

An adjective modifies a noun or pronoun.

A verb expresses an action or state of being.

An adverb modifies a verb, an adjective, or another adverb.

A preposition shows the relation of a noun or pronoun to some other word in a sentence.

A conjunction joins words and groups of words.

An interjection expresses emotion and has no grammatical relation to other words in a sentence.

Let's work our way through a sentence. And as we do let's build the meanings of the words based on their uses as parts of speech.

*Writers write.*

The sentence uses a noun subject, *writers,* and an action verb, *write.*

*Writers write often.*

We still have our noun subject and action verb, but now we've inserted an adverb *often*, that alters the meaning of the verb *write.*

*Prolific writers write often, and they write from compulsion.*

Notice how the meaning changes radically with our addition of words. The word *prolific* modifies or alters the meaning of *writers*. It is an adjective since *writers* is a noun. The word *and* is a conjunction joining the two independent clauses. The word *they,* which begins the second clause, is a pronoun referring to *writers*. The word *write* in that second clause is a verb in the same way that the word *write* in the first clause is a verb. The word *from* is a preposition describing the relationship between *write* and *compulsion*. The word *compulsion* is a noun, in this case the object of the preposition *from.*

*Oh, prolific writers write often, and they write from compulsion.*

Now we've added an interjection, *Oh,* which is apart from the grammatical context of the sentence but which certainly qualifies the meaning of the sentence since now we can hear a voice more easily. In addition, we have some grounding in attributing a potential meaning from that voice, a meaning such as surprise.

What we've done is add words as parts of speech. Words are parts of speech. Parts of speech are words. To know how words interact and lead to meaning you must understand the parts of speech. They suggest the very functions of words.

This doesn't mean, of course, that you need to practice being a grammarian. But it does mean that you need to have a grip on your writing tools. More so, you need to know how to use them. The parts of speech are one of those tools, and an important one. By breaking words down into their parts of speech you're able to discover how meaning evolves. You're able to understand the architecture of the language, to appreciate it and to use it in your writing.

With the parts of speech front and center in your mind, consider the ad copy from the Cover Girl Luminesse Lipstick ad you read previously. Here it is again.

> Nothing else captures the spirit of satin like Luminesse
> Lipstick. The shimmer of it. The fashion and feel of it.
> Rich, creamy color spun with luminous pearl and
> polished to the softest sheen.

Let's take the ad copy a sentence or phrase at a time. For example, the first sentence contains a noun subject, *Nothing,* followed by an adjective, *else,* modifying what the noun subject means. The adjective qualifies the meaning of *Nothing.* This is followed by the verb *captures,* which is followed by the noun object *spirit.* The noun object (it's the direct object of the verb *captures*) is followed by the preposition *of,* which in turn is followed by the object of the preposition, *satin.* Satin, then, is followed by a modifying phrase, *like Luminesse Lipstick.* The word *like* is a simile, but in this case it's also the beginning of a modifier that contains the proper noun *Luminesse Lipstick.* The question is, What is this modifying phrase modifying?

Does the phrase modify or describe satin? If so, the entire phrase being introduced by the word *like* is an adjective since it would modify the noun *satin.* Does it modify spirit? If so, again it would be an adjective since *spirit* is a noun. But as you examine this sentence you should realize that this phrase really doesn't modify either of those two nouns. It doesn't mean the spirit is like the lipstick. It doesn't mean the satin is like the lipstick. It does seem to mean, though, that the act of capturing is like Luminesse Lipstick. Or, nothing else is like Luminesse Lipstick when it comes to capturing the spirit of satin. In the first instance the phrase is an adverb modifying the verb *captures.* In the second instance the phrase is an adjective modifying the noun *Nothing.*

Yes, this all seems very knotty. But it's really not when you think about it. The English language makes considerable sense. It's very logical, very orderly. Some words such as nouns stand on their own. Some words such as adjectives only stand with others since they act as modifiers. The same holds true with phrases or even clauses, which have the same functions as individual words.

In the case of our sentence here, the functions of the words evolve out of their use as parts of speech. These functions are very logical, very orderly. We have a noun subject followed by a modifying adjective and a verb. The verb is followed by another adjective, the article *the,* which qualifies what kind or how much of spirit. The article *the* is followed by a noun object, which is followed by a preposition introducing another noun, the entire prepositional expression or phrase thus modifying the previous noun, *spirit.* And all of this is followed by the word *like,* as a preposition and introducing the proper noun *Luminesse Lipstick.*

Overall, there is considerable orderliness to the sentence. But what might throw us a bit is the position of the final phrase, *like Luminesse Lipstick.* Since it is located at the end of the sentence and follows the noun *satin,* we might be inclined to attach it as a modifier for that noun. But as we analyze it further that attachment doesn't seem to work. It's not the satin that's like Luminesse Lipstick. It's something else, perhaps the *Nothing* else or even the *capture.*

One could argue that to make this meaning clearer, the writer might have written the sentence as follows: Nothing else like Luminesse Lipstick captures the spirit of satin. This would make the phrase *like Luminesse Lipstick* an adjective modifying the noun *Nothing.* Or the writer might have written the sentence this way: Nothing else captures, like Luminesse Lipstick, the spirit of satin. Though that's a clumsy way of handling it, the phrase would then clearly modify the verb *captures.* This would make it an adverb.

Do you understand the point being expressed here? By understanding the parts of speech you can understand the language and how it works the way it does. By understanding the parts of speech you can understand that the very next expression in the copy, *the shimmer of it,* lacks something. It lacks a verb, which means that it's a fragment and not a complete sentence. This often results in low marks for English papers. But it often results in high marks for ad copy.

With this phrase (it's not a clause because it doesn't have a subject and verb) the article *the* is an adjective modifying the noun *shimmer.* The preposition *of* introduces the pronoun object *it.* The entire prepositional phrase, *of it,* modifies *shimmer* and is thus an adjective.

You find this same type of structure in the next fragment of the copy, *the fashion and feel of it.* But following that fragment we're back to a complete sentence with, "Rich, creamy color spun with luminous pearl and polished to the softest sheen."

Notice how the noun subject of the sentence, *color,* is modified by the two adjectives, *rich and creamy.* They provide more precise meaning of color. Meanwhile, the verb *spun* is followed by the preposition *with.* In fairly typical fashion, this preposition is then followed by a noun object, *pearl,* the meaning of which is modified by the adjective *luminous.* The conjunction *and* unites the two verbs, *spun* and *polished.* The verb *polished* is followed by the preposition *to.* Again in typical fashion, that preposition is followed by the noun object, *sheen,* the meaning of which is modified by the adjectives *the* and *softest.*

It all makes perfect sense. And as mysterious as we may believe our language to be at times, in truth it is logical, orderly, and sensible. Notice, for instance, how the parts of speech in the Luminesse copy interact and lend themselves to one another and how the words overall gain meaning, understandable and orderly meaning, based on their action as parts of speech. The word *color,* for example, is indefinite until the adjectives *rich* and *creamy* are added to help flesh out the meaning. Pearl is luminous. Sheen is softest.

Notice, too, that if you were to graph out the parts of speech and their positions in the various sentences or fragments, you would find they offer a pleasant balance to the reading eye and ear. The first sentence of the copy is complete. The next two expressions are fragments, juxtaposed with each other, not separated. The final sentence is again complete, much like the first one, providing a kind of sandwich effect for the middle fragments. Structurally, the copy is neatly packaged and ordered. And make no mistake about it, this particular piece of copy stands as more of a rule than an exception. Examine other pieces of ad copy and you'll find structural sense (perhaps not the same structure, though) based on how the parts of speech are used and positioned in relationship to each other.

Look at this copy closely again and you'll find that the parts of speech within those sentences or fragments are expressed in similar structural ways. For example, verbs follow nouns, and adjective phrases follow verbs. And finally, notice how the careful writer crafting this piece of copy positioned the words as parts of speech. Physically, those words or parts of speech relating to other words or parts of speech are close together so there can be no confusion about what they modify or relate to. Again, very logical, very orderly.

Now, to see at a glance what the parts of speech are and how they are used, let's look at the copy for Luminesse with those parts of speech identified after each word.

*Nothing* (noun subject)

*else* (adjective modifying *Nothing*)

*captures* (verb)

*the* (adjective modifying *spirit*)

*spirit* (noun object of verb)

*of* (preposition)

*satin* (noun object of preposition, with adjective prepositional phrase *of satin* modifying spirit)

*like* (current usage indicates *like* as a preposition)

*Luminesse Lipstick* (proper noun object of preposition, with the entire prepositional phrase *like Luminesse Lipstick* modifying either *Nothing* or *captures*)

*The* (adjective modifying noun *shimmer*)

*shimmer* (noun)

*of* (preposition)

*it* (pronoun referring back to the previous sentence and *Luminesse Lipstick,* which may explain why the writer placed *Luminesse Lipstick* at the end of that first sentence; the adjective prepositional phrase *of it* modifies shimmer)

*The* (adjective modifying *fashion* and *feel*)

*fashion* (noun)

*and* (conjunction joining the two nouns *fashion* and *feel*)

*feel* (noun)

*of* (preposition)

*it* (pronoun referring back to *Luminesse Lipstick*; the adjective prepositional phrase *of it* modifies *fashion* and *feel*)

*Rich* (adjective modifying the noun *color*)

*creamy* (adjective modifying the noun *color*)

*color* (noun subject)

*spun* (verb)

*with* (preposition)

*luminous* (adjective modifying *pearl*)

*pearl* (noun object of the preposition; adverb prepositional phrase *with luminous pearl* modifies the verb *spun*)

*and* (conjunction)

*polished* (verb)

*to* (preposition)

*the* (adjective modifying noun *sheen*)

*softest* (adjective modifying noun *sheen*)

*sheen* (noun object of the preposition; the adverb prepositional phrase *to the softest sheen* modifies the verb *polished*)

Each word with a purpose. And each purpose centered on the word as a specific part of speech. That part of speech dictates how the word will be used and what it carries with it in terms of meaning for the reader.

Regardless of whether you're writing a script or a headline, a classified ad or a brochure, you must write with words. Once you do, and whether you like it or not, you must write the words as parts of speech. If you don't know the difference between those parts of speech and how they interact, far be it for you to have command of your craft. At the same time, the parts of speech aren't that difficult to learn. They're based on the function of words and vital to the logic of our language. There's a definite sense about them, a common sense, one that derives from words as forms of communication. To write well you must know how words work. And how they work depends on their parts of speech.

✍ **WRAP-UP** ✍

What a wonderful thing, words. And you can interpret "thing" however you want. It's wide open.

For the writer, words are everything. Without them the writer is lost. And with them the writer feels at home. This doesn't mean the writer takes them for granted. To the contrary, the writer takes care of them. The writer assesses them, plays with them, polishes them, and hangs them on the writing belt.

In many ways the writer lives inside words, and they live inside the writer. The writer crawls inside words and pays attention to such vital concerns as letters of the alphabet, sounds, gender, age, and tone. Words don't just sit there for a writer. They wriggle and squirm. In fact, the writer loves to watch them do that. A writer even loves to play with them, massage them, bend them this way and that. Like pets, the words love the attention they get. And they reciprocate by making their owner feel wanted and good all over.

When it comes to words there are many things to remember. But that's okay, because a writer doesn't mind remembering them. Take parts of speech, for example. They represent the basic structure of our language. They're the foundation for the meanings that writers convey. And despite how knotty they seem, they make perfect sense. They're very logical, very sensible. They play off of each other, shifting and directing meaning as they interact. To know them is critical. Then once you know them and how they work, you can simply internalize their use and not have to think much about them again. But if you don't know them, and you think you don't need to, then maybe someday you'll write the ad copy line for the bank mailing I received and which we looked at in Chapter 2. Remember? The copy line asked that an applicant complete a questionnaire using the same colored ink as the mailing. It was an example of a misplaced modifier, which is nothing more than not knowing the rule of proximity for parts of speech.

Or worse, if you don't know the parts of speech and how they interact, perhaps you'll also write a headline such as this one for an ad that actually showed up in a major metropolitan newspaper.

19 ENTREES FOR $6.95 OR LESS

The ad was for a well known restaurant. I don't know about you, but after I read the headline I felt like rounding up eighteen people, then having all of us head over to this place, order nineteen fabulous entrees, and thoroughly enjoy ourselves, especially when we got the bill for $6.95, or maybe less.

You see, the word *For* is a preposition introducing the prepositional phrase *For $6.95.* That phrase modifies the noun *Entrees.* And the noun *Entrees* has been modified by the adjective *19.* This means that 19 entrees can be had for $6.95 or less. Now, if the writer knew parts of speech, then maybe headlines such as "Try one of our 19 entrees for $6.95 or less" or "19 entrees, each for $6.95 or less" would have made their way into the ad.

Get it?

## ✍ THINGS TO DO ✍

1.   Read your dictionary. The plot isn't very good. But the characters, the words, are fantastic. Pick out ten of them, five that seem to you to be masculine and five that seem feminine. What makes them so?

2.   Read the copy from an ad in *Modern Maturity, Seventeen, Sports Illustrated,* and any other magazine that you believe targets a specific reader. Jot down a few of those words that seem particularly appropriate for the reading audience. Describe those words according to gender, age, and tone.

3.   Take a pad and pencil with you on your next supermarket shopping trip. Get comfortable in one of the aisles (cereal, cosmetics, or other nonfoods, etc.) and write down a list of brand names within a product class. What do you notice about those brand names that relates to our discussion in this chapter? Do the same with car models. What do the names of those models say about the cars and their prospective consumers?

4.   Break down the following sentence according to its parts of speech: *The dog fetched the bone across the street.* Then rearrange some of the words or phrases (don't add or delete any, though) to change the meaning.

5.   Keep track of your favorite words, words that, as Emily Dickinson said, take the top of your head off. These don't have to be pretentious or haughty words. Just words that grab your fancy. Write them on notecards and display them around your work area. Do at least one everyday. The word I picked for today is *dollop.* Sounds good, doesn't it? It means a chunk or large hunk.

6.   Read over a piece of your most recent writing, preferably a piece of ad copy. Underline all of the "quiet" verbs such as *is, was, am,* or *are.* See if you can replace them with more active verbs.

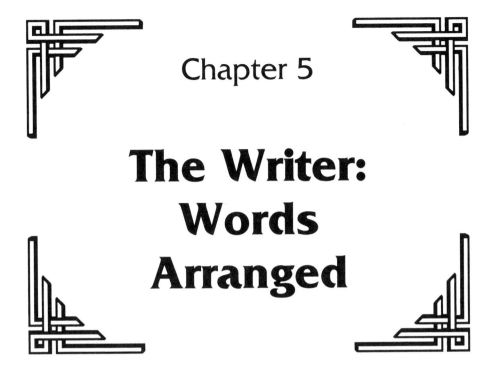

# Chapter 5

# The Writer: Words Arranged

We've said right along that words usually don't stand alone. Not even their meanings stand alone. They're always in contexts. The reader or listener. The writer. The medium. The part of speech. Always these contexts shape the meanings of words. The same holds true for how the words are arranged. This arrangement concerns itself with the actual positioning of words within an expression. Usually that expression is a sentence. Typically the sentence is the bedrock of writing. But the influence of arrangement doesn't stop there. It moves on to other arrangements such as paragraphs, quotes, or punctuation.

We started to enter this area of discussion in our last chapter when we talked about the two fragments in the Luminesse Lipstick ad copy, both of which were juxtaposed against one another and then contrasted with the two longer sentences preceding and following the fragments. For the writer this was a matter of how to arrange the words. The selection and placement of the fragments were really artistic and aesthetic decisions not unlike the decisions of painters or carpenters or landscape architects. In arranging the words as the writer did, certain effects were achieved and certain meanings were conveyed. Both represented the power of word arrangement.

✍ SEQUENCING OF WORDS AS PARTS OF SPEECH ✍

Before we graduate to actual sentences and then on to paragraphs and complete texts, let's start small. Again let's look at the parts of speech and the ways they tend to be positioned in writing. With our Luminesse Lipstick copy, for example, you should notice how the subjects and verbs usually follow a certain order. Also, you should notice how words that relate to other words such as adjectives or adverbs usually are in close proximity to one another. That way there can be no confusion about what the words mean. Here's that part of the copy again.

> Nothing else captures the spirit of satin like
> Luminesse Lipstick. The shimmer of it.
> The fashion and feel of it. Rich, creamy
> color spun with luminous pearl and polished
> to the softest sheen.

First, notice how the noun subjects in the two complete sentences are close to the verbs. In the first sentence we have the noun subject, *Nothing,* only one word away from the verb, *captures.* Following the two fragments we have the final sentence where the noun subject, *color,* directly precedes the first verb, *spun,* and owing to modifiers and the conjunction is a bit further away from the second verb, *polished.*

The order of subject and verb that you see in these sentences is standard fare in writing. Subject + verb, as close together as possible. That is the basic core of writing, though it doesn't mean that all writing needs to follow that structure. For example, it's possible to have a phrase embedded between the subject and verb, such as what we find in a sentence from David Ogilvy's famous Rolls-Royce ad where the electric clock is the loudest noise you'll hear while going sixty miles an hour: "A picnic table, veneered in French walnut, slides out from under the dash." Notice how the noun subject, *table,* is separated from the verb, *slides,* by the adjective phrase, *veneered in French walnut.*

Still, the core of the English sentence is subject + verb, with both being as close together as possible.

Notice, too, how modifiers such as adjective words or phrases are close to the words they modify. For example, the adjectives *rich* and *creamy* directly precede the noun subject, *color.* The writer could have written the beginning of the sentence this way, "Color, rich and creamy, spun...." That would have highlighted the adjectives because of their separation in how the sentence sounded in the reader's mind, but it also would have made for difficult reading because of the even lengthier separation of color from the compound verbs of *spun* and *polished.* In any event, the adjectives are close to the noun they modify.

This same rule of proximity holds true whether you're using a single word adjective or adverb, or an adjective or adverb phrase made up of several or many words. For instance, the phrase *with luminous pearl* modifies *spun*. The phrase *to the softest sheen* modifies *polished*. Both are adverbial phrases modifying their respective verbs. And both are placed in close proximity to the verbs they modify.

Don't undervalue this rule of proximity in writing. For example, imagine if the writer had written the Luminesse sentence this way: "Rich, creamy color spun and polished with luminous pearl and to the softest sheen." Do you see the difference in meaning? Now the product has been spun *and* polished with luminous pearl, all the way to the softest sheen. But based on the original copy, that's not how things work. Instead, the product is spun with pearl. It is not polished with pearl. And, the product is polished to the sheen. It is not spun to the sheen. Thus the value of having your parts of speech, in this case the adjectives, in their proper place so as to convey the proper or correct meaning.

With this in mind, here's a sentence from a piece of copy we looked at in Chapter 2. It was for Schlitz beer, and the sentence read, "So grab for all the gusto you can." Very simple. Very direct. But imagine that sentence rewritten like this, "So grab for the gusto all you can."

Notice how the meaning changes with this rewritten sentence. Now you're urged to go all the way with how you can grab. This doesn't mean the same thing as grabbing for all the gusto, which is the meaning conveyed in the original line. Because the adjective *all* precedes *gusto,* it relates more directly to it. In our rewritten sentence, when the adjective *all* follows *gusto* it squints or points more toward the *you,* meaning that it relates more to you than the gusto. That's not what the writer intended since the product is what contains all the gusto, not necessarily the reader.

This ordering, placing, or sequencing of words as parts of speech in a sentence is extremely important in conveying the right meaning or at least helping the reader gain the right meaning. Shift the position of a word and the meaning changes, sometimes drastically. That's why you must be careful to keep words in close proximity to those words they modify or relate to.

## SEQUENCING OF SENTENCES WITHIN PARAGRAPHS

Just as the sequencing of words within sentences is important to good writing, so, too, the sequencing of sentences within paragraphs is equally important. For example, in our Luminesse Lipstick copy a general statement of capturing the spirit of satin serves as the core of the first sentence. It introduces the focal point for the copy, the satin-like spirit of Luminesse. Then the two fragments that follow elaborate on the satin-like spirit. Its shimmering quality. Its fashion and feel. At that point the copy has become specific, more focused and pointed. With the next sentence the copy retains its specific focus, only now it works its way to the product itself. A two-step process of spinning and polishing creates the rich and creamy color.

Though we've only looked at part of the Luminesse copy, those two sentences and two fragments tell us a great deal about how sentences are often arranged within paragraphs. The first sentence identifies the product and the general theme of the copy. But it also does more. It elaborates on the ad's headline, "Cover Girl Captures the Spirit of Satin." In this way the reader finds it easy to orient herself to the message. Before she leaves that first sentence she knows about the product and the copy to follow. She also knows that Luminesse promises her the capture of satin's spirit. In other words, she knows what the product will give her, in this case a spirit of satin. Then that spirit is qualified and defined. And finally, the creation of the spirit in the product itself is described.

What we can learn from this involves the sequencing of sentences in good writing. Make sure you orient the reader properly so there can be no confusion. Make sure the orientation picks up on the headline or governing theme. Then qualify that orientation. Make it specific and focused. Center it on the product or theme of the copy. And give the reader information about how the product or theme came to be, the benefit to be derived, or both.

In effect, the reader (and it's also the listener with radio and TV) enters the ad with both feet on the ground. Sure, there may be little twists or surprises along the way as the ad develops in the audience's mind. There's nothing wrong with tweeking and raising eyebrows in the process. But overall the orientation is set. And what takes place at the copy's beginning directs the audience in the march toward meaning.

To see how there is this kind of follow-through from beginning to end in the sequencing of sentences, read the entire copy from the Luminesse Lipstick ad. While you're at it, notice how our discussions of words, gender, age, tone, and parts of speech play a part here.

COVER GIRL CAPTURES THE SPIRIT OF SATIN.
LUMINESSE LIPSTICK
Nothing else captures the spirit of satin like Luminesse
Lipstick. The shimmer of it. The fashion and feel of it.
Rich, creamy color spun with luminous pearl and
polished to the softest sheen. So lips look radiant.
Feel satiny. Hour after hour. Cover Girl Luminesse
Lipstick. In a collection of spirited shades. Capture it!

What we get from the copy is a rhythmic swing from the theme of satin-like quality to the product itself (how the satin-like quality came to be), then to the benefit for the consumer (So lips look radiant. Feel Satiny. Hour after hour), followed by another product identification and description (collection of spirited shades), and finalized with a return to the capturing of satin's spirit.

If we had to chart those sentences according to their content, we might be inclined to see the first sentence, two fragments, and second complete sentence as product oriented. They tell the product's story. But with the line "So lips look radiant" we begin to receive a consumer orientation. Now the lines are speaking not so much of the product as what the product will give to the consumer, in this case, radiant lips. This is followed by another consumer-oriented line, "Feel satiny," which in turn is followed by still another, "Hour after hour." Then the copy moves back to the product, its name and description of a variety of colors. Finally, the copy closes with a move back to the consumer and a critical part of the overriding theme, *capture,* complete with the understood *you* (the consumer) as the noun subject.

If you were to follow this copy as a guide to copywriting, then one of the important things to learn is that your body copy should address the product and its consumer or target audience. It should seek to describe the product in terms the audience understands and appreciates. Beyond that it should relate the product's performance to benefits, those meanings that consumers take inside and absorb in respect to what the product does for them.

Still another side to organizing the writing of sentences is the issue of structure. We've already discussed this to an extent when we talked about the fragments in relationship to the complete sentences. Again, though, if you were to follow this copy as a guide to copywriting structure then one of the things to learn is that your copy should combine complete and incomplete sentences. These should be placed strategically for the sake of impact and to make your copy reader-friendly.

You would also vary the lengths of sentences. Notice, for instance, how the last imperative sentence, the call to action, commands the reader in two words, "Capture it!" This is shorter than any other sentence or fragment in the copy and for good reason. It is the final point, the main point, the point to be remembered the most. Use of the word "capture" simply reinforces the governing theme while at the same time inducing action, a strong action. And the action follows on the heels of why, in fact, the benefit of the product (satin-like quality) should be captured.

Still another structural consideration, one that will be addressed more fully in our important Chapter 9 on style, is that of how sentences are weighted around the subject + verb core. For example, notice how the first sentence in the Luminesse Lipstick copy begins with the subject + verb core, but then includes a noun object and two modifying phrases. Structurally this gives the sentence a dominant weight to the left of the subject + verb core.

In giving pleasing variation to their style, accomplished writers know that if they vary such arrangements, their writing will be that much easier to read. In this respect, think of the variations in weighting you could give to the subject + verb core. You could left-branch the weight, in which case the sentence may look like this, _____ subject + verb. Or, you could right-branch the weight, in which case the sentence may look like this, subject + verb _____. Or, you could work within a variety of possibilities such as embedding the weight, in which case the sentence may look like this, _____ subject _____ + verb _____. The Luminesse Lipstick copy line we discussed in the previous paragraph is an example of a left-branching sentence, one where the elements are weighted to the left of the subject + verb core.

Without laboring over this kind of sentence structuring and meaning, it should be clear to you by now that writers write with intention. They have a purpose. Especially copywriters.

With copywriters the purpose is to convey the relevant benefits of why one should choose this product to fill this need or solve this problem. That means the product story becomes important, but only in respect to how it meets the consumer's need or solves the consumer's problem. As a result, when the copywriter writes sentences, these goals are foremost in the mind. They are front and center in that mind. And one of the things that mind knows is that readers or listeners will stay riveted if there's something in it for them. Also, they want information. And they want it as it relates to the supposed benefit derived from using the product.

So, do you want a satin-like look and feel to your lips? One that you can gain while changing color if you wish? If so, then Luminesse Lipstick will give it to you. Why or how? Because it's spun with luminous pearl and polished to the softest sheen. Then it's manufactured in a variety of shades. All for the look and feel of your lips, radiant and satiny.

Think about all of this. I know it's thick. It may even seem tedious and persnickity. But is it really? We're examining ad copy. We have it under a microscope. There's a reason why. It's the way we learn how to write it. Copywriters choose words with intent. Then they arrange the words into sentences, also with intent. By close examination of the copywriters' work we learn why and how they achieve what they're after. We learn their techniques for reaching objectives and actualizing strategies. This kind of close examination is the only way to learn what they do.

Of course, in discussing sentences within paragraphs we've only looked at one piece of copy. To generalize about its structure and apply it to all advertising copy or other forms of writing would be a mistake. There are other structures and methods for writing effective sentences. We will approach them later on, but for now the point to be remembered is that sentences work as units within paragraphs. More so, they work alongside one another, not alone. There is a certain kind of teamwork to a group of sentences, all focused on an overriding goal of communicating particular meanings to a reader. In advertising copy those meanings revolve around the product story and consumer benefits.

## ✍ SEQUENCING OF PARAGRAPHS ✍ WITHIN BODY TEXT

Words as parts of speech are units within sentences. They interact. Sentences are units within paragraphs. They also interact. And paragraphs are units within complete text. Like words and sentences, they interact as well.

The copy for the Luminesse Lipstick ad contained one paragraph, perhaps due to the writer's belief that the copy was relatively short and could be read and understood easily in one paragraph. But as we know that's not always the case with ad copy. Many times it contains more than one paragraph. Many times it contains many paragraphs. Often, as with virtually all writing, these paragraphs signal extensions or tangents of previous ideas. That's why they're expressed as paragraphs and not just as continuing sentences within one paragraph, though the advertising copywriter knows that shorter and perhaps more numerous paragraphs make for easier reading.

Still, for the copywriter the paragraph acts as a unifying structure for a particular copy point. Together, sequential paragraphs act as a means for organization, a means for splicing together an entire theme from the various copy points to be made. In a sense, each paragraph represents a shift or movement to another idea or point. And when taken together in sequence the paragraphs express the totality of the main theme.

So it is when you read the following copy for the Nissan Pathfinder. The paragraph breaks are noted by extra spacing.

THERE ARE NO CITY LIMITS

They've got traffic in Trenton. Potholes in Pasadena.
And noise in New Orleans.

What's a city dweller to do?

Get a Nissan Pathfinder.

It is simply the best combination of power, comfort and
durability of any vehicle on the road. Or off.

And we're not the only ones who feel that way about
the Pathfinder.

Last year, *Four Wheeler* magazine named the
Pathfinder its "Four Wheeler of the year."
And *4 Wheel & Off Road* magazine named
it "4 × 4 of the year."

Which means now, driving will be fun in Philadelphia.
Comfortable in Columbus. And smooth in Smyrna.

You've just read seven paragraphs containing approximately 100 words of copy. That's about fourteen words per paragraph. Not very many. At the same time notice how each paragraph contains its own copy point. Also, notice how all of these individual points link together to form a tidy package of complete text.

In the first paragraph the writer combines a complete sentence with two fragments. The sentence and fragments identify problems faced by city dwellers. These problems are presented through alliteration. Traffic and Trenton. Potholes and Pasadena. Noise and New Orleans. Considerable playfulness here, an important trait of ad copy.

In the second paragraph the writer poses the big question, What's a city dweller to do? To do about what? About traffic, potholes, and noise. Thus the problem is clear. And as we can tell from this paragraph, which asks the big question, a solution is on the horizon.

In the third paragraph the writer presents the solution. Get a Nissan Pathfinder. By this time we've advanced through three paragraphs. Step by step the writer has posed the problem and presented the solution.

In the fourth paragraph the writer makes a bold statement, declaring the superiority of the Pathfinder, specifically in respect to power, comfort, and durability. Clearly, though, such a bold statement of superiority may be suspect. After all, who's to say the Pathfinder is so superior? This leads us right to the next paragraph.

In the fifth paragraph the writer provides us with a transition between the preceding fourth paragraph and the following sixth paragraph. The transition opens the door of support for the bold claim of superiority. Structurally, it acts as a bridge between the fourth and sixth paragraphs. At the same time it tends to ease the minds of any skeptical readers.

In the sixth paragraph the writer notes two pieces of supporting evidence for the claim, both from what appear to be respected magazines.

Finally, in the seventh and last paragraph the writer brings us full circle back to the alliterative touches of the first paragraph, much like the writer for Luminesse Lipstick did with the final copy line of "Capture it!" The main difference, however, between the first and last paragraphs of our Pathfinder copy is striking. In this last paragraph the alliterative touches refer not to the problem but to the result of the reader having purchased the solution. Now we have fun in Philadelphia. Comfort in Columbus. And smoothness in Smyrna.

The writing of paragraphs means the writer must tap away on the typewriter space bar or press the return button on the computer keyboard. It's similar to what we do in our minds. We move to another thought or idea. When we type it (or even write it) we move to another spot on the page. It's the same whether we're writing copy for a print ad or a script for radio or TV. Before the introduction of a new thought or idea, we tap the space bar or press the return button because we know that such a shift needs to be shown.

Of most importance, though, is the understanding of a paragraph as a unit within a larger unit, the complete text, and a unit containing other units, namely, sentences and words. Think of the paragraph (think of a sentence this way as well) as a box within a larger box. The job of the writer is to make certain all of the boxes go together or fit into one another so that by the end of the reader or listener's experience, what's left is a tidy, appealing package of cohesive meaning.

I like what I've just written. No matter how I turn it in my mind, I believe it makes considerable sense. But there's another way to think of this entire matter.

Think of it as art and craft.

Along the way we've made passing references to the art and craft of baseball, painting, carpentry, dancing, cooking, and landscape architecture. Very different arts and crafts, yet they demand the same kind of attention to their perfection as copywriting does. The common ground for the copywriter here is the need to have everything that's written pull together. No hitches in the swing. No foreign elements that don't lend themselves to the totality of the art on the wall. No forgetting one's hammer and how to use it. No not keeping the muscles toned and in harmony with one another. No ingredients that rob the dish of its flavor. No tall flowers in the front of the garden hiding the shorter flowers in the back.

The meaning here is simple. The writer is an artist and craftsperson. As an artist the writer is responsible for creating certain effects and conveying certain meanings. As a craftsperson the writer is responsible for knowing how to use the tools. That's how the art gets created. The tools for the writer begin with the alphabet and end with a complete text, whether that text is a radio script or print ad. In between there are all sorts of considerations. Words acting as parts of speech. The contexts for those words. The audience and its expectations, knowledge, and likes or dislikes. Learning how to work with these considerations is the writer's responsibility.

## ✍ USING PUNCTUATION ✍

Fine. The writing sits on the page, one box in another and tidy as a result. No apparent hitches in the big swing. No ill-fitting boxes. But is that enough? Perhaps not. A final flick of the wrist may help. Possibly a bow on the package. Not much, mind you. But a little something extra to complete the swing or wrapping. Often that can be achieved through punctuation.

There are fourteen different forms of punctuation. Period. Question mark? Exclamation point! Comma , . Semicolon ; . Colon : . Dash — . Parentheses (...) . Brackets [ ]. Ellipsis.... Apostrophe ' . Hyphen - . Quotation marks " ". And the slash /. But let's not bog ourselves down laboring over the appropriate use of various punctuation marks. Let's focus our attention on something more critical to writing, punctuation shaping meaning and creating effects.

### The Importance of Punctuation to Meaning and Effects

Of course, it's important to remember that most often you're required by unspoken but understood rules to toe the line when it comes to punctuation. And there's good reason for that. Like contexts or words themselves, punctuation helps shape meaning. For example, if you don't use a question mark at the end of a question, how is the reader to know for sure that what has been read is a question?

Even when we hear a question we're able to punctuate it with a question mark simply because the inflection in the voice moves us to that punctuation. Leave punctuation out of what you write and you leave what's written open and, perhaps, confusing.

To see how this can work consider Shakespeare's play, *Macbeth*. While plotting the assassination of King Duncan, both Macbeth and Lady Macbeth wrangle with each other. Macbeth's wrangling consists of doubt about committing the deed. Lady Macbeth's wrangling consists of powerful rhetoric to convince Macbeth that the deed should be done. Finally, Macbeth asks, "If we should fail?" And Lady Macbeth replies, "We fail." Now think about what you just read.

Macbeth asks a question signified by a question mark. By its very nature a question asked assumes an answer to come. Lady Macbeth replies with two words, "We fail," almost as if saying, "so what." The meaning is clear, but imagine then inserting various punctuation marks into what Lady Macbeth responds. And consider when you do just how the meaning of what she says changes.

If you insert a question mark after her statement, then it throws into question the strength of her character. In other words, she, too, is unsure. Furthermore, we might assume that she has never considered the possibility of failure before. But now that she does she may have some doubts about whether the deed can or should be committed.

On the other hand, the exclamation point after her statement reinforces her strength. Perhaps it even reinforces her daunting and unswerving single-mindedness regarding the act. In short, she doesn't care if they fail.

Now consider what happens if you break up the two words, "We fail," with punctuation. What happens, for instance, if you place a question mark after "We," followed by another question mark after "fail"? It would read like this, "We? Fail?"

Consider other variations as well. "We...fail." "We fail...." "We! Fail?" "We? Fail!"

No doubt, as you read through each variation you realized that the deep meaning of the words shifted, perhaps dramatically. With the ellipsis following "We," Lady Macbeth seems more hesitant, more unsure. With the ellipsis following "fail," she seems thoughtful, perhaps entranced. With the exclamation point following "We" and the question mark following "fail," she seems focused on their joint strength and outraged or surprised by Macbeth's suggestion of failure. And with the question mark following "We" and the exclamation point following "fail," she seems surprised by Macbeth's suggestion implicating both of them as failures. At the same time she seems boastful, almost disbelieving that failure could result.

All of this because of little punctuation marks on a page. That's how important punctuation can be when it comes to shaping meaning or creating effects. It acts as a final touch, often a touch with large consequences. Consider, for instance, the case for ellipses and parentheses. An example of an ellipses is the three little dots following a word. As we read one word to the next we suddenly come upon those three little dots (or periods) and our reading voice fades like the quieting of an engine. But those dots ask us to continue on in a thoughtful and imaginative way. They ask us to imagine something else said in order to finish the meaning of the preceding words. So, we make something up, hooking the imaginary words to those we've just read.

"Last night she said everything..."

"You'll never know how much..."

"Looking for something quick and easy? Then try..."

In each of these examples the ellipsis pushes us on to create more words, to manufacture or complete meaning in our minds. As a closure device, the use of an ellipsis generates involvement on the part of the reader. An ellipsis asks for the reader's participation in the message. The effect can be powerful on that reader, stimulating the imagination to come alive.

With parentheses there can be an equally powerful effect, only of a different nature. When we come to parentheses in our reading we tend to pause, stopping for a brief moment to gather ourselves and get our bearings. We also tend to snuggle ourselves inside the parentheses. In a weird sort of way we unlatch a tiny door in the opening parenthesis mark and crawl inside to the words. Once inside we get the feeling we had better close the door because the words are secretive and no one else should hear them. Hearing the words is often the effect gained from using parentheses. As soon as we crawl inside the marks a voice seems to speak. It's the writer's voice. It's also a hushed voice, almost a whisper because it's talking only to us and no one else.

In many ways parentheses act like a stage aside in drama. Someone says, "Psst. Come here. I want to whisper something to you." We can almost see that someone beckoning us from afar. Crooking a finger and turning a head side to side to make certain no one else is listening. Then, cradling us around the shoulder, casting furtive glances side to side until the secret is divulged. Of course, this is a bit of an exaggeration, but not by much. Parentheses have that effect on the reader. As a result parentheses can be useful for slipping in pieces of information that are especially important to a message, information that may go unnoticed otherwise. Parentheses are also important for personalizing what's written, conveying the quality of the writer's voice. Material inside parentheses reads like someone speaking, and speaking personally, one-on-one to you with no one allowed to overhear what's being said.

These are some of the effects of punctuation, at times subtle and at other times bold. Depending on what form of punctuation the writer selects, the very meaning of a sentence, phrase, or word can be altered. At the same time and despite its importance, punctuation is generally something we don't dwell on when we write. More often than not it's just there, many times because it seems appropriate. Want to end a sentence? Better type in a period. Want to ask a question? Better type in a question mark. It becomes automatic as we write. Yet, used strategically at key points in the writing punctuation can shape meaning and create effects.

## Trust Your Reading Voice to Tell You When and Where to Use Punctuation

For many writers there seems to be considerable confusion about when and where to use certain punctuation. Sometimes even the rules for that use seem to change. For example, present-day usage leans toward less comma use, particularly after brief introductory phrases such as "by the way," "in addition," "more so," or "after all." Today the trend is toward fewer commas, not more. On the other hand, use of other forms of punctuation such as the period has remained more constant throughout time.

Quite frankly, I'm not one to keep on top of varying rules of usage. I just don't care that much, mainly because I don't think it's that important to live by what at times seem like quite arbitrary rules. Instead, I recommend using punctuation according to the voice you hear while reading. Listening to that voice will guide your selection of what punctuation to use and when to use it. Trust that voice when it speaks to you.

When we read we hear. With quotation marks we hear someone clearly. And if we're really astute readers, we conjure up an auditory and perhaps visual image of that someone we hear. If someone else speaks within a new set of quotation marks we change the auditory and visual image. But all of this takes place in our minds as if there's a mechanism of some type that clicks on, kind of like a cassette tape with voices sounding in our heads.

Even when we read plain sentences we hear a voice. Perhaps less distinct and identifiable than what we hear within quotation marks, but a voice all the same. In fact, as we write we often write from a voice in our heads. A voice speaking to us that then gets transmitted into typed or written words. Similar to what I'm doing right now. The suggestion, then, is to trust that voice while writing. Listen to it speak what it's writing. Listen to it speak what it's reading. And then use punctuation marks accordingly.

If your reading voice wants to pause, but only pause briefly before moving on its merry way through a sentence, use a comma. If your voice doesn't want to pause, don't use a comma. If your voice wants to stop before moving on, perhaps to another thought entirely, use a period. If your voice wants to stop, but only briefly and only to understand that there's elaboration of the point you just made, use a colon or semicolon. If your voice wants to jump up and down with excitement, use an exclamation point. If your voice wants to fill in the blanks, use ellipses. If your voice wants to join two words acting as one, use a hyphen. And if your voice wants to emphasize something and set it apart from the rest of a sentence, use a dash.

Now, these may not be the hard-and-fast rules you'll find in any one of a number of worthwhile grammar books. Certainly those books are worth the reading. And if you read them you'll find the rules for punctuation are not that difficult or complicated. For example, *The Borzoi Handbook for Writers* lists the following as some of the criteria for comma use: to join independent clauses (Read carefully, and you'll take a big step toward being a writer), after a subordinated clause introducing the main clause (Since you want to write, think about reading), after a modifying phrase more than a few words long (In a whirlwind rush of excitement, the writer writes), to separate an interrupting element (The writer, obsessed with how to make words mean, may experience writer's block), and to present quotations (The writer said, "Let there be light").

Notice, however, how the commas in each of the copy lines within the parentheses act as reading breaks. If you sound out those lines you'll find that the commas make you pause. Yes, it's a brief pause. You don't dawdle for very long and then go on. You pause, very briefly, and then go on. So though the rules are clear, they're also fundamentally the same as listening to your reading voice. This is how your reading voice works as a guide. Learn to trust it when it speaks to you.

One important form of punctuation where your reading voice can't be trusted, however, is the apostrophe, primarily because its use avoids sound or rhythm changes. At the same time, incorrect use of the apostrophe can really put off a reader. It's like a wart on the end of a nose attached to a beautiful or handsome face. The viewer has difficulty getting by that wart. Though your writing may be positively gorgeous overall, if it's marred by blatant misuse of punctuation, including the apostrophe, then the reader may be unable to see the gorgeous quality of what you've written. The same, by the way, holds true for spelling.

The most common misuse of apostrophes is to form possessives versus contractions, especially when using the three-letter word *its*. *Its* without an apostrophe shows possession. *It's* with an apostrophe shows a contraction for *it is* or *it has*.

*It's* time to learn the rules of punctuation. (It *is* time....)

Each writer's mind has a reading voice in *its* head (*its* shows possession of head and mind).

This same rule applies to possession when you use pronouns such as *yours, theirs, and ours*. No apostrophe is needed. When you want to show possession by someone or something, however, you'll need an apostrophe. For instance, notice in the last example that the mind belongs to the writer. Because of this the apostrophe is used to show possession, "writer's mind." Of course, there are other kinds of use for the apostrophe such as with plural nouns where the apostrophe comes after the *s*. As an example, consider *the dictionaries' definitions*. Here, we have more than one dictionary. Similarly, *several days' work*. Here, we have more than one day. But if you wanted to show that it was just one dictionary or one day you would write, *the dictionary's definitions* and *one day's work*.

Still another area of apostrophe use is with contractions, one of the most important parts of copywriting. Contractions abbreviate combinations of words and make the reading easy for the reader. They also serve another function, however. They give your writing a conversational tone, almost as if you're talking to the reader in an informal and personal way. In many ways contractions help your writing achieve a quality of voice, simply because they help the words sound like people speak. With this in mind, don't be afraid to use *don't* versus *do not*. Don't be afraid to use *you're* versus *you are*, or *I'm* versus *I am*, or *she'll* versus *she will*, or *it's* versus *it is*. These types of contractions can lend a great deal of warmth to your writing, so use them.

Feeling pestered, you may want to avoid what you perceive to be these mosquitoes of punctuation use. That's why time has been spent here clarifying these areas, at least in a limited way.

To my experience, young writers have an awful time with punctuation, especially in the proper use of commas and apostrophes, and the feeling of freedom to use contractions. Commas and apostrophes are really a matter of abiding by standard rules of use and listening to your reading voice. Contractions, on the other hand, may mean breaking standard rules of use in favor of warmth and conversationalism. This can become a head problem for the young writer. For years, maybe many years, the young writer has been told not to use contractions for the sake of conveying a conversational tone. Instead, the young writer has been told to keep the writing more formal and, in the end, stiffer and more lifeless. In advertising (and other forms of writing as well), stiff and lifeless writing can mean death.

Overall, to have command of punctuation as a means for conveying meaning or creating effects can add a great deal to your writing. It's not the biggest thing, of course. But it is important. Remember, you don't want to develop warts on your writing. They can rob it of its luster. One way to do that is by settling in your mind now the issue of punctuation, especially when and where to use it. Again, beyond what you've read here, you can go to any good grammar book and learn the rules, much the same way you would memorize lists or rules for other interests you may have. You may be surprised at how clear, sensible, and easy those rules are.

✍ **WRAP-UP** ✍

Much of what we've discussed in this chapter relates to style, a subject we'll view more closely and thoroughly in Chapter 9. For now, though, give thought to the stylistic decisions you must make when writing. One of your primary goals is to make your writing coherent and well organized. You can do that by conceiving of written expression as boxes within boxes. A word exists in a sentence. A sentence exists in a paragraph. A paragraph exists in a complete text. And overall, the complete text exists inside your writing goal and the creative idea designed to reach it.

Stylistically, your writing should provide this type of orderly, sequential, and coherent form of expression. It should pay homage to the parts of speech as the bedrock for how your writing leads to appropriate meaning. Sequencing of words, sentences, and paragraphs is important here since it guides your reader or listener from one copy point to another, often, as in the Nissan Pathfinder copy, presenting a problem and then solving it before the ad copy is finished.

A large part of your job as a writer involves this kind of guidance. In effect, you take your audience's hand and show them the way to meaning, the one you want remembered. To do that you must know the path to meaning. It can be a smooth one if your writing pays allegiance to basic rules of grammar, spelling, and punctuation. If it doesn't, however, the journey can be a rough one, with your audience baffled and annoyed along the way. Your job is to avoid that possibility. Or, as we said chapters ago with a different analogy, you try to throw the audience a big fat pitch right down the middle so that they can get the meat of the bat on it. This makes them happy and content. It's the wild curveballs of incoherent writing and errors in the fundamentals of the language that drive them nuts.

### ✍ THINGS TO DO ✍

1.   Select the complete copy from a favorite ad. Pick an ad that contains paragraphs of copy. Then read it over. Carefully. Break down the parts of speech in one of the sentences. Do it again with another sentence. Try to get to the point where you see the words and phrases as units within larger units, each with a function of creating clear meaning.

2.   Using the same piece of ad copy, sound out the lengths of the sentences within the paragraphs. Hum them, approximating their length. If your hum is more of a drone, unvarying and monotonous, cast a critical eye to the copy. It may not be very good stylistically. But if your hum has variation, sort of like this, mmmmmmmm, mm, mmmmmmmmmmmmmmmm, mmm, mmm, mmmmmmmmm, then maybe it's better stylistically.

3.   What's the theme, the "incipient center," of the ad's copy? And how do the specific copy lines help unify that theme?

4.   Notice special effects in the copy. Parentheses, for example. And notice the punctuation and how it helps your reading voice stop and go.

5.    Repeat 1 through 4 above with the following piece of copy taken from an ad for The Nature Company, the manufacturer of a potato-powered clock. We'll look at this ad in its entirety in our later chapters. The copy, by the way, was written as one paragraph.

> At every glance, you'll be hiking, biking, breathing clean air,
> eating sandwiches smashed in the bottom of your pack. You'll
> be birding with Sven, having his children. Or you'll be walking
> with Gwenne in that secret meadow by the creek. Stuff like that.
> A masterful balance of digital watch technology (and isn't *that*
> still amazing) and two russets, white roses, bentjes, or kennebecs,
> this clock will give you honest time. Real time. Tater time.
> It tells month and date, too. It even runs on soda pop
> (if that ruins the karma for you, forget we said it).

6.    Reread a recent piece of ad copy you've written (actually, any recent writing will do). But reread it based on the concepts of structuring we've discussed in this chapter. Be critical of too much repetition of sentence lengths. Be critical also of too much variation. Rewrite the copy including some variations of sentence lengths. Also try to vary the structure of the basic subject + verb core. Include some left- and right-branching sentences in the mix.

# Chapter 6

# The Writer: One Little Ad for Parker Pen

We've been through a veritable forest of tips so far. Let's name some of the trees: The writer's mind. How it works. What makes it tick. Its compulsion. Its need to heal its fragile ego and soul. Its need to find and give meaning. Its courage. Its need to find a time and place. Its process. Its knowledge of the subject.

Others include the prerequisites for writing, even before you begin to put pen to paper or fingertip to keyboard. Understanding surface and deep meanings. Understanding how meaning evolves. From the reader. From the writer. From the contexts.

Still others are: Being able to see. Being visually literate. Not sophisticated necessarily. Just literate. Also, loving words in the same way a professional baseball player loves the bat and ball. The same way a gourmet chef loves ingredients, or the carpenter loves the hammer, or the painter loves the brush. All the way back to the alphabet, then forward to words as parts of speech.

Understanding that words work in combination with each other. Understanding the logic and order of the language. Understanding that the structure of the language is like a box within a box.

These are the tall trees in the writing forest. There are others, to be sure, but these are the tall ones. What they should tell you is that to be a writer you must understand the art and craft. You must devote yourself to it. That devotion begins with how you react when you confront words. Do you pass over them, giving little care to their dynamics? If so, writing's not for you. What you need is a persona, a reading persona, a Sybil of yourself with the passion to read as a writer. Looking for clues. Techniques. Methods. Trying to uncover the mystery of how words *mean*.

It all sounds so grand, and in a way it is. But it's meaningless unless all of us apply these tips. First apply them through reading and then apply them in our writing. With this in mind here's an ad (Figure 6–1) and complete text of what Bruce Bendinger (the author of *The Copy Workshop Workbook*) believes is great writing. It's an ad and copy for the Parker Premier fountain pen. Let's read and view it carefully. And let's read it according to many of the considerations we've discussed throughout the book.

IT'S WROUGHT FROM PURE SILVERAND WRITES LIKE PURE SILK

You will find writing with the Parker sterling silver Premier fountain pen anything but drudgery.

In fact, it's entirely possible you will find it something of an inspiration.

We can't promise it will give you the wisdom of an Oscar Wilde, although holding the solid silver body does lend itself to contemplation. (It's 92.5% pure, as pure as sterling silver comes.)

When you do finally write, the words will flow with such uninhibited smoothness there will be nothing to block the way should a profound thought happen to wander along.

Thank the nib for that. And the extremes we go to making it. The nib takes three weeks to manufacture, because we do it almost entirely by hand.

We fashion it from 18K gold to make it flexible to the touch. Then at the tip we mount a tiny pellet of ruthenium, a metal four times harder than steel and ten times smoother.

The ruthenium tip is sculptured under a microscope—a deft operation any surgeon could envy. But an even more delicate task follows.

The nib must be split with a cutting disc only .004″ wide. Literally fine enough to split hairs.

Finally, the nib is tumbled in walnut shells for eighteen hours to leave the gold incomparably smooth.

Only after all this, not to mention 131 inspections along the way, will the craftsman who made the nib sign the certificate allowing us to sell you this pen.

Buy the Parker Premier and even if you never write anything magnificent, at least you will never write anything but magnificently.

FIGURE 6–1  Copyright Parker Pen USA Ltd. Advertisement reprinted with permission of Parker Pen USA Ltd., Janesville, WI.

## ✍ WRITE WHAT YOU KNOW AND BELIEVE ✍

Is there anything more true than that the writer for this ad copy knew the subject? The writer fills the copy with specifics. But it's more than just specifics tossed in because of arbitrary reasons. These are specifics with a purpose. And the purpose is to support the claim for the pen, that of assured quality writing due to the quality craftsmanship of the Parker Premium fountain pen. Look at how much the writer knows.

The pen is 92.5% pure sterling. The nib takes three weeks to manufacture.

Can you see the craftsman at work? A craftsman mounting a tiny pellet of ruthenium on the tip. Can you see the ad writer at the factory? Can you see the ad writer looking carefully over the shoulder of that craftsman? The writer asking questions? Being a pest about what takes place?

Before reading the copy did you have any idea what ruthenium is or how important it might be to the tip of a pen? I didn't. But the writer tells us. Ruthenium is a metal four times harder than steel, yet ten times smoother. This means the pen tip is strong and smooth. Very strong and very smooth, so that when you write you can press all you want and when the ink flows to the paper, it will flow smoothly and evenly.

But how does the tip get manufactured? And isn't the word *manufactured* a bit too impersonal, too suggestive of an assembly line? Sculptured is more like it. The care and craftsmanship of sculpture. Sort of like fine art. Or more like a surgeon wielding his tools. And this, too, the writer tells us.

Can you see the writer zeroing in on the tip, literally and figuratively? The nib where the action of a pen takes place. This nib is split with a cutting disc only .004″ wide. That's 4/100ths of an inch.

But the writer's not finished with the nib yet. It's tumbled in walnut shells. Not once. Not just for a minute or an hour. It's tumbled for eighteen hours, over and over again, until it's smoothed to a fine, polished finish.

As if that's not enough, the nib and pen undergo demanding inspections a total of 131 times. Only then will the craftsman sign the certificate announcing that the pen is ready to be sold.

Now think about this. How could the writer possibly have written this copy without knowing everything and anything about that pen, especially its nib? At the same time, do you think the writer was given such specific information? Perhaps. But then again, perhaps not. Perhaps the writer had to dig for that information. Perhaps the dialogue between the writer and account person or research director went something like this:

| Writer: | "Well, if the nib's so important, how is it made?" |
|---------|---------------------------------------------------|
| Other:  | "I don't know. Something about ruthenium metal. Very carefully constructed. Very craftsman-like." |
| Writer: | "How so, craftsman-like?" |
| Other:  | "Craftsman-like, you know. One at a time. Painstaking. All that stuff." |
| Writer: | "All what stuff?" |
| Other:  | "Caring kinds of stuff." |
| Writer: | "Like what kinds of caring kinds of stuff?" |

Of course, I've exaggerated a bit here. But maybe not so much, especially if you get the point that the writing and probing go hand in hand. And when not satisfied, the writer probes some more. Eventually it's possible that a trip to the factory might be in order. More so, it's possible that an interview with the craftsman might do nicely as well.

The point overall is that the writer knew the subject. Knew it down to the ruthenium mounting on the nib. Knew it down to the .004″ disc that cuts the nib. A disc fine enough to split hairs. Translated, this knowledge of the writer means the owner of the Parker Premium will receive a grade A pen with a supreme nib, apparently one of the most important parts of a pen's construction.

One of the first things to understand about this ad copy is that the writer knows the subject. And you should take that understanding to heart. If you don't know about what you're writing, don't write about it.

Tangent to writing about what you know, you should also believe in what you're writing. Recall our discussion from Chapter 1 and the importance of sincerity on the part of the writer. Sure, in writing poetry, fiction, or some other personalized genre, the writer has an advantage in sincerity. After all, the writer has presumably made very individual and personal decisions about the subject matter and the way to present it. But with advertising, things are different. Now the writer must work within the constraints of time or space. Moreover, the writer must work within the constraints of a particular product being sold to a particular consumer. No art for art's sake here. To the contrary, strategic controls are needed. Yet, the best copywriters believe in what they're writing.

With this Parker fountain pen copy it should be clear to you that the writer's commitment to and belief in the product peek out from between the lines. Indeed, the writer seems impressed with the fact that the nib is tumbled in walnut shells for eighteen hours. Even in the phrase "And the extremes we go to making it," the writer's self is joined with the craftsmen making the pen. Throughout the copy we gain a sense of the writer enjoying the writing, a sense of commitment to and belief in the product and what it can do for those who choose to buy it.

## ✍ SURFACE AND DEEP MEANINGS ✍

On the surface the copy is clear. It makes some promises. Your writing will be exciting ("anything but drudgery"). It tells of craftsmanship (the nib, the gold crafting process). Stemming from the headline, the copy leaves no room for misinterpretation or misunderstanding. As readers we know exactly what we're going to get should we choose to purchase this product. But beyond that there are reverberative meanings, deep meanings evolving from the subtle use of language.

Notice the writer's choices of words in the headline. This pen is wrought from pure silver. It also writes like pure silk. Think of the writer's choice of the word *wrought.* The writer could have selected other words such as *made, constructed, manufactured,* or *formed.* But those words are sterile. They lack the life, vigor, and precision of the word *wrought.*

Even the surface dictionary meaning of the word reveals a great deal about its deep meaning. Webster, for instance, defines wrought as formed, fashioned, shaped by hammering or beating, made with great care, elaborated, decorated, or ornamented. When something is wrought we attach a deeper meaning to that something than if it is simply made or formed. We know a bit more about that something than if it is made or formed. That which is wrought seems to suggest more value, more care, and more craftsmanship. And isn't that what the copy tells us?

In focusing as we have on this one word, *wrought,* we gain insight into the writer's mind as it carefully selected those words most in keeping with the product and what needed to be said about it. With this one word we learn a lot about the product. We learn that it's crafted, not just mass produced. We learn that it's sturdy, solid, and hard because of the association we make to hard metals such as iron and to the word *wrought,* as in wrought-iron. And because of this learning we read the copy with a particular perspective in mind, that of a handcrafted, quality product whose story is about to be told.

The same holds true for the word *pure.* Used twice in the headline, it suggests the untarnished and impeccable nature of the Parker Premium fountain pen. No defects here. No blemishes. Only perfection. The most perfect silver. And by way of a touch association, a writing experience akin to pure silk. Again, as with wrought, we are predisposed to the quality of the product, even before the story has been told.

Beyond these two words in the headline, notice how other words in the copy reach beyond surface meaning by associating the pen's quality with the quality of language. As precise as the craftsmanship of the pen may be, so, too, the selection of words is equally precise. Words such as *drudgery, inspiration, profound, sculptured, deft, delicate,* and *magnificent.* In their contexts within the copy they tap into our expectations. They cause us to elevate the pen above the ordinary. They impress us with their carefulness and precision, the same way the pen should impress us with its feel and performance.

Of course, we could go to Webster for each word of the copy and gain dictionary definitions to help us construe meaning. But we really don't have to do that. We know close enough what the words mean. And we carry those expectations of meaning into our reading. Like sliding up and down a musical scale, we associate certain meanings for those words. Their tone helps the sliding. When we come across words such as *profound* and *deft* we understand their upscale quality. We understand they're meant to delineate and crystallize meaning. We grant that. That's how we read.

As we read the copy through, one word to the next, we gather the meaning from the individual words, their contexts, and their interaction with one another. Gradually we pile the meanings, one on top of the other, until we have a tidy package of meaning where the individual words blend together. This becomes the deepest meaning for what we've read, all a matter of accrual and association as we move beyond the surface meanings of words.

## ✍ CREATING THE VARIOUS MEANINGS ✍

As we know, meaning doesn't just happen. It's not a magical matter. Rather, it's created, with a number of forces inspiring that creation. You and I, for instance. You and I as readers, that is. Or the writer as another instance. Add to this the contexts for what we read, particularly words surrounding words and a governing theme. And finally, add to everything else the ad's visual presentation. The reader. The writer. The contexts. The visual presentation. Each shaping the meaning of what we read.

### Meaning through Ourselves as Readers

As readers we bring our expectations, knowledge, and likes and dislikes to the transaction of reading. Remember, we give ourselves over to what we read, at least to an extent, and this helps open us up to meaning. With the Parker pen copy we give ourselves over to the pen's story, particularly the story behind the pen's nib. No doubt, we're impressed with the various facts outlining how the pen's nib comes into existence. Perhaps this is due to our own lack of knowledge about pen nibs.

I, for example, had no idea how a pen's nib is manufactured. Nor did I care much. But if I were in the market for a pen, especially a good pen, then I might be interested. Even with that, assuming that I'm interested in a fine pen, I still bring very little knowledge to the subject. And it is here that the writer acts as my guide.

By the time we finish reading the Parker pen copy we know more than when we began. Depending on how much we knew at the outset, we could conceivably know a great deal more. This is most true when it comes to nibs. As we discussed earlier, the writer tells us all the specifics about how the Parker nib is manufactured. At the same time, to read about that isn't something we would expect, unless perhaps we're dealing with a premium pen. Then a story could be told, one which separates this pen from others, even though the others may not be mentioned by name.

The entire notion of telling a story about a pen, especially a pen nib, seems to rattle against our expectations. But still we get the story with this copy. And since we tend to be fascinated with news and information generally, we involve ourselves in the specifics of the copy.

Chances are that if we don't have an interest in pens, then the ad copy won't mean much to us. Thus the importance of the headline as a means for sparking our curiosity. But if we're in the market for a pen, especially a fine pen, or we're simply interested in what we write with, then ad copy for the Parker Premium fountain pen might strike our fancy. Yet not all of us are interested in what will probably turn out to be an expensive pen. If we're not, then again there's little urging us to read on. But if we are or think we might be interested in a somewhat costly pen, and a fountain pen at that, then we'll read on. And as we do we discover that the Parker Premium pen promises us all we could hope for in a quality writing instrument.

Naturally, this has everything to do with who we are as readers. What we bring to the reading act includes our expectations shaped in large part by what we already know and what we like or don't like. If we have an interest in or like pens, especially fountain pens, we'll read. If not, we won't. And as we read we carry into the words that interest and liking.

Given what we've been discussing, it should be clear that this copy for the Parker Premium pen is tailored for a certain type of individual. Maybe that individual isn't you, but even if it isn't, you still need to read it from the targeted reader's point of view, mainly because that reader was critical to the writer's selection of content and style. This is what we meant earlier on when we discussed the importance of creating different reading persona. You read what's written from the perspective of the targeted reader. You read with that reader's eyeglasses on. And you gather meaning through the mind of that reader, in effect transforming yourself into that reader.

Naturally, the transformation to someone or something beyond yourself is no easy matter. It's even eerie at times. We're used to being ourselves, to experiencing life, including reading or listening, according to our personal agendas and priorities. To experience life as someone else experiences it calls for a mammoth and difficult task of selfless-ness. We project ourselves into the other. And we lose ourselves as a result. For copywriters this is all to the good since virtually everything they write belongs to others. It's meant for others. It's written from the points of view of those others. And because it is, with every written word the writer's self dissolves and disappears. Before you know it, you're only a few words into the copy when you realize that the writer is nowhere to be seen. Fortunately, the targeted reader is, especially if the writer has done the writing job well.

With this in mind, what is there about the writing in this copy that casts the reader onto our stage where the light shines brightly?

From what we've discussed to this point we know that the target audience is a certain type of individual. There are giveaways. The upscale language, for instance. A bit uppity at that. In other words, stylistically the copy breathes a more refined air than what we would find in other ad copy, the *TV Guide* VCR+ ad copy we looked at in Chap-ter 4, for example.

Even with the copy's content we gain insight into the target audi-ence. The Parker Premium is a fountain pen. A dead giveaway. This is not a pen you pick up at the supermarket checkout counter, the kind that's packaged in cheap plastic with a slew of pen clones, all selling for less than a buck. This is a fountain pen. Now, who uses a fountain pen? Maybe you don't. I know I don't. But others do. And maybe others will if they bite hard on the ad's copy.

If you had to flesh out this targeted reader, what would he or she look like? How would he or she be dressed? More so, is it a he? Or a she?

Perhaps this reader wears the finest suits. Drives the finest cars. Dines at the finest restaurants. Perhaps this reader not only wants the feel of luxury while holding pen in hand, but also wants others to see the luxury, elegance, sophistication, and class.

If you can accept this brief sketch of a targeted reader for the ad, answer this: What is this reader interested in when reading about a premium fountain pen?

There's no way to answer that question without getting into the mind and heart of the reader. That may take some guesswork on your part. But there's an easier and surer route to take. The copy can be your path to understanding.

We can react to both content and style according to who we are. But again, the ad's copy may not mean much to us if we're not the type to use classy fountain pens. All the hubbub about the nib, for instance, may roll right off or zip right past us. We may end up baffled to the core in trying to figure out why a writer would bother taking up so much valuable time and space with the nitty-gritty story of a pen's nib. If that's the case, it means we've read the copy wrong. We haven't lost ourselves in favor of the words. We haven't kept ourselves open to those words and why they are what they are.

So, let's keep ourselves open to the words, their content and style. And as we do we'll find the reader sitting in our heads in a fine black leather wingback chair, one leg creased across the knee of the other, the Parker Premium fountain pen in hand.

This reader has arrived, or at least has serious plans in that direction. Let's say it's a he, although it could be a she, despite stereotypes to the contrary. He's successful, or perhaps will soon be. And not successful by chance. He's successful by dint of hard work and paying close attention to detail. He's bright, intellectual, or at least fancies himself so. When he comes across words such as *wrought, pure, silver, drudgery, inspiration, contemplation,* and *profound,* he's impressed. After all, that's his language.

But why so much attention to the nib? Well, when this reader writes the last thing he wants is a laggard for a pen. He doesn't want skips and bumps. He doesn't want leaks and scratches. He wants surety, certainty, and silky ease. He wants to feel good about the pen. He doesn't want to ponder the negative implications of toting and wielding a $.99 ballpoint. He wants to impress. Perhaps he needs to impress. Perhaps his very job depends on it. As a result, he takes special interest in the nib. It's like his paintbrush. His hammer. His bat. It's the point where the ink releases itself and becomes one with paper. So it better be good. In fact, it better be the best there is, or else he's not going to buy it. Just like the safety or performance assurance of a Volvo or Mercedes or BMW. No Chevy Geo here. Not for this fellow.

Of course, we've exaggerated a bit here. Or have we? Perhaps we're not too far off. Given what the copy says (its content) and how it says it (its style), our description may be close. And how did we get to that description? By reading the copy. But reading it not according to us, but according to what the words reveal about their targeted reader. That's how we can reconstruct who that reader is and what makes him or her tick. Be assured, it's not everyone who's interested in a premium fountain pen with a nib tumbled for eighteen hours in walnut shells. It's not everyone who expects a pen to be crafted almost entirely by hand, perhaps meant to be sold to select individuals only.

The point that cannot be lost here is that when we read we construct meaning according to who we are as readers. But that doesn't mean we're always the same reader. Especially with ad copy, the task (and it's a difficult one, make no mistake about it) is to read and write as though you don't exist. It's the other who is more important.

Meaning through the Writer

As part of deep meaning beyond words themselves, our assessments of how we're relating to the ad's copy broaden what it means to us. That broadening of meaning carries over as well into the area of the writer of the copy. For us to understand what the copy means in its deepest sense we need to flesh out what the writer had in mind.

Granted, this may not be as important to us as what we give to the copy in the way of meaning, especially if we read through the eyes of an implied reader. At the same time, to do that we must know something about the ad writer's intentions. They're reflected in the writing. That's how we discover what they are, by reading what's written and using that to coax the writer out of hiding. Knowing that the writer selects certain words to express the content and style, we expand meaning by overlaying the words we read onto the writer's intentions.

In this respect, we already know how careful and precise the ad writer was in selecting certain words for the Parker Premium fountain pen copy. The word *wrought,* for example. Such a word tells us of the writer's understanding and knowledge of the product and reader. As we've said, with this copy the reader is a bit upscale, fairly well educated, and holds his or her pen in high regard, either for how it performs or for what it suggests and perhaps symbolizes about the person using it. And based on the selection of such words, the writer gives the intention away, allowing us to discover it as we read.

Combining knowledge of the product (perhaps a must for the writer given the type of reader the writer had in mind) with knowledge about the reader, the ad writer made specific choices of what to write (content) and how to write it (style). Remember, every word chosen suggests many words not chosen. Realizing that the copy space represented valuable real estate, the writer had to be judicious in deciding on content and style. Doesn't it seem likely, for instance, that the writer's selection of the pen's nib as a centerpiece for the copy stemmed from careful consideration? After all, the writer could have selected any one of a number of other product attributes to highlight. The pen's body, for instance. Its streamlined styling. But, no, the copy centered on the nib.

Obviously, in making the nib the copy's centerpiece the writer believed it was important. In one respect it represents a significant differentiating factor for the pen, that which separates it from other competing pens. In another respect it represents an insight into the target audience, the reader. Remember, here we have someone who holds a pen in high regard. Otherwise why would that someone care to know about a nib?

As a centerpiece for the copy the nib stands alone, highlighted for the reader. Yet, it also implies the writer's intention, especially when you consider the contexts in which it is described. Let's see if we can sort through those contexts, aware from the outset that the writer had intentions in choosing what to say and how to say it.

Let's start by answering these questions: Was the writer's intention or goal in highlighting the nib simply a matter of providing specific information about a specific pen part? Or was it something more?

Copywriters know that we don't buy things. We buy abstractions, concepts, ideals, and most of all, benefits. For example, we don't buy perfume. We buy hope. We don't buy word processors. We buy ease and convenience. Well, what about the nib? Was the writer trying to sell us the nib? Or was the writer trying to sell us what the nib could do for us?

This, of course, is a very important part of being a copywriter. Perhaps an important part of being any kind of writer. A writer chooses the content. It's loaded with specifics, with information and detail. But in its own right the content falls short of leading us to understanding the intention or goal of the writing. Instead, it provides us with clues to the intention or goal.

In the case of our Parker Premium fountain pen copy, the nib becomes the pen's reason for being. It is also the nib that leads to the benefit, the ultimate intention of the writer. The nib paves the way for conveying the benefit. Notice that the nib allows us to write magnificently, even if we never write anything magnificent. Realizing this and its supreme importance to this type of target audience, the writer knows that the nib's story will have to be told in order to justify and legitimize the promise of writing magnificently.

Remember, this is an ad we're reading. The overriding purpose of an ad is to sell. But you just can't ask someone to buy your pen because you happened to manufacture it. For someone to buy that pen it must prove itself, especially in respect to what that someone wants or needs in a pen. Since writing magnificently, perhaps smoothly and without apprehension about the quality of the actual penning of words, is important, then the story of how the pen manages to write magnificently becomes all the more important. That's why the nib becomes the centerpiece of the copy.

It's the context of the writer's intention that deepens our understanding of why the nib is featured in the copy. The governing intention here is to convince us that the pen will write magnificently. We should have no fear, hesitation, or apprehension about that. This intention lies beneath the surface of the words or even the entire story of the nib. In fact, it's the strategic reason for the nib controlling the copy.

### Meaning through Contexts

Given this intention or goal of the writer (to sell the pen by convincing us that it will write magnificently), is it no wonder that the entire copy aligns itself so neatly with all of the surrounding contexts? Let's take words around words, for instance.

Notice the selection of words keying into the reader's thoughtful nature. It may even be an intellectual nature. Words such as *inspiration* in the second paragraph. Or, as the story begins in paragraph three, the fact that holding the pen will lend itself to contemplation. Or, as the story begins to unfold in paragraph four, the possibility for a profound thought presenting itself.

These first four paragraphs say nothing of the nib. Rather, they build the promise, the benefit. They reveal the writer's real intention. Writing magnificently, which means writing with uninhibited smoothness. Or even while not writing, the mere holding of the pen lending itself to contemplation. This is how the pen gets sold, simply because the writer understands that this is what the reader needs to know in order to think well of the pen.

To support that promise or benefit, the nib story must be told. And why? Quite simply because the nib is the key to the pen writing magnificently. That's why the next five paragraphs of copy devote themselves to the nib.

As you backtrack through the copy, notice how the theme of writing magnificently controls each and every paragraph. Paragraph one promises no drudgery. Paragraph two promises a possibility of inspiration. Paragraph three qualifies the promise, keeping it realistic and reachable. In other words, the pen won't make you smarter, yet it will help you to contemplate. Paragraph four continues with the promise, now more precise with the smoothness of writing. Paragraph five begins the nib story as support for the promise. This story continues through paragraphs six, seven, eight, and nine. Paragraph ten puts a topping onto the promise. And the final paragraph clarifies where all of the copy has been heading, which is straight to the theme or benefit.

Through the contexts of words surrounding words, the writer's objective and goal, and the singleminded thrust of a theme, we're able to plunge beneath the surface of the copy and discover deeper meanings. Often those meanings lie between lines, even between words. And often they reach deep into the writer's mind as it practices the art, intent on communicating a certain message to a certain reader.

Meaning through Visual Composition

When we discussed the importance of a writer being able to see, we focused on principles of visual composition. We classified our discussion under the rubric of visual literacy: knowing how and why crafted objects (paintings, ads, Mother Nature) look the way they do. As we look at the Parker fountain pen ad (Figure 6–2) we can see these principles in action. Here's the ad again. Stare at it for awhile.

# It's wrought from pure silver and writes like pure silk.

You will find writing with the Parker sterling silver Premier fountain pen anything but drudgery.

In fact, it's entirely possible you will find it something of an inspiration.

We can't promise it will give you the wisdom of an Oscar Wilde, although holding the solid silver body does lend itself to contemplation. (Its 92.5% pure, as pure as sterling silver comes.) When you do finally write, the words will flow with such uninhibited smoothness there will be nothing to block the way should a profound thought happen to wander along.

*Oscar Wilde*

> I can stand anything except the price of everything and the value of nothing.
>
> *Oscar Wilde*

> Man is the only animal that blushes. Or needs to.
>
> *Mark Twain*

Thank the nib for that. And the extremes we go to making it. The nib takes three weeks to manufacture, because we do it almost entirely by hand.

We fashion it from 18K gold to make it flexible to the touch. Then at the tip we mount a tiny pellet of ruthenium, a metal four times harder than steel and ten times smoother.

> He is a self-made man and worships his creator.
>
> *Donald on a fellow politician*

The ruthenium tip is sculptured under a microscope—a deft operation any surgeon could envy. But an even more delicate task follows.

The nib must be split with a cutting disc only .004" wide. Literally fine enough to split hairs.

Finally, the nib is tumbled in walnut shells for eighteen hours to leave the gold incomparably smooth.

Only after all this, not to mention 131 inspections along the way, will the craftsman who made the nib sign the certificate allowing us to sell you this pen.

Buy the Parker Premier and even if you never write anything magnificent, at least you will never write anything but magnificently.

> Be a wit to all; subscribe to many; familiar with few.
>
> *Benjamin Franklin*

### ◈ PARKER

**FIGURE 6–2  Copyright Parker Pen USA Ltd. Advertisement reprinted with permission of Parker Pen, USA Ltd., Janesville, WI.**

On the surface the visual composition of the ad is clear. Visually, it's a fairly uninspired and ordinary ad. We have a product shot of the pen horizontally framing the headline and copy. On a deeper level, however, are visual subtleties that reverberate with meaning, much of it directly tied to what we discussed earlier. For instance, the inactivity of lines and shapes (everything seems at rest because of the broad horizontal framework of the ad) lends itself to contemplation. We're not talking about furious writing here. Even the copy tells us that. We're talking about thoughtfulness, pensiveness, and then some inspiration. But even the inspiration is not the whirlwind kind; at least it's not expressed as such with the visual presentation of lines and shapes.

Notice how the ad's visual elements are strategically shown and placed. For example, the pen's nib is pointing to the left, not the right. Why?

If the pen's nib were pointing to the right, the eye would be drawn in that direction. This means we would have to work our way back to the headline and copy. To make it easier on us, the artist places the pen's nib to the left, just above the headline, almost suggesting that the beauty and stylistic architecture of the copy itself as shown in the ad flowed from the pen's nib.

This positioning of the pen is no accident. It aids the sequencing in the ad. Recall that sequencing is the way elements are positioned so as to help the eye move through an ad. In this case, our eye begins at the upper left of the ad and works its way down.

Notice, too, how the ad is completely balanced. The formal symmetry suggests the sophistication and class of the product and, indeed, the copy. In fact, the formal symmetry may suggest the sophistication and class of the targeted reader. Remember our description of that reader. Sitting in a fine black leather wingback chair with one knee creased over the other. Very formal. Very dignified. Well, the composition of the ad's elements lends to this formality and dignity. We have two columns of copy balanced against one another so that, if you placed a mirror down the middle between the two columns, the images on either side would approximate each other.

At the same time, the artist realizes that the copy is long, so it needs some visual touches to make it more interesting and enticing for the reader. Short paragraphs are one way to keep a reader reading. And so are highlights in margins (you see that often in long direct-mail letters). Here, quotes from magnificent writers are shown penned on paper. We have a quote from Mark Twain, followed by quotes from Oscar Wilde, Benjamin Disraeli, and Benjamin Franklin. As well as being proof of the pen's fine writing, the subtle meaning of these visual additions connects great writers and minds with the reader.

Yes, the copy tones down the promise to make it more realistic. No pen can make the reader smarter or even a better writer than he or she already is. But the penned words of wisdom, often with touches of wit, align themselves in a subtle way with that reader. Moreover, they also help to create unity in the ad. They act as a binding visual ingredient, shown to us in the same way at strategic points beside the paragraphs of copy.

By now much of your reading of the visual composition of the ad has been colored by our discussions of the reader, writer, and contexts. It's virtually impossible for you to view the ad naively or innocently, especially given those discussions. Instead, your expectations have been shaped by what you read earlier. So it goes. But even with that, if you hooked into the principles of visual composition and the importance of visual elements such as line and shape, you probably brought more knowledge into the visual presentation of the ad. Perhaps you may not have viewed it the same way a hundred pages ago. If such is the case, good. That, as they say, is called learning.

Beyond yourself as a viewer, can you see how you can recapture the artist and his or her intention simply based on the visual composition? Obviously, the writer and artist work closely together, sort of like a hand in glove. One knows what the other is doing. In fact, what one does depends on what the other does. With our artist, the task was to stay within the lines of sophistication and class, to match those traits or characteristics of the product with similar traits or characteristics in the reader. That's why the ad looks the way it does. Nothing gauche or rowdy here. Just something a bit understated, somewhat elegant, all the while matching the type of product with the type of reader.

## THE POWER OF THE INDIVIDUAL WORD

Recall back when we took a microscope to individual words. Words meaning as they sound. Words having gender, age, and tone. Let's take that microscope out again and look closely at some of the words in the Parker pen ad copy. We've already taken a close look at the word *wrought*. But let's zero in some more and then listen to the sound of that word, the sound of *rawt*.

What does the sound suggest to you? The dominant letters, *r* and *t*, should suggest a hardness in the word and what it means. Perhaps a fullness in the word as well. As we've said before, when something is wrought it's not just made. It's built. And we tend to think it's built tough. The letters *r* and *t* help us build that very meaning.

That which is wrought is not crocheted or sewn or glued or pasted. It's built. With the sound of the word we conjure up images of fire and ice. A steely workman, hard hat and goggles in place, scarred about the face, shirtsleeves clumped above the elbows, forearms like Popeye. He's the one who will wrought, and he'll do it with his trusty hammer in hand.

*Wrought* is a masculine word. It's a word of experience, of age. In fact, it carries with it the quality of age, as if something wrought has endured the test of time. It also carries with it the tone of hardness or firmness. It's an oak of a word, wrought.

Beyond the contraction of *it is* in the headline, wrought is the first word we read. When we read on we carry in our minds all of these filings of meanings about wrought. They attach themselves to the magnet in our minds, much like the bits of meanings from other words found in the copy.

Think of the word *sterling,* for instance. Something sterling is pure. There's a ring to that word, a clear, crystalline ring, perhaps due to the *-ing* sound combined with the *-erl* sound. It peels. It's a clarinet. Not a tuba. A piano. Not an organ.

Or the word *drudgery.* Drudge sounds like sludge. Slow. Lazy. Impure. Sticky. That's what you won't get if you write with the Parker Premium fountain pen.

Or the word *flow.* FFFFFFLLLLLOOOOOOO. Nice and easy does it with this pen. You won't find the words bouncing or skipping. They'll be flowing. Here, the mixture of masculine and feminine. We don't expect something wrought to flow. Pound, maybe. But flow? Yet, the pen is wrought so that its end result is the flow of ink.

Or the word *smoothness.* SMOOOOOOTHNESS. Like flow, smooth rolls off the tongue. It sounds like it means.

Notice the writer's mixing of hard and smooth words. Contrasting words in sound, gender, and tone. *Smoothness* versus *block* in paragraph four. *Harder* versus *smoother* in paragraph six. *Tumbled* versus *smooth* in paragraph nine. Such combinations operate at extremes in the reader's mind, breathing life into the writing and making it more vivid and vigorous for the reader.

And what of the word *ruthenium*? Sounds like something straight off the periodic table. Scientific. Metallurgic. Like kryptonite. Something with unearthly powers. Something mystifying, yet intriguing. We want to know about that word, simply because it sounds the way it does.

Individual words can have such effects on a reader. Our reading voice sounds the words out. We hear them, however silent that may be on the outside. We hear them inside, in our minds. Their various shadings of gender, age, or tone echo inside us. Then we crystallize them and attach them to our minds.

### ✍ THE POWER OF PARTS OF SPEECH ✍

Recall our discussion of parts of speech, the network of our language. Recall that the verb represented the most important part of speech, simply because it creates the action in the reader's mind. As a writer, your best friend is action verbs. Adverbs and quiet verbs such as the state-of-being verbs (*is, was, am, were,* etc.) are your enemies. With that in mind, let's look at the structure of sentences in terms of how the parts of speech are used, with emphasis on the verbs.

Beyond noticing the headline where the action verbs, *wrought and writes,* control the sentence, the parts of speech in the first copy line set the stage for the remainder of the copy. The line reads, "You will find writing with the Parker sterling silver Premier fountain pen anything but drudgery." The subject is "You," a magic word in advertising copy. Often, no other word can match it for impact since it relates to the reader in no uncertain terms. The verb, *will find,* is future tense. A promise of things to come, though given the sophisticated copy to follow, one could possibly build a case for substituting the verbs *discover* or *experience* for *find.*

The word *writing* is a gerund, meaning it has noun and verb qualities. In this case it's a noun acting as the direct object of the verb *will find.* It answers, "Will find what?" Following the noun *writing,* the prepositional phrase *with the Parker sterling silver Premier fountain pen* reaches back to modify that noun. Notice, however, how the phrase has been placed close to the noun so that there is no confusion in what it's meant to modify.

Also notice the capitalization of Parker and Premier, the pen's name. But notice that capitalization in contrast to the words embedded within the name so as to give more pointed description of the pen. For instance, before we know the pen's name in its entirety we know that it's made of sterling silver and that it's a fountain pen. Now go back to the headline and notice that the pen's name isn't mentioned at all, perhaps because the headline is meant to tease us into reading the copy in order to find out what is wrought from pure silver and writes like pure silk. By the way, all of the words preceding the word *pen* in that first sentence act as modifiers. Parker and Premier modify *pen.* Sterling modifies *silver.* Silver modifies *pen.* And fountain modifies *pen.*

Finally, the adjective *anything* reaches all the way back to modify the gerund noun *writing.* You will find writing anything. In a way it looks through the gerund *writing* to the verb *find,* attaching itself to both words. It also qualifies the noun object, *drudgery,* which as a noun relates to the verb and action status of the gerund *writing.*

Of course, we don't want to bog ourselves down nitpicking parts of speech. But almost as a game, you can go through each sentence trying to sort through the words, then classifying them according to their parts of speech. If you do that you're sure to find some interesting combinations used by the writer. For example, in contrast to the structural combination of subject + verb + object + modifying phrase + modifying word + object, look at the final sentence in the next to last paragraph. It reads, "Only after all this, not to mention 131 inspections along the way, will the craftsman who made the nib sign the certificate allowing us to sell you this pen."

This sentence is a mouthful, to be sure. But don't be intimidated. Take it a step at a time. First, where's the subject? You'll have to search through more than half of the sentence to find it. It's *craftsman.* Where's the verb? Again, you'll have to search. The verb is *will sign.* In other words, the "craftsman will sign." Within that basic subject + verb structure you have a subordinate clause, *who made the nib,* embedded. You also have a host of modifying phrases including "Only after all this," "not to mention 131 inspections along the way," and "allowing us to sell you this pen."

Naturally, within each of the modifying phrases (themselves units within units) you have individual words functioning on their own. For instance, in the phrase "along the way," *along* is a preposition introducing the prepositional phrase, complete with its noun object, *way,* which modifies the noun *inspections.*

This kind of sophisticated writing doesn't happen by chance. It happens as a result of paying homage to the language and the potential in what can be achieved when the language is understood. This takes time. It takes practice. And it takes focus. But if you're intent, if you have but one main vocational goal in life which is to write, then the time, practice, and focus should not intimidate you.

## ✍ THE POWER OF WORDS ARRANGED ✍

As important as the individual word is to your writing, remember that the word doesn't stand alone. It stands beside other words, usually in phrases, clauses, and sentences. They, in turn, stand beside each other in paragraphs. As you work with these various units your goal is to arrange them so that your writing is coherent and enjoyable to read.

As you look at the Parker pen ad copy you should notice the variations in how the words, sentences, and paragraphs are arranged. For example, notice that the first four paragraphs contain complete sentences. The first two paragraphs contain one sentence each, both approximately the same length and structured in the same way. Subject

+ verb + object and modifiers. But in the third and fourth paragraphs the structure changes. Here, we have much longer sentences containing expanded modifiers in the form of phrases and clauses.

Think about this. In re-creating the writer's intentions, there must be a reason why the first two paragraphs contain fairly simple sentences and the next two paragraphs contain fairly complex sentences. Perhaps, for instance, it has to do with the writer not wanting to intimidate the reader early on. By writing simple sentences to begin the copy, the writer promises the reader some ease in reading. In effect, the reading journey won't be that difficult. Now, if the writer began the copy with long, complex sentences, then the invitation to partake in the copy may have been met with apprehension. Long and complex sentences may have scared off the reader.

Notice, too, how the first two paragraph sentences focus on the reader, making two promises of benefits. The third paragraph expands the promise, while at the same time beginning to shift attention to the product. In fact, parentheses in this paragraph contain words exclusively product-based. But in the fourth paragraph, the writer guides the reader back to self-interest with more of a promise, a benefit.

When we get to the fifth paragraph we're fully into the product and its story, especially the story of the nib, yet notice how this story is introduced by two fragments. Quick. To the point. And acting as transitions to the nib's story.

Let's chart out these first five paragraphs, approximating the sentence lengths, so that we can see the shifts in rhythmic and stylistic patterns for each sentence Notice as we do, however, that the copy avoids monotony by creating various sentence lengths. This makes the reading more enjoyable.

_____.

_____.

_____.

( _____ ).

_____.

_____._____.

If you were to sound out the copy (and you should, by the way), then it will sound anything but boring. As with the promise in the copy itself, the arrangements of the words according to length and the variations of subject + verb + object structure avoid drudgery and create easy, enjoyable reading.

Even in terms of punctuation, the copy conveys a sense or tone of warmth and personalism. Not that the copy is too personal or friendly. In fact, it's not. That would put off this particular reader. Instead, it's a bit distant, but it still carries with it a light air of personalism. Notice, for instance, the use of contractions in the second and third paragraphs. These contractions convey a voice to the reader, almost as if there's someone speaking one-on-one across the table. At the same time, there are instances where contractions aren't used, thus keeping the copy a bit more formal and dignified. After all, given the product, creative idea, visual composition, proper tone, and this particular reader, you wouldn't want your copy to get too comfy, too down home or friendly. Better it should remain somewhat dignified, perhaps even slightly aloof at times.

## ✍ WRAP-UP ✍

One little ad for the Parker fountain pen. But so much to see in it. So many valuable lessons to learn from it.

Write what you know. And believe in what you're writing. This means you must learn all you can learn about your product and your audience. Fill your head with knowledge. Keep probing and digging until you find the most important match between your product and audience. Then write about it in a believable and personable way. To do that you'll need to be committed to what you're writing.

Be sensitive to how meanings accrue and develop. Through the audience. Through the writer. And through contexts. Then pay attention to the individual word. It has considerable power. At the same time, remember that the individual word doesn't stand alone. It stands beside other words. Combined together, these words guide your audience to meaning. But even in that combination of words, you must make decisions about how they're arranged.

Will you rely on the standard subject + verb + object structure? Will you vary it along the way? Will you write all complete sentences? Or will you embed a few choice fragments to ease the reading flow or create emphasis? And how will you get from one copy point or paragraph to the next? What transitions will you use to achieve this? Will you vary your sentence lengths? And when is the right time to do that? Finally, will you tell a story? If so, how will you shape it? How will you begin and end it?

These are important questions for you as copywriter. But you need to address them. As we move through our next chapters we'll focus on the strategic underpinnings to help you with your ad copy. Eventually we'll get to the questions asked here. Still, though, you can begin thinking about them now. In many ways to answer them means you must think like a writer. Certainly the writer for the Parker fountain pen ad did. The ad copy proves it.

**THINGS TO DO**

In previous sections of "Things to Do," you've been asked to play your way through a variety of exercises. But here, let's get more involved with the nitty-gritty of ad copy. Take a close look at the two ads, one in Figure 6–3 and the other in Figure 6–4. Then give both of them a good read, meaning a read that applies all that we've discussed, including a read that looks between or behind the lines and words. And have fun while you're doing it. You'll see and read these ads again before you're done with this book. When you do, the discussions surrounding them should be no surprise, especially if you give them a good read now.

By the way, the copy for each ad is shown separately, with extra spacing given so you can take notes, doodle, or just practice reading better between the lines.

*Copy for Timberland*

Don't get us wrong. If you want to use our new boat shoes with the

Interactive Grip System to fox-trot across the yacht club dance floor,

that's your choice. We guarantee you and your blazer will look good, and

we promise to accept your money.

Just be aware that we engineered these shoes so you dance on a very

different surface. The storm-blackened foredeck of a boat that's bucking

like a rodeo bull.

On so wet and treacherous a playing field, one slip of the foot could be

one slip too many. Preventing it is what the Interactive Grip System is all

about.

As its name implies, the System starts where the foot interacts with

the boat. At the sole. Our new design gives you such a profusion of siping

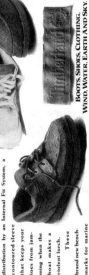

FIGURE 6–3 Advertisement reprinted courtesy of The Timberland Company.

(razor cuts for traction) that the number of leading edges exceeds the traction capacity of traditional boat soles by a good 50%. What's more, the edges are clustered in an exclusive quadrant cut pattern. (Competitors beware. The Timberland quadrant cut sole so outgrips standard wave cut soles it may cause mutiny at the yacht club.)

Part Two of the Interactive Grip System makes sure that your foot stays in the right place so the quadrant cut sole can do its work. Your foot is secured for proper balance and energy distribution by an Internal Fit System, a contoured sleeve that keeps your toes from jamming when the boat makes a violent lurch.

These brand new benchmarks for marine footwear aren't just high-tech, but true high performance for the 1990s. A new definition of authenticity that puts our imitators in an embarrassing place.

Overboard.

*Copy for Royal Viking*

THERE ARE NO MAPS TO STEER YOU EAST OR WEST. Yet it is possible to get there, and perhaps the best way is by ship.

But not just any ship. It should be one filled with the elegance and little touches that make a vessel worthy of being designated five-star-plus. We have not just one, but an entire fleet of such remarkable crafts.

FIGURE 6–4   Advertisement reprinted courtesy of Royal Viking Line. Reprinted with permission.

Each of our ships is equipped with candlelit dining rooms that offer unhurried single seating. Aboard every one, you'll find kitchens where 33 European-trained chefs will prepare fine delicacies. In the staterooms, fresh flowers appear magically each morning. Surrounding each vessel are the most spacious, most strollable decks.

At every turn, you'll witness the alert, gracious service that inspired the readers of *Travel-Holiday* magazine to vote us the Most Courteous Cruise Line for three years running.

So in the end, it is not a question of whether you can arrive at the proper state of mind by way of our ships. It is merely a question of how soon you will choose to do so. Your travel agent will help you decide, or call us at (800) 426-0821. We look forward to your call and to seeing you on board.

# Chapter 7

# Strategy Considerations

In a simplistic way, think of ad writing like this. You want to say something, and you want to say it in a certain way. The something is the *content,* and the way is the *style.* Content generally revolves around a theme, that "incipient center," often expressed as a benefit. Style generally revolves around an idea, the vehicle that carries the theme and content. Very simple. Very understandable.

Of course, things aren't always as simple as they seem, especially when we probe beneath the surface. For example, the content in an ad can range far and wide, depending on the type of product, the medium, and the objective. Even the targeted audience has influence here, as we've seen with our ruthenium nib as content matched to a specific audience. Remember, nothing stands alone, not even words. Everything is in context. Change a part of the contextual mix and everything changes with it. Change certain factors such as the product, the medium, the strategy, or the audience, and your ad changes as well.

The consideration you give to the various factors and contexts influencing your ad leads directly and immediately to your strategy. Despite the fact that we're not trying to do what most other copy books do, which is emphasize advertising creative strategy, the importance of strategic considerations cannot be undervalued. That's why when you pick up virtually any advertising copywriting book you find most of it devoted to creative strategy.

Although there are many varied formats for creative strategy, all of them focus on one primary goal, how to sell the product to a specific customer. The strategy outlines the way to do that, with a large part of the selling job dependent on matching something about the product with something about the consumer. Every product has features and corresponding selling points, sometimes called *product benefits*. Every customer has wants and needs to be filled and problems to be solved. Your job is to match the two.

## ✍ THE MIX OF STRATEGY CONSIDERATIONS ✍

Obviously this is much more a book about how to write than it is about how to conceptualize a creative strategy. Again, you can turn to any one of a number of other texts for strategic preplanning to write an ad. At the same time we'd be remiss (worse, misleading) if we ignored strategic considerations. Actually, we've dwelled on some of those considerations already in our discussions about readers, words, and especially the Parker pen ad copy. Still, there are specific components that go into the ad mix.

### The Product

There are all kinds of products. Just look through the stores the next time you visit the shopping mall. There are so many kinds of products they boggle the mind. As if the mall isn't enough, the next time you visit just about anywhere look carefully around you and you'll see products.

A dentist's office? All the instruments, the chairs, the technology, the filing systems, the computer at the front desk, the coat rack in the waiting room, the dentist's lab coat and mask. Products everywhere, and each one had to be sold and bought.

A golf course in the middle of Mother Nature? Fertilizers. Sprinkler systems. Poles with flags. Grass-cutting equipment.

On a daily basis we're flooded with an absolute torrent of product life. And every part of that life is different, even products known for their parity. Something about them still makes them different. Perhaps it's the color. Or the shape. Or the container. Or the price. But rest assured, something's different. And the same also holds true for services or stores. Now, if there's a match between that difference and a customer's need, want, or means for solving a problem, then the match is made in heaven, and the ad will almost write itself.

Sounds easy, doesn't it? Of course, it's not. Not at all. Many variables enter the picture, complicating it along the way and making the writing of an ad anything but easy. Not the least of these variables is the consumer whose need today may not be the same one tomorrow.

Still, there are certain ways of relating with your product that will help you map out a strategy for your ad. More than anything they involve a life beyond your own skin. They involve living the life of the product. They involve making lists and answering questions. No short-cuts here. The only route to a good ad is knowing everything that can be known about your product, especially as it compares to the competition and relates to your target audience. Everything.

*Getting Inside Your Product and Its Competition.*   Get out of yourself and inside the product. Become the product. Dissolve into it. Feel it. Taste it. Learn what it's all about, whether it's an actual product or a store or service.

Let's go back briefly to the Parker Premium fountain pen. We spent considerable time analyzing the ad copy, but do you remember how the analysis began? It began by discussing how the writing mirrored the writer's knowledge of the product. To become knowledgeable about the pen the writer had to crawl inside. Especially inside the nib. And even inside the pen's competition.

Be assured, a good copywriter is a good detective. A bloodhound. A busybody. A good copywriter won't leave the product and its competition alone, constantly hovering around both, inquiring, probing.

Let's say you have to create and write an ad for Cheerios. Do you think you could do it without knowing all there is to know about the product? Sure, you'll also have to know what the ad is supposed to achieve and who it's targeted toward. But first and foremost you'll have to know about the product. You'll even have to eat a few bowls of it. Then, to know it well and in its proper context, you'll have to compare it to the competition, which means you'll have to eat various bowls of cereal.

Recent Cheerios ads tout the theme of "Plain and Simple." As simple as that theme is, don't be misled. Read behind the line. What does that reading tell you about the strategic considerations of the writer, particularly as they relate to the product? Is Cheerios a fancy cereal? Is it one of your combination cereals filled with assorted fruits and nuts and flakes? Of course not. Or at least it's not based on the theme, that "incipient center" around which all elements of the ad revolve.

Imagine the writer for Cheerios sitting at a table reading the side panel of the cereal box. Then reading other side panels from other cereal boxes, those of the competition. Then pouring the contents of the boxes into bowls. Then tasting the cereals and drawing comparisons, not to mention taking careful notes. Not too farfetched, is it? Or that same writer standing at the supermarket checkout counter with a dozen or so boxes of assorted cereals filling the basket. Then that writer seated at a breakfast table looking as though he or she is conducting some sort of weird experiment.

The message here? Get inside the product and its competition. Learn what makes both tick. Will the customer get a cereal that's unadorned, unglitzy, and loaded with all the plain and simple ingredients of Mother Nature? Cheerios. Will the customer get a cereal that contains more nutrients per bowl than other cereals? For example, Total cereal promises just that. Total. Will the customer get a cereal whose sound differentiates it from the sound of other cereals? Rice Krispies and Grape-Nuts.

There's no other way to reach important conclusions about a product unless you know all there is to know about that product, particularly as it competes with others in the marketplace. You can guess and risk being wrong, very wrong. Or you can do your homework and immediately improve your chances of being right, very right.

Of course, to recommend that you get inside your product is easier said than done. After all, you're you, right? But remember that if you're a copywriter then you are secondary. You're more a chauffeur for the product, driving it to the consumer. So you absolutely need to lose yourself in favor of the product. You also need to lose yourself in favor of the consumer, your target audience.

## The Target Audience Consumer

Consumers are people, too. That's important to remember. If you don't remember it the consumers lose their individuality and importance. They become faceless blobs merging into one another and losing their identities. That's why you should think of consumers as people— in fact, as one person complete with all the networks of beliefs, attitudes, and emotions that make us human. If you can't think of the consumer that way, then your ad copy will ring a false, flat note. It will sound hollow, generic, and artificial.

There are various ways to describe a target audience consumer. Chief among these are demographics, psychographics (VALS), and behavioristics. As disciplines in their own right, these umbrella terms of audience description provide you with a means for profiling your consumer. The result is a composite picture of that consumer according to criteria such as age, sex, attitudes, values, and behaviors toward your product or the general product class. Such information helps you see the target audience as a person complete with human traits, needs, wants, and problems to be solved. The information can't do everything that needs to be done, however, especially in fostering a complete understanding of what makes a particular individual tick. In effect, there are gaps and blank spots along the way, and it's up to you to fill them in.

   *Getting Inside Your Target Audience.*   A large part of your responsibility as a copywriter hinges on your ability to understand your target audience. Because you're writing for one person, you can't expect your writing to be effective unless it taps into that person's needs or wants. Through your writing you must prove to the individual that you understand his or her world, that you're on the same side, and that there's common ground between you. To do that you must think and feel like that person, much the same as you thought and felt like the product.

   This ability to think and feel like another person is common to creative individuals. It's known by such terms as *empathy, negative capability,* or *projection.* It means you lose yourself in favor of someone else. We do it often in daily life, though to varying degrees. For example, haven't you seen someone else so sad or glad that for a moment, however brief, you experienced the same emotion? You cried or laughed, not necessarily for yourself but for that other person. For that moment you lost yourself in the emotion of that other person. It is this awareness and, even more, this empathy for the other that often separates good copywriters from bad. Indeed, it may even separate good people from bad.

   Once again, as with our discussion of the product, to become someone else is much easier said than done. But you must do it. You must crawl inside that other skin and leave yourself behind. Only in that way will the other person come to life, and in the process, bring the understanding of how to communicate.

   Recall our discussion of the reader for the Parker pen ad copy. A successful and aspiring male expecting the finer things in life. Literate. Contemplative. Perhaps a bit haughty. So that when the copywriter wrote, that reader was right beside, urging the writer to tailor the copy carefully with words joining the product and reader on a common ground.

   Change the target audience for the Parker pen and the entire ad's copy and layout change as well. In fact, if you change the target audience you're obliged to change the pen's features and selling points within the copy. Bound together as they are, the copy and target audience become inseparable.

   There's really no other way to achieve this kind of bonding than by knowing your target audience. Yes, demographics, psychographics, and behavioristics build your knowledge. But it's your ability to lose yourself and become the other that makes the ultimate difference. Through the understanding that results you can then select the appropriate product features and theme to govern your copy.

   Think back to all of the chapters you've read thus far and try to characterize the various people we've discussed as readers or receivers of messages. Even with Marx and Engels there was a specific reader in mind. For the passage from Dr. Seuss there was another reader in mind. The same holds true for the Schlitz "Gusto" ad, the Cover Girl Luminesse ad, the health care ad, and, of course, the Parker fountain pen ad. Very different people with very different ways of viewing life. They coat the things they see or hear with vastly different colorings of likes and dislikes, values, attitudes, and lifestyles. At the same time, the writers behind those words wrote for those people, stimulating the most probable effects and responses. Those writers couldn't achieve that without understanding the hearts and minds of their readers.

Again, to get inside a product or consumer is easier said than done. We are who we are, and we're often locked inside who we are. But to make the task a bit easier, the following list of exercises should help.

## Ways to Get Inside Your Product and Target Audience

1.    Make a list of the product's features. Make the list inclusive. Take every possible point of view with the product. On top of it. Under it. Beside it. Inside it. Use your senses here. How does the product taste? Feel? Smell? Sound? For example, if you were making a product feature list for Cheerios some of the notations might be round, sugarless, hole in the middle, tan, light, oats, oat bran, fiber, and natural.

2.    Answer the 4 W's and the H. What? When? Where? Why? And How? And answer those questions as they relate to the product itself and its movement through the channel of distribution. What is the product made of? When is it made? Where is it made? Why is it made? How is it made? These provide answers of production. What is it sold in? When is it sold? Where is it sold? Why is it sold? How is it sold? These provide answers of buying. What is it consumed with? When is it consumed? Where is it consumed? Why is it consumed? How is it consumed? These provide answers of consumption, and as with the buying questions, they tilt toward the customer. In my idea-generation book you'll find some valuable questions as well in the section on behavioristics.

3.    Make a list and answer the same questions as they pertain to key competition or your product as it compares to the key competition.

4.    Talk with your product. Take a piece of paper, draw a line down the middle, and hold a dialogue with your product. On one side of the paper ask the product questions. On the other side of the paper write the answers as the product would state them. Considerable imagination is needed here because you're asked to play two roles. One can be

you, but it's better if it's the consumer. And the other is the product. That can be hard, but try. For instance, what would Cheerios answer if it were asked, How do I feel after I eat a bowl of you?

5.  Talk with your consumer. Take another piece of paper, draw a line down the middle, and hold a dialogue with your consumer. On one side of the paper ask how the consumer feels at the point of purchase and at the point of consumption or use of your product. How does the consumer feel after consumption or use? Ask the consumer what he or she likes or dislikes about the product. Expand the dialogue by asking questions about the consumer's wants, needs, and problems, especially as they relate to your product or product class.

6.  Expand the dialogue exercise by interchanging the roles. Have the product ask the consumer questions, for example. Or, have the consumer ask the product questions. While you are doing this, keep an attentive ear to "buzz" words and insightful and innovative perspectives. When they pop up, jot them down.

7.  Play "before and after." Write down your consumer's beliefs, attitudes, or feelings before buying or using the product. Then write them down during or after buying or using the product.

8.  Still role-playing as your consumer, walk yourself through the points in time when your product is bought and used. Actually imagine yourself at those points in time. How would you stand, sit, behave, or talk? How would you be dressed? What would your surroundings be? In fact, it wouldn't hurt to walk through a part of the consumer's daily life, listing as you go the consumer's various interests.

9.  Play psychiatrist. Make your consumer comfortable and probe about his or her problem regarding the product or product class. Imagine what the responses would be.

As you can see, the means for getting inside your product or consumer depend to a large extent on the liveliness of your imagination. Are you able to lose yourself in favor of something or someone else? That's the key. And your imagination holds that key in its hand. Use it to open the door to your creative strategy.

Searching for the Nib

The match between product and target audience holds complete sway over your creative strategy, let alone your ad's success. But to find those elements or concepts to be matched often requires considerable probing and thought on your part, especially since the right elements or concepts aren't always obvious. Take the Parker fountain pen, for example. No doubt, research had a great deal to say to the ad's writer. The information passed along examined the product, its competition, and the target audience. But that information never said to the writer that the copy should be written the way it was or that the copy should focus on the nib the way it did. Those selections were the writer's responsibility. And making those selections led the way to the creative strategy and eventual ad.

Of course, if you know just about everything there is to know about your product and target audience, then the match will be that much easier. At least you won't be pulling things out of the dark, hoping as you do that they'll be compatible. In knowing just about everything, you shed light on elements or concepts worthy of the match. You discard some others, quickly realizing that they're not meant for each other. And others you set aside because you can see their promise. Ideally, what you're after are differentiating factors for your product, those features or selling points that separate your product from the competition.

To shift this important concern out of the theoretical and into the practical, let's consider an example from real life, perhaps one all of us have experienced, the buying and selling of a used car.

For as far back as I can remember, my family always bought used cars. I was raised believing that to buy a new car was foolish. That in itself sounds foolish, but let me explain. My father believed that new cars, short of some new cars costing extraordinary amounts of money, began to lose their value the minute you drove them off the lot. He considered them horrendous investments, so he always opted for used cars, believing all the while that he could save money in the long run and still get whatever it was he was looking for in a car. As we know, buying a used car isn't always a wise choice. You can get burned. Then again, you can also get burned buying a new car.

In any event, the point of this little digression is that used cars are in my blood, and in my pocketbook, so that's what I buy. This means that when I'm in the market for a used car I read the used car classified ads, perhaps as conscientiously as others read the sports or fashion pages of their newspapers. And when I expect to turn one used car over for another, I place a classified ad. It just so happens that this is going on right now as I write this chapter. I'm looking for a used car, a second car for my family, and attempting to sell one existing second car, this only months after having bought and sold our main family car.

In searching out a used car I apply a common reading strategy. I look for certain cars. Not all. Just a few models. And what I've found recently are some interesting twists by the sellers in respect to matching their cars with buyers, matches that remind me of the seller's innate searching for differentiating factors.

Now, I'm just one buyer, so I carry my own personal set of likes and dislikes into my reading and eventual auto selection. Still, a few things have grabbed my attention and sit well with me, especially since I'm aware of how you can get burned buying a used car. For example, several ads have noted that service records are available, clearly a copy point that differentiates some car ads from others. I like that. A lot. And I like it because of what the copy point suggests on a deep level more than what it says on a surface level.

Yes, in buying a used car you take your chances. But if the service records are truly available, then this says something important about the car and its owner. It says the car has been cared for, no doubt a major concern for those buying used cars. In other words, this may well be the major problem one confronts when deciding whether to buy a used car or not. It is for me at least. And I would guess it is for many others as well.

To me the availability of service records suggests there may be nothing to hide about the car, assuming of course that the records haven't been doctored or selectively chosen to be shown. It also suggests that the owner believes in the vehicle's quality and isn't afraid to substantiate it. It suggests the owner's organization. And it suggests the owner's treatment of the car, which in all likelihood is probably good, otherwise the service records wouldn't be noted in the ad.

Would you consider service records an important feature to advertise when selling a used car? Would you consider it important if you were in the market to buy a used car? What other information would you consider important? For instance, what would you think if you saw the copy line, "One owner," as you searched for a used car? That's another feature I like to see because of what it suggests in the way of deep meaning and because of how it cuts the risk of having a car abused by more than one previous owner.

I recently looked at a used car whose ad claimed "One owner." It turned out that the owner was a leasing company and that the vehicle had been leased by one person for all of its 30,000 miles. That amount of mileage on a used car is not enough to warrant serious wear and tear or damage. But when those miles are put on by someone leasing and not owning, all of a sudden they seem like 100,000 miles in my mind.

Even when you respond to ads for used cars and test-drive the vehicles you can see persuasive strategies and tactics at work. For example, most car ads include the mileage (not gas mileage). I responded to an ad where the mileage was listed at 39,000. When I drove the car I noticed that the mileage was in the high end of the 39,000 range. In fact, it was a hair from turning 40,000. Now that's not a big deal to be sure. But I was very much put off by that. It seemed like misleading advertising. I could understand the 39,000 miles claim as the result of a persuasion strategy, but I didn't like it.

On the other hand, there are some things you notice that go a long way in selling you the car. As I mentioned earlier, a few months ago I bought a used car. A Mazda 323. It had good reviews in all the important books. The price wasn't great, but it was decent. The ad didn't say very much to convince me to call. But the owner lived close to where I live, so I decided to take a look. Here's what I found. First, the car had a babyseat in it. Second, the car's owner, perhaps twenty-eight to thirty, had been an archaeology major in college and was now in the business of restoring old buildings in the area. Third, there were service records available. And fourth, it was a one-owner car.

Each of these factors convinced me to buy the car with the hope that it was cared for. But when looked at as the means for selling a car, they reach deep into the groundwork of advertising creative strategy. Remember, we don't buy things necessarily. We buy what things can do for us. We translate product features into selling points and benefits. We translate the tangible into the intangible. For example, a car with a babyseat suggests to me that the owner might not be reckless in his driving. The fact that he was an archaeology major and was now restoring old buildings suggests to me that he may have taken care of the car. The fact that there were service records available suggests to me he did take care of the car. And the fact that he was the sole owner suggests to me that there may be less risk of the car having been abused.

If you look at used car ads and then go test-drive the cars you'll find this type of product description, which, in the mind of the sellers, matches their cars with prospective buyers. Even to write a used car ad takes that kind of strategic thinking, that kind of searching for the key copy points.

Boiled down, that thinking is not unlike the thinking that goes into national advertising. Yes, it's far less sophisticated, and not as pointed or organized, but still, the same concerns plague the seller. What do I say to get someone to call and buy? What are my prospective buyers thinking? What do they believe? What's important to them? What does my car have that matches well with those prospective buyers?

Again, the answers to these questions aren't always easy. In fact, they can be very difficult, and they often hide beneath the surface. Let me give you another example. The American Academy of Advertising (AAA) and the International Newspaper and Marketing Executives (INAME) groups jointly sponsor a national student advertising competition, always for a socially redeeming cause. During the 1991/92 year the task was to create a newspaper campaign raising awareness of environmental waste and convincing people to participate in cleaning up the environment. As part of the preparation for strategic thinking I asked students to write me a letter convincing me not to use Styrofoam coffee cups. I told them that I used a Styrofoam cup everyday and did so without remorse. They were to convince me that it wasn't a good idea to continue that behavior.

The letters I received were interesting and appealing in many respects. Most of the letters chastised me for my behavior, then launched into heavy-handed statistics of how there were mountains of discarded Styrofoam cups threatening the planet's life. These mountains were being added to daily, and I, among others, was responsible. Usually the letters closed by telling me how dangerous these mountains were and urging me to take action.

During class discussion it was clear that a few letters stood out in their method for convincing me not to use any more Styrofoam cups. One of the letters, in particular, reflected a unique strategy that class members agreed had the most promise. This letter never mentioned the heavy-handed statistics such as the zillion tons of this or that mounting up somewhere and threatening us all. And it never blamed me for my actions. Instead, it spent its time explaining to me how easily I could change my behavior and how such a change would benefit me, my children, and my children's children.

Now think about this. No doubt some of you reading this book participated in the AAA/INAME competition. Before you conceive of your ads do you conceptualize a strategy? As you read through our discussion on the competition devoted to the environment, did you consider that the casual tossing around of mountainous statistics could backfire? How is one likely to read those statistics on a deeper level? What will the statistics mean on that deeper level? Perhaps the reader will say this, "A zillion tons of this or that. No way that what I do will make any difference." If this is what readers were liable to think, then ads conveying gargantuan worldwide problems with little individual responsibility attached to them were sure to fall on deaf ears.

That strategic consideration became the rallying cry for the students in the class. Now, at this point I don't know whether it worked. That's up to assorted judges. But I was convinced by the tact. I believe it makes considerable sense. An avalanche of numbers that buries the individual reader's sense of responsibility and hopefulness could easily backfire. To keep things personal and within reach, however, could work. As a result, when numbers were a vital part of the student ads, those numbers tended to be personalized. They tended to be numbers reflecting the actions or behaviors of one individual, the reader.

Looked at strategically, this tactic regarding the use of numbers stemmed from the class's conclusion that people don't believe they can make a difference in the environment. Though people believe something needs to be done, they're content to continue their old ways without taking much responsibility for their actions. Of course, these are bold generalizations, and we know that not everyone fits into this mold. At the same time, however, there is strategic sense to this overall view, and it really wouldn't have materialized if there weren't considerable probing and digging by each of the students. And much of this probing and digging unearthed differentiating factors that could be used as key copy points.

We've called this unearthing "Searching for the Nib." What it means is finding the right product feature or selling point, preferably the one that's different and the one with the most appeal to the target audience. Again, sometimes it's obvious, but don't expect it to be, at least not very often. Instead, expect that you'll have to do some clever and insightful matching of the product and target audience. And the product features and selling points you use might not always be so tangible, such as what we just discussed with the environmental campaign. Or what we'll look at now with Avis and Hertz ads in Figures 7–1 and Figure 7–2, respectively.

With these Avis and Hertz ads, the themes reflect the competitive and comparative nature of the strategy. As Bruce Bendinger describes in his book, *The Copy Workshop,* the two car rental companies often run advertising stemming from a strategic "Against" position.

Notice how both ads use the competitive position of the advertiser as a means for conveying the benefit to the customer. For Avis the benefit is that you'll receive more attention and service because of the company's number-two ranking. This ranking translates to the need for Avis employees to try harder on your behalf. For Hertz the benefit you'll receive is low cost, at least compared to Avis, which helps explain why Avis is number two.

For Avis the theme of number two became a real plum for the company's advertising. But if you unpeel that theme and look behind it, you'll find the strength of strategy. Avis knew it was number two. Many other companies would have considered that a disadvantage. Not so, Avis. As a differentiating factor separating it from its competition, particularly Hertz, Avis used it as a key copy point. In fact, Avis used it as a governing theme, the "incipient center" of its advertising, realizing all along that service is a key factor in the rental car business. In short, it used its position in the marketplace as an advantage. In so doing it also touched a sympathetic chord in the target audience, that of rooting for the underdog. It's a very American thing to do.

At the same time, Hertz realized the power of being number one. After all, most people understand that you don't get to be number one because you're lucky. You get to be number one by dint of good value and service, at least in the car rental business.

Look behind each ad you see or hear and you'll discern a strategy governing the ad's content and style. That strategy matches something about the product, store, or service with something important in the

# Avis is only No.2 in rent a cars. So why go with us?

We try harder.
(When you're not the biggest, you have to.)
We just can't afford dirty ash-trays. Or half-empty gas tanks. Or worn wipers. Or unwashed cars. Or low tires. Or anything less than seat-adjusters that adjust. Heaters that heat. Defrost-ers that defrost.

Obviously, the thing we try hardest for is just to be nice. To start you out right with a new car, like a lively, super-torque Ford, and a pleasant smile. To know, say, where you get a good pastrami sandwich in Duluth.
Why?
Because we can't afford to take you for granted.
Go with us next time.
The line at our counter is shorter.

© 1963 AVIS, INC.

FIGURE 7–1   Advertisement reprinted with permission of Avis Rent A Car System, Inc. and its affiliate Wizard Co., Inc.

consumer's network of needs, wants, or problems to be solved. Often the match takes place between something different in the product that satisfies a specific need or want. Sometimes deciding what to match can be easy. Usually it's not, however. Instead, it requires both the results of thorough research and the thoughtful, perceptive, and often innovative insights of you as copywriter.

FIGURE 7–2   Copyright Hertz System, Inc. Advertisement reprinted with permission of Hertz System, Inc.

We've surrounded this concept of searching for the nib because of its importance to the success of your strategy and ad. It acts as the hub, the core of what you will say in your ad. It forms the foundation of the theme or benefit, and your choices of story line or even individual words tend to revolve around it, keeping close to its "incipient center" of gravity.

In Figure 7–3 you'll see a popular ad idea for Eveready® Batteries. As you view the storyboard for this television commercial, search for the nib, for the controlling center of the ad. This doesn't mean the center or theme necessarily lays claim to a specific physical attribute. Especially with television, you don't have the luxury of crafting an involved case supporting your theme. Quite simply, you don't have the time. But still, notice how the Eveready commercial focuses on a single theme.

No doubt, you recall seeing this or similar Eveready® Battery commercials. They earned acclaim for their originality. People in and out of the ad business buzzed about them. And indeed, the one you see here lends testimony to that originality. Yet, as original as this Eveready Battery commercial is, solid strategy forms the foundation for that originality. Notice, for instance, how the voice-over announcer repeats, "They keep going and going and going and...." In effect, the center or strategic theme for the ad focuses on the long-lasting quality of the Eveready Energizer® battery. In reading between the lines and seeing behind the images, the entire point of the commercial can be summed up in one word, "long-lastingness." The repetitive phrasing carries that theme, and the very idea of the Energizer bunny breaking through a bogus commercial reinforces the

**FIGURE 7–3** Advertisement reprinted courtesy of Eveready® Battery Company, Inc. Eveready and Energizer® are registered trademarks of Eveready Battery Company.

theme, almost as though the bunny has kept going and going and going from one commercial to the next to the next and so on.

Can you see the strategic mind at work here? Can you see it searching for the right slant, the right theme, the one that links the product with the audience's need or want or problem to be solved? Can you see it testing and retesting the Energizer® compared to its competition, constantly searching for the most appropriate theme to govern the creative idea? To do that, the strategic mind understood the importance of knowing the product, all the way to the point of how the selling point of "long-lastingness" came to be. Much like the strategic mind behind the Parker Premium fountain pen ad understood the nib to convey the theme of writing magnificently.

## Product Features, Differentiating Factors, and Benefits

As part of your preplanning for an ad, searching for the nib requires that you concentrate your attention on appropriate product features, differentiating factors, and benefits. This means you're focused on what the product has or does, which corresponds to the consumer's need, want, or problem to be solved. In short, you're looking for the importance in the product, at least as far as the consumer is concerned.

Bear in mind that product features often include physical attributes such as the nib for the Parker Premium fountain pen or the full-bodied flavor of Schlitz beer. These attributes then lead to the benefit, often the theme of the ad, such as the theme of writing magnificently with the pen, grabbing gusto from the beer, or using a battery that keeps going and going and going, as in the case for the Eveready® Energizer®.

At the same time, much of the thought involved in pinpointing the most appropriate product feature and theme includes the search for the differentiating factor. This is the point of difference separating your product from its competition. Of course, that's a large part of what we discussed in "Searching for the Nib." The nib differentiates the Parker Premium fountain pen from competing pens. And, if such a differentiating factor leads to the key benefit or theme, then it should be the centerpiece of the copy.

At the close of Chapter 6 under "Things to Do," you were asked to read carefully the copy from two ads, one for Timberland and one for Royal Viking. Let's take another look at the Timberland ad and copy, all the while focusing on how the differentiating factor acts as the centerpiece. The ad can be seen again in Figure 7–4. And if you need a closer look at the ad's copy, remember you can find it under "Things to Do" at the close of Chapter 6.

Notice how the copy for this Timberland boat shoe ad concentrates on the interactive grip system as the centerpiece for the copy. In fact, much like the explanation of the nib for the Parker pen ad, this copy

# BOAT SHOES SHOULD BE JUDGED BY HOW THEY GO WITH A BLACK SKY. NOT A BLUE BLAZER.

Don't get us wrong. If you want to use our new boat shoes with the Interactive Grip System to fox-trot across the yacht club dance floor, that's your choice. We guarantee you and your blazer will look good, and we promise to accept your money.

Just be aware that we engineered these shoes so you could dance on a very different surface. The storm-blackened foredeck of a boat that's bucking like a rodeo bull.

On so wet and treacherous a playing field, one slip of the foot could be one slip too many. Preventing it is what the Interactive Grip System is all about.

**INTERACTIVE GRIP SYSTEM**

Quadrant cut sole has 50% more leading edges than standard wave cut soles.

Quadrant cut exceeds wave cut for traction, providing 360° of grip.

Internal Fit System keeps foot in correct position for comfort, balance and grip.

© 1992 The Timberland Company. Timberland and ⬤ are registered trademarks of The Timberland Company.

As its name implies, the System starts where the foot interacts with the boat. At the sole. Our new design gives you such a profusion of siping (razor cuts for traction) that the number of leading edges exceeds the traction capacity of traditional boat soles by a good 50%. What's more, the edges are clustered in an exclusive quadrant cut pattern. (Competitors beware. The Timberland® quadrant cut sole so outgrips

standard wave cut soles it may cause mutiny at the yacht club.)

Part Two of the Interactive Grip System makes sure that your foot stays in the right place so the quadrant cut sole can do its work. Your foot is secured for proper balance and energy distribution by an Internal Fit System, a contoured sleeve that keeps your toes from jamming when the boat makes a violent lurch.

These brand new benchmarks for marine footwear aren't just high-tech, but true high performance for the 1990's. A new definition of authenticity that puts our imitators in an embarrassing place. Overboard.

**BOOTS, SHOES, CLOTHING, WIND, WATER, EARTH AND SKY.**

FIGURE 7–4   Advertisement reprinted courtesy of The Timberland Company.

164

explains the importance of the grip system, even to the point of highlighting and explaining the term "siping," a somewhat technical term describing razor cuts on the sole for better traction. In addition, the shoe also has an internal fit system, one "that keeps your toes from jamming when the boat makes a violent lurch." In other words, the shoe's construction, especially in respect to these two features, leads to the ad's theme, the benefit of safe traction and comfortable wear. Even the creative idea overall pays allegiance to what these product features mean to the consumer.

Important to your understanding of the Timberland ad, however, is the recognition that the key product features are also differentiating factors. They separate the Timberland shoe from its competition, and the writer skillfully and subtly makes that known in the copy's close. In turn, these features as differentiating factors exist only by way of providing a benefit to the consumer, one that's needed and wanted so as to avoid the worry, if not the disastrous prospect, of going overboard.

## Audience Expectations and Involvement

Given all of this discussion about nibs, bunnies, and Interactive Grip Systems, it might seem as if the product itself rules the ad's roost. In many ways this is true. Often the product, or some feature about the product, acts as a hero in an ad. But don't be misled. A large part of strategy development centers on the prospective consumer, the target audience. In fact, as you think back to the Parker, Eveready®, and Timberland ads, it should be clear that the very themes of those ads were meant to meet a consumer need or want, or solve a consumer problem. Indeed, in the largest of ways your strategy considerations should always be grounded in the target audience. Your job overall is to match something important about the product with the consumer's need, want, or problem to be solved.

If you recall our discussion from earlier in the chapter, we highlighted the various ways a target audience can be described. Demographically or psychographically, for instance. Still, there's more you need to understand about your audience, and that understanding relates to matters of audience expectations and involvement toward your product.

When we speak of audience expectations we're really talking about the network of knowledge, likes, and dislikes the audience brings to your product and ad. Recall our discussion in Chapter 2, for instance, about how we bring certain expectations to the messages we see or hear, expectations rooted in what we know and what we like or dislike. They represent a belief system we have toward something outside of ourselves, in this case a product. Certain expectations are brought to the purchase or use of that product. And depending on the nature and intensity of those expectations, your strategy will take on various points of emphasis.

Tangent to a network of expectations toward your product, audience involvement also exerts influence on your strategy. Conceptualize involvement like this. Based on various beliefs or perceptions, your target audience relates to products in certain ways and with varying degrees of enthusiasm or commitment. The degrees of enthusiasm or commitment are simply another way of describing involvement. For example, if the audience is enthusiastic and committed toward your product, then high involvement exists. If the audience isn't enthusiastic or committed, then low involvement exists.

For copywriters, knowledge of the audience's expectations and involvement weighs heavily on the creative strategy. In fact, it weighs heavily on the eventual crafting of copy. Take the Timberland boat shoe ad again, for example. Clearly the writer knew the importance of a boat shoe as a fashion statement for the audience. And clearly the writer also knew the importance of a boat shoe to the safety of that audience. This knowledge shaped the writer's task, to convince the audience of Timberland's benefit in terms of safety first and fashion second. This means the writer tried to raise the knowledge and involvement level of the audience toward the shoe as a safety device, relying for the most part on a fear appeal intent on securing the audience's safety.

Bear in mind that when we commit to purchases, products, or even each other, decisions have been made. These may or may not be rational decisions. Often they're emotional or a combination of emotion and reason. And generally they're made based on gaining something that we perceive has more value than what we will give up in return. In addition, the more involved we are with the decision, the more important it is to us, so the more thought we'll put into it. We may fact-find more than we would if we weren't so involved. This means we'll pay closer attention to the factors weighing on that decision, factors such as product features or selling points.

On the other hand, if we're less involved, we may not be inclined to think about it. We'll just decide and that's it. Sort of like selecting chewing gum at the checkout counter. Very little thought. Very little information processing. Obviously, however, deciding on a chewing gum is very unlike how we decide on what college to attend or what car to buy. And in knowing the complex system of expectations and involvement levels we bring to such purchases, the copywriter crafts the strategy and copy accordingly.

## The Media

Still another strategy consideration for the copywriter includes the medium used for the ad. Sure, you may have a wonderful match between a product selling point and a consumer need, but that match means nothing unless it's advertised. And to advertise it means you'll need a vehicle, a medium that reaches out to your target audience.

Change one part of your strategic mix and everything else changes. This holds true as well for media. Not that you decide which media will be used. You're told that, though you may have some input on the decision depending upon a host of variables. Still, expect to be told which media will be used. And once you're told, expect to write your copy with the media front and center in your mind.

There are many ways to have your message carried to the target audience. Newspapers. Magazines. Radio. Television. Outdoor. Direct mail, among others. All of them are different. All of them require or allow certain types of copy tactics, depending on the characteristics of difference for the individual media. Each medium is unique in itself. Though there may be similarities of characteristics medium to medium, by and large the similarities fade when compared to the differences. This is especially true when you consider the most important of all media contexts, your target audience.

In the same way that an understanding of your target audience helps you focus on the appropriate product feature, selling point, or benefit, an understanding of your target audience helps you focus on the appropriate means for using the media. For example, imagine how differently people behave toward the various media, say magazine versus radio. Then imagine having to write an ad for both media. Realizing that your target audience doesn't behave the same way toward magazine as toward radio, what will change? Perhaps everything. And certainly how much you say in your ad will change.

If you knew your target audience would give your ad undivided attention, wouldn't that change what you say in the copy? Conversely, if you knew your target audience's attention were split, wouldn't that also change what you say? The answers should be obvious. And that's why you must consider the media beyond their raw characteristics such as the printed word versus the fleeting image. More important is the understanding of how the consumer behaves toward or uses the various media.

Newspapers are used for news, often an entertaining kind of news. Often, too, a local news. Readers spend time with newspapers. Readers are riveted when they read newspapers, at least to varying degrees. Readers rely on newspapers. They trust them, some more than others, of course.

Magazines may be used for news as well, but it's a different kind of news. It's more focused. Perhaps business news. Or sports news. Or fashion news. Usually with an individualized slant of the writer. Readers relate more personally to their magazines. They see themselves more easily in their magazines. They spend time with their magazines.

Radio is used for entertainment. Unlike newspapers and magazines there's relatively little information processing that goes on with radio, at least music radio. The message is here and gone, perhaps never to be recaptured again, and the listener knows that. The listener is predisposed to not paying riveted attention to radio. The listener keeps radio in the background as a kind of mood-setter or entertainment fix. The listener is driving, reading, cleaning house, or doing any one of a thousand activities while the radio is on.

Television is used for both news and entertainment. The viewer spreads out in front of the TV and says, "Take me, I'm yours." Sight and sound bombard the consciousness. The viewer picks and chooses the spots, now easier than ever with remote controls.

Direct mail is used for news. Personalized news direct from your own mailbox. Even your name is on it. If not chucked right away, it gets read. The reader reads with a strict personal interest, unwavering and colored by the personalism of other mail such as letters from friends or payment notices.

Outdoor advertising is used for news and entertainment scaled down to a few words and images. Viewers are doing other things when they meet outdoor ads. They're driving, walking, or looking at the many images in their field of vision.

An important idea to keep in mind here is that the best ads are different. This means they may contradict or fly in the face of basic media rules such as only putting six to eight words on a billboard. Remember, for instance, that Ed McCabe advised doing all words when others do all pictures. McCabe's advice holds true for media as well. For instance, since newspapers contain a great deal of words, then maybe a bold picture should be the tactic. If television contains color, then maybe black and white is the tactic. Often with ad ideas, rules are made to be broken.

Still, consideration of how the media are used by your target audience leads to insights about what you should or should not do in your ad. Should you say as much in your radio spot as in your magazine ad? Perhaps not. Perhaps you can't, simply given the time limitations. Again, though, rules are made to be broken. But this doesn't mean you shouldn't craft your copy according to how your target audience is using the media. In fact, you should. That way you'll align yourself with certain expectations. If you need a bold idea to break through those expectations in order to gain attention, fine. But more often than not, the supporting copy should tailor itself to those expectations.

As you can tell, a great deal of what and how you write depends on the various contexts influencing the strategic mix. Whether influenced by product or medium, the job of the copywriter is to key the copy to the audience, especially as the audience relates to the elements in the mix. There is no magic formula available. No cookbook to follow. But thinking helps. And what you're thinking about has everything to do with establishing a strategic plan, one that centers on creating a common ground between your product and audience.

## ✍ THE STRATEGIC PLAN ✍

The result of research and your innovative insights is called *creative strategy*. Generally that strategy is simple, many times able to fit on one side of a piece of paper. As we know already, however, deciding what to put on that piece of paper isn't so simple. And it's always important since the strategy guides the making of a creative idea. Ultimately it bears responsibility for whether the right message is delivered in the right way to the target audience.

There are many varied formats for creative strategy. Each advertising agency tends to have its own way of articulating the strategy's key components. For example, the creative strategy format for the Young and Rubicam ad agency (Y & R) is shown in Figure 7–5. It's known as the Creative Work Plan.

**FIGURE 7–5   The Creative Work Plan.**

THE CREATIVE WORK PLAN

1. Key Fact:
2. Problem the Advertising Must Solve:
3. Advertising Objective:
4. Creative Strategy:
   A. Prospect Definition:
      Product Usage
      Demographics
      Pyschographics
   B. Principal Competition:
   C. Promise (We've termed it Benefit):
   D. Reason Why (We've termed it Support):
5. Mandatories and Policy Limitations:

Regardless of how different the strategy formats may be from one agency to another, there are still the tried-and-true components that manage to overlap. We'll focus on a few key components beginning with the objective. Notice its placement in the Y & R Creative Work Plan.

### Objective

Think of your *objective* as the desired effect you seek from the target audience. It should answer the question, What do I want my ad to achieve? Yes, sales or market share increases are usually the ultimate desired effect. But sales or market share increases qualify more as marketing objectives. An advertising objective is more tailored to the communication side of things. It tends to rely on the steps of persuasion as desired effects. It avoids the hard-and-fast marketing numbers and focuses on a shift or reinforcement of the target audience's network of needs, wants, or problems to be solved. Bruce Bendinger, for instance, claims the objective often states the solution to the problem.

Usually the objective contains three parts embedded within one concise statement. The first part identifies the desired communications effect of the ad. As we've said, that effect tends to stem from steps in the persuasion process. These steps begin with gaining attention or increasing awareness. They then move to building understanding, then establishing preference (perhaps the Avis and Hertz objectives), to creating conviction and desire, and ending with some type of attitudinal or behavioral movement such as changing an opinion about a car model or shopping at a store during certain times in the day. Beyond these steps, there are other types of key terms familiar to objectives such as reinforcement and name recognition. Still, the steps in the persuasion process provide a catalog of terms governing the first part of the objective, the desired effect. You can see the progression of those steps in Figure 7–6.

Overall, the objective guides the creative strategy and its key components. It tells the copywriter what is to be achieved or, in essence, the desired effect. Increase awareness. Convince. Build preference. Improve name recognition. All of these effects would be found as the first part of

**FIGURE 7–6  Steps in Persuasion.**

---

—From William J. McGuire, "An Information-Processing Model of Advertising Effectiveness," paper presented at the Symposium of Behavioral and Management Science sponsored by the Center for Continuing Education, The University of Chicago, July, 1969.

PRESENTATION—ATTENTION—COMPREHENSION—YIELDING—RETENTION—BEHAVIOR

—From Robert J. Lavidge and Gary A. Steiner, "A Model for Predictive Measurements of Advertising Effectiveness," *Journal of Marketing*, October (1961), p. 61.

AWARENESS—KNOWLEDGE—LIKING—PREFERENCE—CONVICTION—PURCHASE

—AIDA Formula

ATTENTION—INTEREST—DESIRE—ACTION

---

the objective. Notice how they are action-oriented, conveying a shift or alteration in the target audience's state of mind. In other words, some effect on awareness or attitude or belief results from the ad.

The second part of the objective is a general descriptive statement of the target audience. College students. Executives with families. Working mothers. Such descriptions are the kind you might find as the second part of the objective.

The third part of the objective is synonymous with the ad's theme, the main message you want conveyed. For the Eveready® ad the theme might have been that the Energizer® battery will last a long time. For the Parker fountain pen ad the theme might have been that the pen will write smoothly, with an even and elegant flow.

Again, all three parts of the objective are expressed in a single statement that answers what you expect your ad to achieve in terms of impact on the attitudes, beliefs, problems, or perhaps knowledge of the target audience. In essence, the objective states what the match between product and consumer should be.

The overall strategy for your ad originates with the objective, moving beyond the expectation of what you hope to achieve and into the area of how you hope to achieve it. In effect, the strategy explains what you need to do to meet the objective. It contains the objective, which is but one element within the strategic mix. Other elements such as *tone* and *support* expand the strategic base. They broaden your understanding of what you should or should not be doing in your ad. They exist as a floorplan for your theme and creative idea. In essence, they represent the foundation for your tactical thinking, which is the actual conception and writing of the ad.

Once again, there are many formats for creative strategy. Each ad copy book you read describes at least one, sometimes more. Whichever one you follow doesn't matter so much since the formats, despite different jargon, tend to focus on the same things such as objective, benefit, tone, and support.

The best way to round out your understanding of objectives and strategy is to unravel some ads, looking all the while for the objectives and strategies. The objective is what you want the ad to achieve. The strategy is how you plan to achieve it. Just like your life as a college student. Your objective is to do well in your classes. But the strategy is the plan you conceptualize to meet that objective.

## Benefit

Throughout our last two chapters you've seen this word *benefit* a great deal and in several contexts. For example, we've referred to it in conjunction with the theme of an ad. We've referred to it as a promise, as something intangible that fills a need or want, or solves a problem. In many ways, the benefit represents the lifeblood of an ad's success or failure. If it's clear and strategically right, then chances for success sky-rocket. If it's not clear or right, however, then chances for success plummet. The benefit. It's that important.

In essence, the benefit answers the question "What's in it for me?," meaning the audience. Beyond paying attention to ads because they may be entertaining, most often we pay attention to them in the hope that they promise us something of value. That something of value is the benefit. Think, for instance, of some of the ads we've discussed in this text. With Schlitz you get the benefit of gusto. With the Parker Premium fountain pen you get the benefit of writing magnificently. With Eveready® you get the benefit of "long-lastingness." And with Timberland you get the benefit of not going overboard by accident.

Of course, it's one thing to state the benefit in an ad and let it go at that. But since we know that most people are skeptical of ads, then there's a big chance the benefit won't be believed. It may simply sound like raw salesmanship, vested for the purposes of the advertiser. That's why the benefit often needs to be substantiated.

### Support

There are many head games you must try to win as a copywriter. Chief among those games is the assumption that your audience waits breathlessly for your ad to appear, and when it does, there's happiness all around. Nothing is further from the truth, despite the fact that there are understandable reasons why this assumption takes hold. You live with the product. You live with the strategy. And you live with the evolution of the ad. This means you're involved in it. You're committed to it. You may even love it. But the result of that involvement, commitment, and love can be a disaster.

Because you're so involved with your ad, there's a tendency to forget the target audience, especially how the audience perceives the ad. In all likelihood that perception includes skepticism, apathy, and maybe even hostility. How the audience relates to your ad is a far cry from how you relate to it. That's why you must take special pains to overcome your audience's potential skepticism. You must make your ads friendly and personal. And you must be sensitive to providing support for your bold promise.

Recall the Parker Pen ad copy. The bold promise, the theme, was a fountain pen that wrote magnificently. Plain and simple. But the copy elaborated on that promise or theme. The elaboration contained a number of copy points, with the dominant point centered on the pen's nib. Its construction. Its durability. Its overall performance. In essence, the nib became the theme's support. It provided a foundation for the theme, a solid and irrefutable mass of evidence for why the pen would write magnificently.

Like the Parker Pen copy, much of what you'll write demands supporting evidence. Remember, the audience isn't sitting out there waiting for your ad to appear. And when the ad does appear, the audience doesn't plunge right into it. Instead, the guards are up. That's why you need to prove your theme, whether by copy points or pointed visuals.

Naturally, if you've done your homework and immersed yourself in the product and audience, your research and innovative thinking will have generated supporting evidence. It's up to you to recognize it, and the way to do that is by asking yourself this question: What makes the promise or theme believable? This doesn't mean the creative idea needs to be believable. It means the ad's promise or theme needs to be believable. And believability starts with the building of a case on your product's behalf. That building of a case centers on the support you provide.

### Tone

Often undervalued by students, *tone* represents a core strategy consideration. All messages have a tone. Some are cynical. Some are straightforward. Some are light and airy. Others are serious and weighty. Even in this book you've probably recognized the shifting of tones in various passages. At times we've pored over discussions, and they've carried with them a tone of seriousness and heaviness. At other times we've breezed our way over points, and they've carried with them a tone of warmth and lightness. All messages have a tone, even a combination of tones at times. But with ads, which are brief and to the point for the most part, the tone is singular.

Think of tone as personality. Think of it as you would think of a person. In fact, picture someone in your mind. You know that person. Perhaps a loved one, a friend, or an acquaintance. How would you describe that person's personality? Is it outgoing or reserved? Is it flamboyant? Sophisticated? Down-to-earth? Friendly? Warm? Lighthearted? Laid back? Exciting? Fun? All of these adjectives fit with tone, the personality of your ad.

If you consider that all messages, whether visual or verbal, have a tone, then it's easy to understand the importance of tone to your ads. The tone lets you know how to write. Not necessarily what to write, the content. But how to write, the style. The tone moves your writing in certain stylistic directions. It sets your course for word choices, sentence arrangements, and, in the case of radio and television, dialogue and lyrics. Overall, it keeps you on track stylistically.

Recall, again, the Parker Pen ad copy and how the word choices and sentence arrangements conveyed a sophisticated, literary, and stylistic tone, at times spiced with a more personal and conversational tone. In essence, the tone acted as a coating for the copy, striking a responsive chord in the reader's mind. It invited the reader into the copy content, in a sense opening the door for the description of the product's primary feature, the nib.

Once you've discovered the tone for your ad, your copy should follow suit. It should reflect the ad's personality. For example, if the ad's personality is brisk, light, and peppy, then the copy should contain shorter sentences and brisk, active words. If the ad's personality is serious and informative, then the copy should contain longer sentences and slower, more straightforward words.

Naturally, your knowledge of the product and target audience contributes to your setting of the proper tone. Since the job is to match one with the other, invariably you'll be forced to make decisions about tone. Insights into the product and consumer behavior toward the product lead to those decisions. For example, if there is low involvement toward the product, and if the product fills more of an entertainment, impulsive need, then the tone will be different from one in which there is high involvement and a product filling more of an informative, thoughtful need.

## ✍ WHY AREN'T POTATOES CONSIDERED VEGETABLES? ✍

As we've done right along, let's look closely at an example to flesh out the essence of our discussion. To this point we've covered the major elements in strategy considerations and the formulation of a Creative Work Plan. Most important are the product, audience, and media. However, it's the audience that influences the copywriter's decisions about an ad's content and style. It's the audience that acts as the most important context for those decisions. We can see this in Figure 7–7.

Think back to all we've discussed in this chapter. Can you apply your learning to the potatoes ad?

Look behind the ad to the creative strategy. What do you see? For instance, do you see a product whose research told the copywriter about consumer misunderstanding? Do you see a product attempting to position itself in a new way? Do you see a product attempting to attach itself to the consumer's belief that vegetables are good for you?

Obviously, the Potato Board had a problem. Potential consumers weren't perceiving the potato as a vegetable, typically perceived as a nutritious food. Perhaps the potato's shape, color, size, or texture had something to do with that. I know that I have trouble thinking of the potato as a vegetable. In any event, the ad reflects that problem. But it also reflects the strategy and tactics to solve the problem. For instance, if we imagine the workings of the strategic mind behind this ad, we can re-create the Creative Work Plan.

Based on the Y & R Creative Work Plan the key fact might read something like this: Consumers don't think of the potato as a vegetable,

FIGURE 7-7    Advertisement reprinted courtesy of The Potato Board.

yet vegetables are generally considered a desirably nutritious food. The problem to be solved then is to change the key fact, which exists because potatoes aren't green, and to convince consumers to think of the potato as a vegetable. This translates to the ad's objective as well.

Look again at the ad. Unravel it. Look behind it. Read the copy, which elaborates on the governing theme of the potato as a vegetable. Notice how the writer states key copy points in the second paragraph. Those copy points act as support for the claim that the potato is a vegetable. In the third paragraph notice, too, how the writer keys into the consumer's problem. Simply stated, the problem is that potatoes aren't green. And the creative idea picks up on the problem. Indeed, it becomes the driving force for the ad since the visual expresses the painting of the potato. In the fourth paragraph the writer continues to work on the elimination of the problem by stating that other vegetables aren't green, yet they are considered vegetables.

Now stop and look at the ad again. Given the extreme importance of visuals to advertising, notice how the visual conveys all of the elements in the strategy. The key fact is that potatoes aren't considered vegetables. The problem is that consumers relate vegetables to green, and the potato isn't green. The objective is to convince the target audience that potatoes are vegetables, thus attaching all of the health benefits associated with vegetables to potatoes. The benefit is that the audience will add to its healthy diet when it eats potatoes. The support centers on nutrition, calories, and a shifting of audience predispositions regarding the color of vegetables, all the while substantiating the benefit. But what of the tone?

Might we consider the tone flip, personal, and conversational? I think so. There's a certain off-handedness about the ad and the copy. A certain cleverness and inventiveness. A certain personalism and conversational tone. You can almost see the writer writing. And as unintentional and innocent as the first copy line in the first paragraph sounds, you know it's not. You know it's bent toward the tone of the ad's copy, that of cleverness, personalism, and "conversationalism."

Notice how the copy reads as if someone is speaking. Notice its conversational and personable turns of phrases such as "We can't figure it out," or "maybe it's because we're not green." As well as fitting in with the theme and idea, such phrases also fit in with the tone of the ad. They warm up the copy and make it more appropriate to the audience. They also lend themselves as mortar for the theme's foundation of support. In effect, they help build the support for that theme, conveying the impression of genuine sincerity on the part of the Potato Board.

## ✍ HOW MUCH CAN ONE AD DO? ✍

Taking all we've discussed in terms of strategy, you should know the importance of a solid and tight creative plan before you craft your gold-plated copy or even come up with a sterling creative idea. The plan sets the stage for that copy and idea. However, to round out our discussion of strategy, let's look at a number of ads that attempt to achieve differ-ent communication objectives and goals. Remember, the objective acts as the rudder for ads, directing the crafting of the various elements, copy included. Remember, too, that the objective avoids marketing goals and centers on communication goals. This means you're more interested in achieving shifts or reinforcements in the audience's state of mind.

Shifts in states of mind can range widely. For instance, perhaps you're trying to convince the audience to believe something, maybe prefer it, even solidify it, or change it altogether. Obviously, the more of a shift you're after, or the more change you seek, the harder the copywriting job. And often the more you'll have to say in your copy, simply because you may have to build the product's case in order to justify the audience tak-ing on a new belief or changing an old one. Recall, for instance, our dis-cussion earlier about audience expectations and involvement.

With this in mind, notice the spectrum of objectives in Figure 7–8. It highlights the extreme ranges of what an ad or campaign of ads can achieve.

A SPECTRUM OF OBJECTIVES

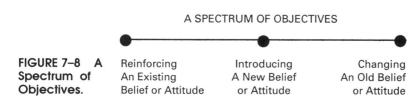

| **FIGURE 7–8  A** | Reinforcing | Introducing | Changing |
| **Spectrum of** | An Existing | A New Belief | An Old Belief |
| **Objectives.** | Belief or Attitude | or Attitude | or Attitude |

### Reinforcing an Existing Belief

At the far left end of the spectrum of objectives, reinforcing an existing belief represents a fairly easy task for the advertiser, especially when compared to ads that try to change an old belief. Often there are times when an advertiser wants to remind the audience that an exist-ing belief is worth holding. Not having to change the audience's mind is the easy part of the job. But you still must be careful to highlight the right theme. For example, Frank Perdue has been an advertising celebrity for many years. During that time he's been the successful and memorable spokesman touting the quality of his product. That claim to quality has been expressed in many variations. But each one reinforces the existing belief in the minds of the target audience. The ad shown in Figure 7–9 is one variation building on an existing belief.

To reinforce an existing belief you may have to provide a new slant to the old theme and idea. Frank Perdue's theme is quality. Extraordinary quality, especially when compared to the competition. But there are many ways to convey Perdue's quality, some of them more indirect than others. You can say, "Quality." That's too bold and bland, however. So you tie into

# MY CHICKENS EAT BETTER THAN YOU DO.

*Frank Perdue*

The problem with you is that you're allowed to eat whatever you want.

My Perdue chickens don't have the same freedom. They eat what I give them. And I only give them the best. Their diet consists mainly of pure yellow corn, soybean meal, marigold petals — you'd call it health food.

My chickens drink nothing but fresh, clear water from deep wells.

The reason I'm so finicky about what goes into my chickens is simple: a chicken is what it eats. And because they eat so well, Perdue chickens are always tender, juicy and delicious. And have a golden-yellow glow that separates them from the rest.

If you want to start eating as good as my chickens, take a tip from me.

Eat my chickens.

**PERDUE**
F R E S H
Young Chicken

IT TAKES A
TOUGH MAN TO MAKE
A TENDER CHICKEN.

FIGURE 7–9   Advertisement reprinted courtesy of Perdue Farms Inc.

the various ways the product results in quality, such as the food a chicken eats. Then the reader translates that to the benefit of a quality product.

This same reinforcement of an old belief can be found in the Maytag ad in Figure 7–10.

For years the Maytag repairman has been perceived as a symbol of the product's quality, simply because he's rarely busy. The fact that he's rarely busy translates in the audience's mind to a product selling point, which, in turn, evolves to the benefit of not having to be inconvenienced by repairs. Maytag products last. They're durable. At the same time, Maytag has found many ways of saying that over the years.

Sometimes, too, you may want to reinforce something more basic about the product, such as its name. You realize that most everyone knows the name and thinks well of it, but your objective is to solidify that name in consumers' minds. In Figure 7–11, the Doublemint gum ad attempts to do just that.

Notice how the Doublemint ad copy concentrates on the letter *D* and word *double*. The headline states, "Double delicious." The copy repeats those words twice. In fact, the copy repeats the product name twice, once in the first copy line and once in the last copy line. Moreover, the word *double* is repeated in the subhead, "Double your pleasure." Clearly, the use of the *D* sound reinforces the product name in the audience's mind.

### Introducing a New Belief

At the middle of the spectrum of objectives the copywriter's task changes. Now, the goal is to introduce a new belief, such as what might exist for a new product. Since the audience may not be open to newness if it's presented in an ad, the copywriter may have to explain the newness, particularly as it relates to the audience's self-interest.

Of course, a daily check of your local newspaper or a recent edition of one of your magazines will provide you with many ads trying to introduce a new belief. That belief can range from a new product to a special sale going on at a store in the mall. As you focus on the copy for those ads, however, notice how the ads invite action on the part of the audience. After all, something new must be tried, or it won't be in the marketplace very long. And this goes for existing stores or products that offer something new to the target audience. Take, for example, the Hunt's ad in Figure 7–12.

For years, Hunt's has satisfied the needs of its consumers by providing a range of canned tomato products. But given the health craze of the 1980s and the consumer movement to cut down on salt, Hunt's obliged the new need by offering tomato products without added salt. This ad alerts retailers to the new products. It is an example of a trade ad positioning Hunt's as a health-conscious company.

# CHAIRMAN OF THE BORED.

Maytag made this man what he is today. We did it through hard work and determination. We did it by building washers that last longer and need fewer repairs. And by making sure every Maytag dryer, dishwasher, range, microwave and disposer meets our rigorous quality standards. Our standards are so high that we make many of our own parts, so you get Maytag quality, inside and out. Every appliance Maytag makes is individually tested to prove it can meet those standards— before it leaves our door.

It's true, not all Maytag repairmen have reached these heights of loneliness. But through hard work and dedication, Maytag is making sure every one of our repairmen will have a chance to find out how lonely it is at the top.

MAYTAG
THE DEPENDABILITY PEOPLE
©1985 The Maytag Company

**FIGURE 7-10** Advertisement reprinted courtesy of the Maytag Company.

180

Still washing, still drying, still cooking,

still cleaning, still innovating, and still lonely.

**MAYTAG**
THE DEPENDABILITY PEOPLE
One Dependability Square, Newton, Iowa 50208

© 1986 The Maytag Company

FIGURE 7–10 Advertise-
ment reprinted courtesy of
the Maytag Company
(*continued*).

Given the parity of the marketplace today for most businesses and products, an important advertising goal is to differentiate one product from another. As we've discussed, this differentiation can be found in product features or selling points. Something separates the product from its competition. And when that something controls the theme in an ad, it tries to introduce a unique way for the audience to perceive of the product. The Volkswagen ad in Figure 7–13 is a classic example of honing in on a new belief in the car buying process, that of smallness.

Notice how the Volkswagen ad centers on one word, *smallness*. This is its theme. Yes, the car is small, and the creative idea overall emphasizes that smallness. But the copy elaborates on the basic theme by explaining how a Volkswagen leads to such benefits as smaller fuel bills, smaller repair bills, and smaller insurance premiums. In other words, the ad separates Volkswagen from its competition. It creates a unique position for the vehicle in the audience's mind. And it supplants old information or beliefs about cars and the Volkswagen with new information and beliefs.

**FIGURE 7–11    Advertisement reprinted courtesy of the Wm. Wrigley Jr. Company.**

Creating Preference and Changing an Old Belief

At the far right end of the spectrum of objectives we have advertising's most difficult job, to create preference or change an old belief into a new one. Conceive of change like this. We know everyone is different, and one of the things that makes for differences in people is their system of beliefs or attitudes. All of us carry around our individualized systems. They get activated on a daily basis as we react to the stimuli around us. For example, if we're conservative in our beliefs, chances are we'll carry that conservatism into many areas of life. But at the risk of stereotyping, whether we're liberal or conservative, that individualized way we have of viewing life acts as a magnet for assessing many of the realities we experience each day. In other words, we draw the many diverse parts of reality into the slot of our individualized systems of thought.

Once something enters that slot it's hard to move it to another slot, particularly if that other slot is a long distance away. So, if someone believes something, especially if the person strongly believes it so that the slot gets closed and locked, then to change that belief is much more difficult. Think of it as tucking beliefs in a safe somewhere and then hiding the key. Not only that, think of it as protecting that safe, especially if the belief is central and irrefutable to us.

**FIGURE 7–12**    Advertisement reprinted courtesy of Hunt-Wesson, Inc., Consumer Advertising Division.

Fortunately, for many advertisers ultra-strong beliefs aren't the rule. Generally when it comes to brands, particularly those with low involvement and existing in a crowded parity marketplace, we tend to have fluid beliefs. They're not so rock hard.

# Think small.

Our little car isn't so much of a novelty any more.

A couple of dozen college kids don't try to squeeze inside it.

The guy at the gas station doesn't ask where the gas goes.

Nobody even stares at our shape.

In fact, some people who drive our little flivver don't even think 32 miles to the gallon is going any great guns.

Or using five pints of oil instead of five quarts.

Or never needing anti-freeze.

Or racking up 40,000 miles on a set of tires.

That's because once you get used to some of our economies, you don't even think about them any more.

Except when you squeeze into a small parking spot. Or renew your small insurance. Or pay a small repair bill. Or trade in your old VW for a new one.

Think it over.

**FIGURE 7–13    Advertisement copyrighted by Volkswagen of America, Inc. Advertisement reprinted with permission of Volkswagen of America, Inc.**

As far as you're concerned, all of this translates to how your objective and strategy influence the theme, creative idea, and ad copy. If you're attempting to combat an existing belief, for example, then your copy will have to convince the owner that what has been tucked away is less valuable than what will replace it. Not an easy task, to be sure. Quite frankly, what you hope to achieve is to kick the competition out and replace it with your product.

Earlier in the chapter we looked at ads for Avis and Hertz. These were examples of preference ads. They were directly competitive, with the overriding goal behind both being a shift in what the audience believed about the competition. We can see the same tact in the classic Wendy's ad in Figure 7–14.

**FIGURE 7–14   Advertisement reprinted courtesy of Wendy's International, Inc.**

# THE
# WENDY'S
# NATIONAL
# ADVERTISING
# PROGRAM,
### INC.

TITLE: "FLUFFY BUN"

LENGTH: 30 SECONDS
COMM'L NO.: WOFH-3386

CUST. #1: It certainly is a big bun.
CUST. #2: It's a very big bun.

CUST. #1: A big fluffy bun.

CUST. #2: It's a very...big...fluffy... bun.

CUST. #3: Where's the beef?
ANNCR: Some hamburger places give you a lot less beef on a lot of bun.

CUST. #3: Where's the beef?

ANNCR: At Wendy's, we serve a hamburger we modestly call a "Single" — and Wendy's Single has more beef than the Whopper or Big Mac. At Wendy's, you get more beef and less bun.

CUST. #3: Hey, where's the beef? I don't think there's anybody back there!

ANNCR: You want something better, you're Wendy's Kind of People.

Though we can laugh at the humor in the memorable "Where's the beef?" copy line, we shouldn't forget what the line means. Remember, the beef is lost in the competitor's big bun, and it's lost because of its smallness. The voice-over announcer tells us that at Wendy's "you get more beef and less bun." In fact, the announcer compares the amount of beef in Wendy's burger to Burger King's Whopper and McDonald's Big Mac. Of course, the comparison speaks in Wendy's favor.

Sometimes, as in the Wendy's ad, it pays to meet the competition head on. For example, another ad, this one for Volvo in Figure 7–15, does just that.

The Volvo ad's theme concentrates on the car's safety in comparison to other cars, notably subcompacts. Using a fear appeal, the writer highlights Volvo's safety record and asks the reader to decide how much one's life is worth. Is it worth the pittance of money you'll save on gasoline with a subcompact car? It's a leading question, of course, but one with its own irrefutable logic behind it.

Still another situation occurring at the end of the spectrum of objectives involves a noncompetitive preference appeal, but one that seeks to change an old belief. Here, research would tell you that the target audience believes something about your product that is misleading or perhaps untrue. Thus, your ad seeks to change the audience's misconception. The Price Pfister Company had just such a problem on its hands, and its advertising sought to correct it with ads such as you see in Figure 7–16, a sequence of four frames from a television commercial.

Notice how the ad attempts to achieve name recognition for the company, similar to the technique used in the Doublemint ad. However, this striving for name recognition for Price Pfister was based on a consumer misconception, one that confused the Price Pfister name with names of other companies such as Fisher Price toys and Pfizer pharmaceuticals.

We've briefly scanned a number of ads reflecting certain objectives and strategies. But by no means have we exhausted the variety of objectives and strategies available to direct the copywriter to the most appropriate theme, idea, and copy. What an individual advertiser hopes to achieve with an ad or campaign of ads is as diverse and numerous as the individual advertisers themselves. The ads you've just seen are new to this text. You haven't seen them before, and we haven't discussed them in detail. Yet, you should be able to see the governing strategies underpinning those ads, particularly the objectives. In fact, if you think back to the ads we have spent more time discussing, you'll find they, too, depend on solid strategies. For example, providing new and complete information about a pen. Hooking into an audience's need for long-lasting batteries. Or convincing an audience

# IS IT WORTH RISKING YOUR LIFE FOR 45 MILES PER GALLON?

Tiny little subcompact cars may be great for saving gas. But as accident statistics show, they're not particularly safe.

A Volvo on the other hand gets a very respectable 29 m.p.g. highway—19 m.p.g. city.* But ultimately, we put a much higher premium on life than we do on gasoline.

The roomy passenger compartment of a Volvo is surrounded by six steel pillars, each one strong enough to support the weight of the entire car.

Crumple zones, front and rear are designed to absorb the impact of a collision, rather than passing it on to the passengers.

As a matter of fact, the federal government is so impressed with Volvo's crash worthiness they've become one of our biggest customers. They bought more than 60 Volvos, many of which have been crashed into each other at closing speeds of up to 90 m.p.h. in an effort to establish safety standards for cars of the future.

So before you buy your next car, weigh carefully what you have to gain and lose.

A big substantial Volvo can not only save gas. It could end up conserving something much more precious.

VOLVO  ©1978 VOLVO OF AMERICA CORPORATION. LEASING AVAILABLE
*EPA estimates based on 240 Sedans with manual transmission. Mileage may vary on other models or because of your driving habits, cars condition and equipment.

## VOLVO. A CAR YOU CAN BELIEVE IN.

**FIGURE 7–15**  Advertisement reprinted courtesy of Volvo Cars of North America.

that boat hazards can be avoided. Each ad grew from a strategy. And each ad reflects that strategy, particularly the objective, benefit, support, and tone.

FIGURE 7–16    Advertisement reprinted courtesy of Price Pfister.

### 🖎  WRAP-UP  🖎

As usual, we've covered a lot of ground in this chapter. But it's important ground. It should not be undervalued, despite the fact that this book focuses more on methods for actualizing your writing self than it does on strategy development. At the same time, a large part of that actualization involves strategic considerations. Writing for writing's sake is fine. It has its place. But that place is continents away from ad copy.

As a purposeful writer, one with specific goals and someone else's money to back your words and ideas, strategy plays an important part in your writing life. This means you need to dwell on the elements in the strategic mix. There are really only three, but they expand into complex territories. Product. Audience. And media. Of the three, the audience should dominate your thinking, particularly in respect to how that audience relates to your product, its competition, and the media.

Still, there are other important considerations for you to ponder. Differentiating factors, for instance. What does your product have that others don't? What makes it different? And is that difference important to the audience?

Expectations and involvement suggest still another instance. What does your target audience bring to the ad by way of knowledge and likes or dislikes toward your product? Or what is your audience's degree of commitment, enthusiasm, or involvement toward your product and the media?

Each of these concerns leads to your strategy, synthesized into the Creative Work Plan. The key fact comes from research. It leads you to the problem to be solved. This in turn leads you to your objective, perhaps the most important part of your thinking. From here you sketch out support for the theme of your ad, that promise you'll make to the target audience, the all-important benefit. To close the plan you decide on the ad's tone, its personality, flavor or atmosphere. This goes a long way to matching your idea and copy with the audience.

Finally, you need a theme and idea. One should match or mirror the other. They should be inseparable. The theme is the idea. And the idea is the theme. The difference between the two is that one is relatively staid and uninviting. The other is exciting and arresting. Again, this doesn't mean they're different. To the contrary, in the most important respect they're the same.

This concern over theme and idea is where we're going in our next chapter as we focus more tightly on the actual crafting of ad copy.

## ✍ THINGS TO DO ✍

1. Go back to the early parts of the chapter where suggestions were made for getting inside your product and consumer. Now pick a product. Pick a consumer. Then work your way through the exercises. You'll find them helpful.

2. Read one of the ads in this chapter closely. Read between the lines for strategy. Then, following the format for the Creative Work Plan, re-create the plan as you think it would have been developed by those responsible for it.

3. Go into the kitchen cabinet where your cereals or other breakfast foods live. Take them out and display them on a table. Then, sit with a pen and pad and list the potential "nibs" for each. Stare at the packaging (itself a form of advertising) and jot down a rough plan for your favorite. Include the objective, benefit, support, and tone.

4. Create an imaginary dialogue between a potato and a consumer. Try to embed key elements of our discussion about the Potato Board ad into the dialogue. See if anything turns up in the way of an insightful revelation about how you might develop the strategy for this problem if you had the chance.

5.   Go back to your favorite breakfast food and list its main features, differentiating factors, and benefits. Then list the expectations you bring to that product. Try to form combinations leading to potential headlines for print ads. Finally, change who you are. Become someone else, a different consumer, and do the same thing.

# Chapter 8

# Crafting the Ad: Content

What to say in an ad depends on the contexts inherent to your strategic thinking. The context of your objective and strategy. Of the theme and idea. Of the audience. And of the medium. To a large extent these contexts represent the core of your primary considerations in ad writing. Each requires your attention, simply because each helps determine what you'll want to say about your product and how you'll say it. Change one, and your copy will change.

Beyond the prospect for change, your concern and thought for each of the contexts generates insights to your copywriting problem and may suggest solutions for how to solve that problem. For instance, if your objective is to convince the target audience to remember your product's name, then your theme and idea should include the name prominently. And if the ad is a print ad, perhaps the headline should be dominant and include the name. David Ogilvy, for instance, believes the name should be in the headline.

This, of course, seems like a simple situation. But it's not unlike what you'll face in the ad copywriting world. Often, however, we tend to complicate rather than simplify, simply because we know so much about the product and want to do such a great job with its advertising. So, we build layer upon layer of copy points and appeals, perhaps complicated with multiple themes and ideas. That's part of the head game for you to avoid. In advertising the idea is to simplify, not complicate.

In any event, what you say in an ad and how you say it depend to a large extent on these contexts. As you think about them you should try to tie them together. Part of your job as a copywriter is to create unity in the ad so that everything blends together into a meaningful whole for the audience. You can't do that if all of your concerns and thoughts are separated, almost as if one context is removed or separated from the other. Instead, you should try to unite them and in the process create a sense of order and simplicity. This will guide your copy and help make it unified and orderly.

At the same time, once you have your strategy considerations in order, you should begin to conceptualize and write your ad. Guided by the blueprint of your strategy, conceptualization and writing mean the actual crafting of the ad. Still, there are basic understandings that go into that crafting, understandings that reach to the core of what you can say, your content, and how you can say it, your style. Taken together they should become part of your writing arsenal helping you wage battle against the blank page. They should also relate directly to your content and style.

## ✍ THEME AND IDEA ✍

We've referred often to theme and idea, generally in the context of other discussions. But let's concentrate our attention on them exclusively, especially since they represent the very essence of an ad.

By the time you've planned your strategy you should know your theme. Remember, the theme is the "incipient center" of your ad. It's the ad's core, the heart and soul of what you want to say or show. And usually what you want to say or show is the benefit you wish to convey. On the other hand, the idea is the vehicle for expressing the theme. Ideally, the theme and idea should be inseparable, even though the idea may seem at first glance to be far removed from the theme. This is because the idea is often a unique and original way to express the theme.

Since your audience may be skeptical, apathetic, or even hostile, you need an idea that turns heads. You need an idea with originality, enough originality to lift the ad out of the ordinary and into the extraordinary. And often you need an idea that rocks reality. For instance, the potato ad shows a paintbrush painting a potato green. This isn't something you're likely to see in the real world. What you'll see instead are potatoes in clumps of mountainous brown stacked on supermarket shelves. But for the creative mind, this mundane and ordinary way of showing the product gives way to the more imaginative and innovative application of a paint brush to the product.

Imagine being the creative mind behind the invention of this idea. You knew the research findings. You knew the potato was perceived as a nonvegetable. You knew your target audience perceived vegetables as nutritious food. And here was the rub, the problem. How to convince the audience that the potato is a vegetable.

Well, you could have just said that the potato is a vegetable, perhaps overlaying the headline onto a mountain of earthy potatoes flanked by more traditional vegetables. But not so for the creative mind behind this ad. Instead, a quirky, imaginative step leads to an idea of having the potato painted green. It's not an ordinary step. It's not even a step with both feet in reality. After all, when was the last time you saw someone painting a potato green? But it is an example of how the creative mind thinks. That mind strains and stretches reality. It elasticizes it. It may even explode it. And all this for the purpose of yoking attention, realizing this as a necessity for an audience with its guard up, ready to ward off selling messages.

As inventive as the creative idea may be in the potato ad, notice how it doesn't drift from the theme. Rather, it mirrors the theme, making the theme and idea inseparable. Moreover, the creative idea attacks the very problem plaguing the consumer. In essence, that problem boils down to one word, green. And though potatoes seem removed from the artist's paintbrush, for the advertising creative mind they're not. Anything goes here, as long as it mirrors the theme. In fact, many great advertising campaign ideas do just that. They mirror the theme. Quite often as well, those ideas and themes can be reduced to single words or phrases. Fast and Federal Express. Slow and Heinz Ketchup. Gusto and Schlitz. More beef and Wendy's. Number Two and Avis. One or two words representing the essence of theme and idea. That controlled. And that single-minded.

## Theme and Idea in One Little Ad

Look at the photoboard for a television commercial from the Partnership for a Drug-Free America in Figure 8–1. The commercial was created as part of a campaign to prevent drug abuse, especially among today's youth. Let's try to unpeel the layers of words and images as they relate to the governing theme and idea.

The theme of the ad is simple. Drugs destroy your brain. No ifs, ands, or buts. But imagine how dull and boring the ad would be if it simply had the man in the commercial saying that drugs destroy your brain. Instead, a unique idea that mirrors the theme provides the arresting quality in the ad. The idea stems from an analogy of an egg and skillet to brain and drugs. This analogy forms an association of meaning for the viewer, one grounded in reality but that also makes a quantum leap into the unreal. In reality, your brain is not an egg. Drugs are not a hot skillet. Yet, for the

This is your brain,

this is drugs,

this is your brain on drugs.

Partnership For A Drug-Free America          N.Y., NY 10017

FIGURE 8–1    Advertisement reprinted courtesy of the Media Partnership
              for a Drug-Free America. Figure 8–1a portrays print
              advertisement.

creative mind searching for the unique idea, your brain can certainly be an
egg, and drugs can most definitely be a hot skillet. The comparisons made
result in the analogy controlling the creative idea.

As Leo Burnett advised, it's easy to be unique or different. All you
need to do is come downstairs in the morning with a sock in your

Partnership for a Drug Free America
ANY QUESTIONS? :30

Is there anyone out there who still isn't clear about what "doing drugs" does?

Okay. Last time

This is your brain.

This is drugs.

This is your brain on drugs.

Any questions?
(SILENCE)

Partnership for a Drug-Free America

**FIGURE 8–1** Advertisement reprinted courtesy of the Media Partnership for a Drug-Free America (*continued*). Figure 8–1b portrays television spot.

mouth. But in advertising, difference doesn't matter if the ad's theme and idea are wrong. In this respect you need to be right or on strategy, perhaps best conceptualized in William Bernbach's advice that you can certainly show a man standing on his head as long as your product keeps things from falling out of his pockets.

Do you get the point of Leo Burnett's and William Bernbach's advice? In and of itself, different doesn't translate to better. But matched with strategic rightness, especially in the most appropriate theme, it will translate to better. So, as a creative idea you can show a man standing on his head. That may be different enough to qualify as an innovative, unique idea. And if the product keeps things from falling out of the man's pockets, then the idea is not only unique, it's also right.

With our drug-free ad we have a similar situation. The relevance or rightness of the idea occurs in its immediate link to the theme. Virtually everyone knows how to fry an egg. But with a fairly small imaginative step on the part of the viewer, the frying of an egg can be likened to frying one's brain with drugs. It's an easy step for the viewer to make since the act of frying an egg is so common. A little crossover thinking and the viewer gets the theme immediately.

This match between theme and idea is critical to your success as a copywriter. The theme should be right or on strategy. And the idea should mirror that theme. Simultaneously, however, the idea should also grab attention, often by being different. Once the idea grabs the attention, then it's the ad copy's job to hold it.

Given the bold starkness of the drug-free ad's creative idea, notice how the writer matches and unites the copy strategically with both the theme and idea. The man speaking projects an authoritative, yet kind and fatherly appeal. Shirt sleeves rolled up, he projects strength and firmness. Still, there is also quiet gentleness about him, a caring, soft-eyed look to counteract the strength and vigor of his words. And what he says relates directly to the theme and idea. In fact, he states in no uncertain terms what the analogy really means. Very concise. Very firm. And very single-minded.

If you reflect on the ads we've discussed, you're sure to find coordinated themes and ideas. In the Eveready ad, for instance, the creative idea of the bunny interrupting a bogus commercial suggests the ongoing nature of the battery. In the Parker fountain pen ad, the straightforward formality of the creative idea suggests the dignity of writing magnificently. And in the Doublemint ad, the creative idea of the twins, combined with the *D* words, suggests name recognition.

Sweeping meaning into a tight and concentrated single-mindedness, the joining of themes and ideas allows the audience to grab onto something. The audience can easily understand what is being sold (remember, it's not a product per se, it's a benefit) while at the same time having that message reinforced through an arresting creative idea.

## ✍ TO SELL ✍

As much as we've been discussing artistic decisions in creating a single meaning through what you say and how you say it, it's important to understand that those decisions should be focused on selling. Again, no ad copy for ad copy's sake here. Your job is to sell. And if you don't like to sell don't become a copywriter. Because that's what your theme, idea, and copy should do.

Then again, if you're not sure if you like to sell, but you know you like to write, consider this. Selling's not bad. In fact, in many ways selling through ads is cleaner and more wholesome than much of the selling that goes on right under our very noses each and every day of our lives. People sell each other all the time. Our loved ones sell us all the time. We sell them all the time.

We're not talking about products being sold here, but about selling, persuading, or convincing others to believe something the way you want them to believe it. Unfortunately, in real life the selling, persuading, and convincing often seem like something else. Something not as vested, for instance. Or something innocent. The wholesomeness in selling through ads is that everyone knows they're ads. Before the ads are done, the person reading, seeing, or listening to them knows they're ads. It's too bad we can't say the same thing about real life.

What it comes down to is that the word *sell* has taken on negative connotations for some people. But those same people do it all the time, often without realizing it. So get your head on straight about selling. And then pay careful attention to how it's done. Even down to selling a friend on going to the big bash Saturday night.

Once again, however, it's easy to say "Go sell." But the problem of how to do it lingers in the foreground. Still, if you think about how selling gets done in life generally, this can open the door for understanding how selling gets done in ads. For example, how about bringing yourself and other people together? How do you do that? Well, you do it by being nice when the occasion calls for it. You do it by being authoritative when the occasion calls for it. You may even threaten when the situation calls for it. And most of all, you do it by a genuine concern for others, those being sold. Otherwise they won't buy what you're selling for a minute.

And how does what you say, your content, fit into the selling? Initially it may extend a hand to the audience. That hand suggests concern and understanding. It lets the audience know you care. Most of all, your content fits in by way of promising something. That promise is the benefit. It fills a need or want, or solves a problem. But since this is advertising, which means it's vested in its interest, people aren't so willing to take your promise at its word. They're not so willing to accept your extended hand. So, you have to support that benefit. You have to make it believable. By weaving relevant features and selling points into the product's story and making certain that your story relates to your audience, you make your promise, your benefit, believable.

Conceptualize the entire matter of selling as trying to link up with your audience on a common ground. Ordinarily your audience is distant from you. The distance may be long or short, depending on how the audience perceives you. Your job is to shorten that distance and bring your audience to the common ground.

## ✍ CLOSING THE DISTANCE BETWEEN ADVERTISER ✍ AND AUDIENCE

Product on one end. Consumer on the other. The product wants to be accepted. The consumer's not sure. In fact, the consumer may be skeptical, apathetic, or perhaps even hostile. Your job, again, is to close the distance and bring the two together on a common ground. In a nutshell, this is your primary task. And you start bringing them together through the appropriateness of your theme.

Recall back to our discussion of the Partnership for a Drug-Free America ad. We identified the theme as drugs destroying your brain. A plain and simple statement. It says exactly what it means. But think of all the prospects for failure in such a statement.

If you were a teenager or young adult and someone walked up to you on the street and told you that drugs destroy your brain, what would you think? Would you nod yes and think of a snide comment such as, "Like I never knew that. Thanks for telling me"? Would you be totally put off by the statement? If you were a teenager or young adult who's been experimenting off and on with drugs, what would you say then? Or if you were a teenager or young adult who's been even more involved with drugs, what would you say?

Sometimes we don't allow messages inside us, especially if we just don't want to hear them. Then, someone can be shouting in our ears, and it won't make much difference. That could have happened with our drug-free ad. So the ad's creators had to be careful. They had to focus on their target audience, and they had to blast their way through all the shields and defense mechanisms of that audience.

Remember, the theme controls an ad. Once you determine what it should be, the objective and strategy articulate it. They keep you focused on that theme. When you sit down to generate the ad idea, all tactical considerations bend toward the theme. Later on, after you crystallize your creative idea, the tactical considerations of your copy lean toward expression of the ad's content, an important part of which stems from the support section of your creative plan.

Again, the content is what you say in an ad. And that content should match the theme with the consumer. But that's not all it should match. It should match the theme and idea with the strategy, especially the objective, such as we saw in the ads in the previous chapter.

No doubt, in the drug-free ad consideration of the target audience's perception about drugs led the ad's creative minds to a creative way for conveying the theme. Once again, simply to state the theme might put that audience off. It might sound preachy or dictatorial. It might lengthen the distance. And the audience might react according- ly. Thus, the ad uses an analogy to carry the theme, an analogy that closes the distance between the audience and theme, in this case the fact that drugs ruin one's brain. If you go back and look at the ad again, you'll notice how the distance between the advertiser and the audience closes.

The analogy of an egg frying in a pan to suggest your brain being fried with drugs represents the creative mind's ability to form new real- ities as ideas. Combining realistic elements together in odd ways often leads to new ideas. Here, a brain frying on drugs as one realistic ele- ment, and an egg frying in the pan as another, coalesce into an entirely new reality known as the creative idea. The comparison being made is clear and simple. No one can mistake it.

This ad is an example of how the idea, that which carries the theme, should be unique and attention-grabbing. Remember, your audi- ence isn't waiting for your ad. And when it reaches them, they confront it with skepticism, apathy, or even hostility. Thus the need for originali- ty. But this doesn't mean the originality exists for its own sake. To the contrary, it should mirror the theme. It's simply that the idea is an orig- inal, attention-grabbing, and thought-provoking way to do it.

With our drug-free ad the governing idea of frying an egg is some- thing everyone has done. It's relevant to all of us. Because of this it clos- es the distance between audience and product. We can relate to it, sim- ply because it's so common to us. But notice how the core governing idea is fleshed out in the commercial.

As we've observed before, the man frying the egg projects an authoritative yet kind and fatherly appeal. Shirt sleeves rolled up, he projects strength and firmness. Yet there is also a quiet gentleness about him. A caring, soft-eyed look to counteract the fire in his words. And listen to those words. "Is there anyone out there who still isn't clear about what 'doing drugs' does? Okay. Last time. This is your brain. This is drugs. This is your brain on drugs. Any questions?"

As content for the ad, what he says is direct and firm. Coiled tight- ly around the creative idea, each word builds the relevance of that idea, which, in turn, blends with the theme. Overall, the ad's dramatic crisp- ness intensifies the effect for the audience. But that crispness results from the singularity in theme, idea, and content. There is no scattering of shot here, no drifting from the strategy or from the single-minded purpose exemplified in theme, idea, and content. All aspects comple- ment each other.

The common ground in the drug-free ad may have been difficult to establish, given the potential backlash from a sensitive audience. But closing the distance of that ground is a necessity for an ad's effectiveness. Naturally, your advertising and consumer research evaluates the distance and ground for you. But it's the correct theme and appropriate idea that begin to close the distance. And it's the content that should join you with your audience.

### Closing the Distance to the Common Ground, Student to Student

If you think about the ways we manage to shorten the distance between ourselves and others so that we join together and commit ourselves to one another, you can learn a great deal about what to say and how to say it in an ad. For example, pay close attention the next time you've been sold something. Chances are the salesperson spent a great deal of time shortening the distance between you and what was being sold. The means for doing that probably included letting you know how important you were, perhaps through a sensitive understanding of your problems.

In an introductory copywriting exercise students were divided into pairs and asked to sell their partners a breakfast food. First, though, the partners had to interview each other. Do some crude consumer research, in effect. Research that would guide them to the common ground between the product and audience. In making inquiries of each other, they were sure to determine the distance that had to be covered to establish that common ground.

Understand, this wasn't an advertising assignment per se. Or was it? We've said right along that the best way to be a writer is to start from the ground up, meaning living and thinking like a writer first and being a writer second. Well, the way to be an ad copywriter is similar. You start from the ground up, which means you understand the entire mix of what you're writing and who you're writing it to. More so, you understand that advertising communication or persuasion isn't different from most forms of communication or persuasion taking place in real life each day. This includes how we relate to others and how they relate to us. A great deal can be learned by paying close and careful attention to how this happens.

So, given this assignment and following their interviews, the students wrote personal letters to their partners. The letters were meant to convince the partners to try a particular breakfast food. Here's the text of one of those letters.

As a fellow commuter to campus I know how stressful a daily drive into town can be. Late starts and traffic tie-ups on top of an already exhausting courseload can leave you feeling really run down. This is when daily nutrition becomes essential.

A good breakfast can be a crucial factor in deciding your success in school. It wakes you up and keeps you up. Most of us don't have time to wake up every morning and cook ourselves a healthy breakfast. And many breakfast cereals can be messy or full of sugars and preservatives that are bad for you.

A tasty alternative for you can be Kellogg's Eggo Waffles. A few minutes in your toaster, then your favorite toppings and you've got a quick, hot, and delicious breakfast that's perfect to get you going in the morning. An Eggo's breakfast will leave you more time to prepare for more important things. You can even eat them right in the car on the way to school on those days when you're really in a rush.

With no preservatives and fortified with seven essential vitamins, an Eggo's breakfast might be one of the smartest choices you can make all day. With Eggo's it's easy to start your day fast and right.

Now, we can take some issue with what was selected for the letter's content and how it was expressed on occasion. But remember the assignment. Then read between the lines to discover what the writer found out about common ground.

Obviously, the target audience for the letter lacks time, especially in the morning in getting to school. Notice how the student writer creates that common ground in the very first copy line. In fact, the writer joins with the audience, a sure means to shorten the emotional distance between one and the other. An elaboration of that drive to school reflects how the writer understands the audience's problem.

From here the writer moves to breakfast and how essential it is for success in school. And before you know it we're into the story of Eggo Waffles, including why they're good for you and how you can eat them.

Understand that this letter has no governing theme or idea. It's not an ad per se. But it does what ads are supposed to do. Bear in mind, too, that there was very little instruction to write the letter the way the student did. The student simply wrote a personal letter after having considered the issue of common ground and the distanced relationship of the partner to the product. From this point the student wrote the letter the best way he knew how.

What I like about the letter is how it warms up to the audience, how it begins to bridge or shorten the distance between the product and that audience. Immediately there's a link between the product and audience. And that link relates directly to something important about the audience's life as it pertains to this product.

Obviously, as it now stands this letter is totally inappropriate for noncommuting students. It's inappropriate for me. In fact, it's inappropriate for anyone not a student. At the same time, this is a targeted letter. The audience is clear. And the message is tailored specifically for that audience. In this way it closes the distance and makes the selling job that much easier. So it is with ads. Just remember our Parker fountain pen ad, for example.

## Closing the Distance to the Common Ground, Ad to Ad

A great deal of what to write in an ad centers on closing this distance between your product and audience. It can be a distance of belief, attitude, thought, or emotion, all as they pertain to your audience's perceptions of your product. As with any selling, if you shorten the distance, the completion of the sale is that much closer. And when you make a sale, it's generally the beginning of your contact with the customer that sets the tone and gets things off on the right foot.

In ads, getting off on the right foot relates to contact with the first things seen or heard. Headline perhaps. Or visual. Overall, the creative idea, which, again, should mirror the theme. But after this initial contact the copy takes over, especially what it says at the beginning.

Think of it like this. The idea, including the headline, gets the audience looking or listening. But the audience won't look or listen very long unless there's a common ground established. That's the job of the ad copy. Notice, for instance, the first copy lines from some of the ads we've seen throughout the book.

> Schlitz beer—You only go around once in life. So grab for all the gusto you can.
>
> Parker pen—You will find writing with the Parker sterling silver Premier fountain pen anything but drudgery.
>
> Perdue—The problem with you is you're allowed to eat whatever you want.
>
> Hunt's—The time is right. Millions of Americans have made the decision to cut down on salt.

Notice how these first copy lines focus more on the audience than they do on the product. In this way they act as a bridge to the remaining copy, which often works in reverse, focusing more on the product than the audience.

Obviously, however, we've picked our spots here. Not all of the ads we've looked at spend time at the copy's beginning trying to close the distance between product and audience. Then again, research may have determined there was little distance to be closed. But if there is, then you will need to do it. And what better way than by talking less of yourself and more of your audience. Victor Schwab, advises, "Tell me quick and tell me true/Or else my love, to hell with you,/Less, how the thing came to be/More, what the thing can do for me." We've termed this the theme or benefit. But it takes time to build a case for the theme or benefit in the ad copy. Meanwhile, it takes no time to build your interest in the audience. Just some genuine sincerity regarding their problems and concerns, expressed immediately or soon after the copy's beginning.

One of the problems with many ads, it seems to me, is that they don't follow Victor Schwab's advice. Often they seem more intent on waving the product's flag, even though their audience may have walked away a long time before. Common selling sense says that the audience is number one. Your job is to reaffirm that and then make it clear and believable that your product fits an important audience need or want, or solves an important problem. This, I believe, is the essence of what you should say in your ads.

With this in mind, many variables influence your content, all of which serve to create the common ground. Your strategy, for instance. And, of course, your theme and idea. Given the importance of unity to an ad, your content cannot stray from the strategy or from the theme and idea. Everything needs to be working together, playing its own role and not trying to do more than it was meant to do. Sort of like a successful team. Each team member in position and knowing the role to be played.

In Figure 8–2 is an ad with all team members in sync with each other. You first saw it in our last chapter.

We've discussed this Potato Board ad at length, mostly from the perspective of strategy considerations. Here, though, let's discuss it from the perspective of closing the distance between product and audience.

We know that the creative idea goes hand in glove with the theme. We know that the theme stemmed from the strategy. Consumer perceptions indicated that potatoes are considered nonvegetables. That's a problem for the Potato Board since vegetables are considered nutritious, and there is a movement afoot to consume more vegetables. To overcome both the consumer's and the advertiser's problem, the ad seeks to change the consumer's perception.

Because it's not enough simply to state the theme, the creative idea must grab the attention. It must be original in some way. Painting the potato green is certainly original. But it also mirrors the theme. From here, the writer must close the distance between product and audience. In effect, the writer must convince the audience that the claim being made is believable and in the audience's best interest. The support and tone are important means for achieving this goal.

Overall, the ad conveys a personal tone. But it's personal in a lighthearted way, one that emphasizes the relative insignificance of the product in the audience's life. After all, we're not talking about extreme involvement here. This is not a product that demands considerable thought. And it's not one that should be taken too seriously. It is, in the end, a potato.

**FIGURE 8-2    Advertisement reprinted courtesy of The Potato Board.**

In selecting what to write about, the writer must consider these perspectives. As is, the beginning of the copy pretty well writes itself. You have a creative idea expressing a theme, and the copy's beginning must begin to establish the common ground while relating back to the idea. That's exactly what the copy's first line achieves in this ad. It's almost as if the writer is talking with the audience. But it's not a lecture. It's a conversation, one on one and in an informal setting. At the same time, the copy relates to the creative idea.

With the second paragraph we begin to get the explanation óf why the audience's problem shouldn't be a problem at all. This is part of the support for the ad's claim, support specific to the health values of a potato.

In the third paragraph we find ourselves yanked back to the creative idea and an explanation as to why it exists. Very personal. Almost a self-disclosure on the part of the advertiser, one conveying sincerity and honesty. A kind of keyhole look into why the ad is the way it is.

In the fourth paragraph we encounter more support through reasons why our perception about potatoes might be wrong. The support is called carrots, squash, and cauliflower. Imagine the writer thinking of ways to support the ad's theme or promise. One of those ways is to consider what the audience already perceives as vegetables, which may be similar to potatoes.

Finally, in the last two paragraphs we receive more of the conversational and personal tone that serves to keep the copy warm and appealing.

Overall, what is actually said by way of content in the ad's copy can be broken down as follows. Response to the headline question, linking the idea and theme with the copy. Copy claims of health value. Statement of the perception problem. Explanation of the creative idea expressed as a self-disclosure to shorten the distance of liking between product and audience. Comparison to commonly accepted vegetables as support, almost as a critique of the audience's perceptions but certainly not expressed harshly. Then a wrap-up of the main message.

If you really think of this ad as closing the distance between product and audience, certain insights should emerge. For example, through consistency of theme, idea, support, and tone, the audience isn't expected to understand or accept too much. There's very little threat here, either in terms of changing a rigid belief or working hard at a change. The ad is clear and to the point. Also, not too much is made of the theme. It's not overplayed or expressed in a way that challenges the core of what's believable about potatoes in the audience's mind. Finally, there is no condescension here, no vaunting claim and boast, even though the potato is positioned higher in the audience's mind. Instead, there's a kind of warmth about the copy, and a light touch of how simple it is for the audience to change its mind. Even more, there is support for why the audience should do that.

As you look at ads, pay attention to how the writers close the distance between advertiser and audience. Usually it's by placing the audience front and center, even more front and center than the product.

This is especially true at the beginning of the copy. As a gate opener, it allows you to tell the product's story. Of course, the story should be centered squarely on the theme and idea in the same way the theme and idea were centered squarely on the strategy.

Overall, what you say in your ad depends on these many contexts and variables. You can strive to eliminate the audience's problem, such as in our Potato Board ad. You can strive to fill a need with the product, such as in our student letter for Eggo Waffles. You can strive to reveal an important differentiating factor for your product, one that leads to filling a need, such as in our Parker pen or Timberland ads. Or, you can strive to entertain the audience, while at the same time creating meaning relevant to your advertiser as it matches with that audience. For instance, the following radio spot for Saint Mary-of-the-Woods in Terre Haute, Indiana, does just that.

*60-Second Radio Spot*

| | |
|---|---|
| Chorus: | (young female voices singing softly as if in echo hall, and continuing underneath throughout) La-La-La, La-La-La, |
| Sister Teresa: | Sister Marguerite? |
| Sister Marguerite: | (respectfully) Yes, Sister Teresa. |
| Sister Teresa: | About the Saint Mary-of-the-Woods recruitment brochure you've written. |
| Sister Marguerite: | Yes, Sister. |
| Sister Teresa: | (as if shocked) Some of the language. |
| Sister Marguerite: | Yes, Sister. |
| Sister Teresa: | I realize no one loves our school more than you, but must we refer to Saint Mary-of-the-Woods as so-o-o-o-o awesome? |
| Sister Marguerite: | No, Ma'am. |
| Sister Teresa: | Totally tubular? |
| Sister Marguerite: | No, Ma'am. |
| Sister Teresa: | A mondo cool place to be? |
| Sister Marguerite: | I'll change that, Sister. |
| Sister Teresa: | And right here where you talk about attracting serious, well-rounded students? |
| Sister Marguerite: | Yes, Ma'am. |
| Sister Teresa: | Do you have to say no zods, airheads or space cadets need apply? |
| Sister Marguerite: | I'll work on it, Sister. |
| Sister Marguerite: | Another thing. When you come to Saint Mary-of- |

|  | the-Woods you'll be enriched, fulfilled, enlightened, but Sister Marguerite, you will not be blown away. |
|---|---|
| Sister Marguerite: | No, Ma'am. |
| Voice-over: | (soft, reassuring male voice) Saint Mary-of-the-Woods in Terre Haute is a career-oriented liberal arts college providing women with leadership skills and self-direction. For more information contact the admissions office. |
| Sister Teresa: | Really, Sister, this whole recruitment brochure just kinda freaks me out. |
| Sister Marguerite: | It's a bummer? |
| Sister Teresa: | Totally. |
| Sister Marguerite: | It's grody? |
| Sister Teresa: | To the max. |
| Sister Marguerite: | Should I rewrite it? |
| Sister Teresa: | Please do. |
| Sister Marguerite: | Fer sure. |

Advertisement reprinted courtesy of Saint Mary-of-the-Woods College.

Notice how the language in this clever radio spot hooks into the language of a younger audience in an entertaining way. That language, most identified with the mid-1980s and California, creates a common ground between the school and its audience. As the essence of the creative idea, it does so in a playful way. At the same time, notice how the message, the theme, is clear. Saint Mary-of-the-Woods is a place where young women can become enriched and fulfilled in what promises to be a youthful and contemporary environment.

What should come from this, of course, is the importance of tailoring your content to your audience, particularly as your audience relates to your advertiser. We've referred to this relationship as distance and common ground. And one thing's certain. As you decide what to write about and then begin to write it, you must keep your eye on the audience's relationship to your advertiser. Your goal, after all, is to join them together on a common ground.

## Closing the Distance by Being Positive and Nice

Here's one sure way to help close the distance to the common ground. Be positive. And be nice. Notice, for instance, how many ads are just that, positive and nice. Think about it. Based on research, your theme is positive and nice. It states what good someone will get when that person buys and uses you. There's something positive and nice about that. In fact, there's something positive and nice about most ads. By the time you leave them you feel pretty good. Life seems good. All you have to do is buy the yogurt or whatever else is being sold. Small price to pay, really.

Then again, positive or nice can have various meanings. What's nice to one person might not be so nice to another. Still, we humans tend to agree that some people are nicer or more positive than others. Those who care about us, for instance. We consider them nice. Those who don't claim and boast. They have a good chance of being considered nice. Those who give us something we want without expecting too much in return. They're nice. Those who don't talk down to us. Or up at us. In short, those who talk eye to eye with us. They're nice. Those who understand us, who sympathize with us. They're nice. Those who are sincere with us. They're nice.

Of course, we could go on about what constitutes positive or nice, even in ads. Our Potato Board ad, for instance, was positive and nice. Recall how we discussed the ease with which the writer criticized the audience. Tactfulness goes a long way in advertising copywriting, let alone life. So positive and nice count. Often they count a lot.

If you review the ads in various textbooks, including those devoted to creative strategy or the creative side of the field, you're sure to find that many of them are positive and nice. They're friendly. Yes, positive and nice can mean different things. But if we think of positive and nice as friendly, uplifting, and personable, then you'll find it in ads. For example, in reviewing the ads from Bruce Bendinger's delightful and insightful book *The Copy Workshop Workbook,* many of those ads are nice. Here are headlines and copy lines from some of those ads.

The Joint Is Jumpin' (for the San Diego Zoo)

I Love New York (for New York City)

Buy the Parker Premier and even if you never write anything magnificent, at least you will never write anything but magnificently (our familiar Parker pen ad)

Set a Shining Example (for Cascade dish detergent)

Saturday Morning Car Tunes (for KSJN/1330 AM Radio)

S'Alternative (for Sunkist lemons)

When You Need It Bad, We've Got It Good (for Florida)

Give A Toy A Child For Christmas (for Kay Bee stores)

But to be positive and nice doesn't mean you have to be gooey or soppy. Just pleasant. Or personable and fun. And most of all, friendly, as in this advertising copy taken straight from the package containing a

Nelson Rainshower 55 water sprinkler for lawns. You see it in Figure 8–3. For the sake of brevity, not all of the copy is transcribed below. Copy from the back of the package is shown in Figure 8–3 (there are eight columns of copy on the backside of the package alone).

*Copy Excerpts for Nelson Rainshower Sprinkler*

**FASCINATING INSTRUCTIONS FOR YOUR FASCINATING NELSON RAINSHOWER LAWN SPRINKLER.**

See this NELSON RAINSHOWER Sprinkler. It's going to do absolutely fantastic things for your lawn. But there are a few things you've got to do first before you see that luscious neighbor-envying green carpet appear.

**START HERE**

Let's face it, nothing is going to happen until you open the box so that's step one.

Lately there's been a huge surge of interest by many in the exact science of lawn watering. For those watering buffs, the NELSON RAINSHOWER has 59 positions so you can experiment until you make some sort of scientific discovery.

**THRILLING TIPS FOR WATERING YOUR LAWN**

If your lawn is brown, it's probably too late. If it's soaking wet, it's probably too soon. If you can see footprints on the grass, that's the right time to whip out your NELSON. However, if the footprints are either very large or very strange, you may want to call the police before watering.

Notice how the copy closes the distance between the product and the audience, and does so in a playful way. Remember, the product is a lawn sprinkler, and watering one's lawn carries with it a certain amount of fun. It's the lighter side of life, given the fact that there are so many serious sides. Not so with lawn watering. Here, we have the lighter side. You mosey out to the yard on a leisurely Saturday morning and proceed to get yourself in touch with Mother Nature. All the while you feel the wonder and beauty of making things grow, taking an almost childish pleasure in hooking up your sprinkler. Then, a cool glass of iced tea in hand, you sit back and watch the soothing arcs of water sweep back and forth across your lawn. What a treat! And the copy for the NELSON RAINSHOWER Sprinkler matches with the treat in a positive and lighthearted way, the same way the audience member feels when it comes to watering the lawn.

This is not to say that all of the ads and their copy in the Bendinger book are nice. Many, in fact, are not. Many rely on caustic wit and crisp but not nice plays on words. Even then, though, there is a sense of playfulness to those ads. They tend to joke with the audience, even if their wit is caustic. As we'll see in a bit, not all ads are so nice at

# NELSON

# RAINSHOWER® 55
## non-puddling sprinkler

**FASCINATING INSTRUCTIONS FOR YOUR FASCINATING NELSON RAINSHOWER LAWN SPRINKLER**

See this NELSON RAINSHOWER Sprinkler. It's going to do absolutely fantastic things for your lawn. But there are a few things you've got to do first before you see that luscious neighbor-envying green carpet appear.

**START HERE**
Let's face it, nothing is going to happen until you open the box so that's step one.

**DIALING INSTRUCTIONS**

On your lawn, as in life, you need to have a plan. Random sporadic sprinkling is tacky especially when it's so easy to do it right with the RAINSHOWER. The major point is — you'll save money if you only water what needs watering. That's what the special Dial-A-Rain® coverage control is all about. It lets you control the coverage.

If you want to water the right side of your lawn, you switch the dial to the right. To water the left side, you turn the dial to the left. To water the center only, turn to center, and for the whole shebang, switch the dial to full.

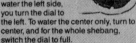

**Left      Right      Center      Full**

Lately, there's been a huge surge of interest by many in the exact science of lawn watering. For those watering buffs, the NELSON RAINSHOWER has 59 positions so you can experiment until you make some sort of scientific discovery.

**LOOK NELSON, NO PUDDLES!**

The RAINSHOWER sprinkler feature that's just going to knock your socks off is that you won't ever have to worry about puddles. Your RAINSHOWER sprinkler has something quite technical and quite extraordinary called the Turbo-Heart™ cam which keeps the sprinkler moving all the time so there's no way a puddle can form. No Pause=No Puddle. It's one of those big principles in life like $E = MC^2$.

**SOME THINGS YOU'VE PROBABLY BEEN WONDERING ABOUT**
Q. Is the RAINSHOWER an oscillating sprinkler?
A. Yes.
Q. What's an oscillating sprinkler?
A. An oscillating sprinkler sprays upward and moves back and forth rather than some other way which we aren't going to talk about now.
Q. What's so hot about an oscillator?
A. It throws the water up and drops it like a shower of rain. That's why we call a NELSON oscillator a RAINSHOWER. It gives very even gentle, careful coverage. You might say it's the sensitive, caring watering system. That's why it's such a perfect parent for new grass seed.
Q. How do I adjust my sprinkler?
A. Two ways — on the sprinkler and at the spigot.
Q. Why do I adjust my sprinkler?
A. Let's not get philosophical.

**A LITTLE HELP FROM A FRIEND**
Your NELSON RAINSHOWER sprinkler is going to perform wondrous feats by the square feet for you so you want to be good to it in return. Here are some tips for the care and feeding of your NELSON RAINSHOWER sprinkler.

**FIGURE 8-3    Reprinted courtesy of L. R. Nelson Corporation.**

first glance, but before the copy ends, they're certainly positive and friendly in their own unique way.

Still, in advertising overall, nice is good. Positive is good. Of course, to be positive and nice have a great deal to do with the ad's style, our major concern in the next chapter. But they also have a great deal to do with the ad's theme, idea, and content. Having evolved through research, the theme is positive and nice automatically. At least

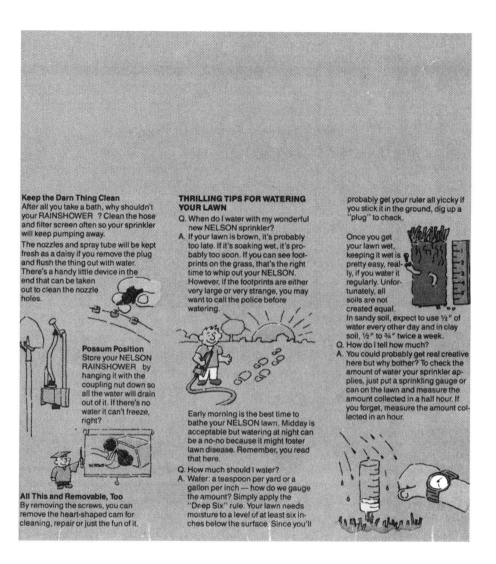

**Keep the Darn Thing Clean**
After all you take a bath, why shouldn't your RAINSHOWER ? Clean the hose and filter screen often so your sprinkler will keep pumping away.

The nozzles and spray tube will be kept fresh as a daisy if you remove the plug and flush the thing out with water. There's a handy little device in the end that can be taken out to clean the nozzle holes.

**Possum Position**
Store your NELSON RAINSHOWER by hanging it with the coupling nut down so all the water will drain out of it. If there's no water it can't freeze, right?

**All This and Removable, Too**
By removing the screws, you can remove the heart-shaped cam for cleaning, repair or just the fun of it.

**THRILLING TIPS FOR WATERING YOUR LAWN**

Q. When do I water with my wonderful new NELSON sprinkler?

A. If your lawn is brown, it's probably too late. If it's soaking wet, it's probably too soon. If you can see footprints on the grass, that's the right time to whip out your NELSON. However, if the footprints are either very large or very strange, you may want to call the police before watering.

Early morning is the best time to bathe your NELSON lawn. Midday is acceptable but watering at night can be a no-no because it might foster lawn disease. Remember, you read that here.

Q. How much should I water?

A. Water: a teaspoon per yard or a gallon per inch — how do we gauge the amount? Simply apply the "Deep Six" rule. Your lawn needs moisture to a level of at least six inches below the surface. Since you'll

probably get your ruler all yiccky if you stick it in the ground, dig up a "plug" to check.

Once you get your lawn wet, keeping it wet is pretty easy, really, if you water it regularly. Unfortunately, all soils are not created equal. In sandy soil, expect to use ½" of water every other day and in clay soil, ½" to ¾" twice a week.

Q. How do I tell how much?

A. You could probably get real creative here but why bother? To check the amount of water your sprinkler applies, just put a sprinkling gauge or can on the lawn and measure the amount collected in a half hour. If you forget, measure the amount collected in an hour.

FIGURE 8–3    Reprinted courtesy of L. R. Nelson Corporation (*continued*).

it better be. And with the playfulness and originality evident in many ads, the ideas are also positive and nice, though perhaps a bit offbeat. With the content, positive and nice come through in the friendly nature of what you choose to say. Not how you say it. That's style. But what you say. That's content.

To be positive and nice in your content means you keep your main eye focused on your audience. Think of it like this. You write for an

**FIGURE 8–3** Reprinted courtesy of L. R. Nelson Corporation *(continued).*

advertiser. We've referred to the advertiser as the product, understanding that it can be a service or store as well. When you write for that advertiser there's a danger of keeping your writer's mind so fixed on the product that you don't even see the audience. Right away, train your mind to avoid that. Common-sense selling should help convince you in this respect. Train your mind to look through the product to the audience. Train your mind to talk about the product only in terms of your audience.

Think back to many of the ads and much of the ad copy we've discussed in the book. Schlitz. Cover Girl Luminesse Lipstick. Nissan Pathfinder. Parker pen. Avis. Potatoes. Saint Mary-of-the-Woods. To varying degrees the content of the ad copy in those ads was positive and nice. Sometimes hopeful. Or endearing. Or cute. Or uplifting. What was said in the copy made the audience feel good. It gave the audience something to think about. New and relevant information, perhaps. Or the promise of something good to happen if you drank this, beautified yourself with that, drove this, wrote with that, rented here, ate this, or attended this school. Translated, these good things to happen are benefits. And benefits, or at least the substantiation and support of benefits, should control what you say in your ads. Simply put, that's meeting your audience on the common ground by being positive and nice, as in the Royal Viking ad you see in Figure 8–4, the same one you saw and read at the close of Chapter 6 in "Things to Do."

If need be, refer to the ad's copy at the close of Chapter 6 and notice how it conveys a positive image of the cruise line, one that links together with the needs or wants of the audience. Candlelit dining rooms. Unhurried single seating. Fine delicacies. Fresh flowers appearing magically in the morning. Spacious and strollable decks. Alert, gracious service. And at the copy's close, just prior to the call to action with the 800 phone number, we have the familiar circle back to the theme and idea, that of arriving at the proper state of mind.

Positive and nice. Two words that reveal themselves often in the best of advertising. Two important words. So important, in fact, that despite the pounding headache or the seemingly unsolvable problem facing you when you sit to write your copy, your responsibility won't change. You will still need to be positive and nice.

## Closing the Distance with an Imposing Creative Idea, but Getting Real Positive and Nice During the Copy

Not all ad ideas are so nice. Yes, all ad themes are nice. But not all ad ideas. Some, such as our familiar Timberland ad in Figure 8–5, rely on other attention-grabbing methods that are more imposing than nice. Often these ads are meant to yank a response from the audience, something like, "Yikes, what is this?" This response should be followed by another, "I better get into this to see what it means."

In this ad for Timberland boat shoes the idea jolts. Right away you pay attention. Obviously, the first job of any ad. But it will take the ad copy to close the distance between advertiser and audience. It will take the ad copy to prove to the audience that Timberland boat shoes are, well, nice.

Shown here but also transcribed at the close of Chapter 6, the ad copy comprises four columns. Notice how the copy in the first column

FIGURE 8–4    Advertisement reprinted courtesy of Royal Viking Line. Reprinted with permission.

# BOAT SHOES SHOULD BE JUDGED BY HOW THEY GO WITH A BLACK SKY. NOT A BLUE BLAZER.

Don't get us wrong. If you want to use our new boat shoes with the Interactive Grip System to fox-trot across the yacht club dance floor, that's your choice. We guarantee you and your blazer will look good, and we promise to accept your money.

Just be aware that we engineered these shoes so you could dance on a very different surface. The storm-blackened foredeck of a boat that's bucking like a rodeo bull.

On so wet and treacherous a playing field, one slip of the foot could be one slip too many. Preventing it is what the Interactive Grip System is all about.

As its name implies, the System starts where the foot interacts with the boat. At the sole. Our new design gives you such a profusion of siping (razor cuts for traction) that the number of leading edges exceeds the traction capacity of traditional boat soles by a good 50%. What's more, the edges are clustered in an exclusive quadrant cut pattern. (Competitors beware. The Timberland quadrant cut sole so outgrips

### INTERACTIVE GRIP SYSTEM

Quadrant cut sole has 50% more leading edges than standard wave cut soles.

Quadrant cut exceeds wave cut for traction, providing 360° of grip.

Internal Fit System keeps foot in correct position for comfort, balance and grip.

standard wave cut soles it may cause mutiny at the yacht club.)

Part Two of the Interactive Grip System makes sure that your foot stays in the right place to do its work. Your foot is secured for proper balance and energy distribution by an Internal Fit System, a contoured sleeve that keeps your toes from jamming when the boat makes a violent lurch.

These brand new benchmarks for marine footwear aren't just high-tech, but true high performance for the 1990's. A new definition of authenticity that puts our imitators in an embarrassing place. Overboard.

BOOTS. SHOES. CLOTHING,
WIND, WATER, EARTH AND SKY.

© 1992 The Timberland Company. Timberland and ⊕ are registered trademarks of The Timberland Company.

**FIGURE 8–5** Advertisement reprinted courtesy of The Timberland Company.

seeks to build a story explaining the jolting ad idea. At the same time, notice how the copy begins to woo the reader, "Don't get us wrong" and "we engineered these shoes so you could dance on a very different surface." Notice how the imposing danger inherent in the visual is softened in the third paragraph with "one slip of the foot could be one slip too many." Yes, the threat is there, but "one slip too many" softens the potential disaster.

Overall, the paragraphs in this first column explain the creative idea, especially in terms of how it relates to the product and audience together. But in the second column there is a shift away from the audience to the product itself (remember our Parker pen ad copy). In fact, the third column continues the product story, now focusing more on comfort than safety. And in the fourth column the copy closes with a one word paragraph, "Overboard."

In circling back to the creative idea, this one word, *overboard*, helps unify the ad. It helps create the ad's Gestalt. Yet the copy overall concentrates on the advantages of the product, expressing those advantages in the context of what's good for the audience. For example, in the third column the writer even expresses concern for the comfort of the audience's toes. All positive. All nice. And this despite the fact that the threatening and imposing visual suggests potential disaster.

Think back to our Drug-Free ad, for example. It, too, seemed imposing at first glance. Bold. Brash. Authoritative. But remember our man. Soft-eyed. Caring. And also firm and strong. Also, remember the audience for that ad. Young people, primarily teens. Sometimes a threat can work with teens, especially when it's in their best interests. Sometimes fear has its place in selling and in closing the distance between the salesperson and the customer. But in the end, the threat or fear appeal has niceness attached to it. Remember being disciplined by your parents and being told that it was for your own good? There's truth to that. And as an end result, it's nice to know that someone's willing to watch out for you and your best interests. Why?

Because so much is riding on your tires, that's why.

### ✍ WHAT TO SAY ✍

Say enough and no more. Enough so that the theme, the message, is clear and unmistakable. Enough so that the theme can be believed. Enough so that the audience knows you're on its side. Enough so that audience members know you understand them, perhaps even sympathize or empathize with them. Enough so that they know what your product can do for them, all the while reflecting that understanding, sympathy, or empathy.

There are many ways to say what you want to say. And each of these ways is mediated by various influences, the contexts weighing on your ad. We've considered them all to varying degrees, but let's elaborate on them.

## The All-Important Strategy Leading to Theme and Idea

Obviously what you say depends on your strategy, especially the objective. Evolving from your strategy, the theme and idea then start you on your way to copywriting. Because one of your primary goals as a writer is to unify the ad, you must keep your pen centered on the theme and idea. As you work through your ad's copy, what you say revolves around the theme and idea reflecting the strategy.

In Figure 8–6 you'll see a Nissan ad created and written by a student who won a first-place award in the annual Nissan competition. Let's look at the ad as an example of how the content revolves around the theme and the idea reflecting the strategy.

Based on the strategy, with emphasis given to the objective and benefit statements, it was determined that the ad's theme included the extraordinary fun one could have in owning a Nissan Hardbody 4 × 4. As we know, however, simply to state that theme can be boring, so a creative idea is needed to carry the theme. Here, the creative idea hinges on missing class to drive the Nissan Hardbody 4 × 4. Notice how the idea's irreverent tone matches with the audience. You wouldn't have the same tone in an ad for senior citizens, would you?

With the theme and idea in place, the student writer immediately begins by linking the copy with the idea. This acts as a bridge for the reader, allowing the mind to travel from idea to copy without interruption. By the time we get to the second and third paragraphs, however, the writer transports the reader to another line of thinking, that of product features, which are the real reasons why someone can have fun with the 4 × 4. In effect, these features are the support for the theme. They make the theme true and believable. Recall, for instance, the nib, the Interactive Grid System, or the fresh flowers every morning. All features supporting the theme, the benefit.

In the final paragraph, the writer introduces a call to action, "test-drive." Certainly the writer could have stopped there, true? But he didn't. Instead, he went on to include copy relating back to the idea. Meanwhile, he makes sure to reinforce the theme, "fun," in that last paragraph.

Think back to the ads we've looked at closely and recall how the copy never drifted too far from the theme and idea. For instance, recall painting a potato green and then writing copy to explain why. Or, recall including literary quotes and then writing copy with touches of literary excellence.

# Ever wonder why the kid who sits next to you is always absent?

If somebody you know drives a Nissan® Hardbody™ 4x4, you might as well disregard all their bogus reasons for not showing up to class. Because the real reasons are a whole lot more interesting.

For starters, there's an optional fuel-injected V6. Plus your choice of 5-speed manual or overdrive trans- mission. Which gives you power to get wherever you want to go. And have a great time getting there.

And with its 1400-pound capac- ity, the Nissan Hardbody 4x4 can help you carry much more than a heavy course-load.

Stop in and test-drive a Hardbody at your nearby Nissan Dealer. And see how much more fun you could be having in school. Espe- cially during your most boring classes.

Built for the Human Race.

*This advertisement is based on a concept submitted by Joseph Zukowski, Temple University*

**FIGURE 8–6    Advertisement reprinted courtesy of Nissan Motor Corporation in the U.S.A.**

As you create your ads, the theme and idea provide you with a tar-get of sorts. The content of your ads should always be focused on that target. A common practice in ad copywriting is to hit the target at the beginning and end of your copy. In between, in the copy's middle, you elaborate on the support for the ad's promise. And all the while you keep a watchful eye on your strategy, certain not to divert the content from the ad's primary objective.

## The Media

As you know, our goal here is not to replay the types of formats you need for preparing radio scripts, television storyboards, or print ad copy. Instead, our goal is to highlight other considerations for you as an advertising copywriter. Yet media considerations are critical to your copywriting success. Let's highlight the essence of those considerations.

To a large degree, what you say in your ad depends on the medium in which it is carried. Naturally, all of the other considerations we've been discussing influence your decisions as well and, in fact, influence your concerns about the media. Again, nothing stands alone. Everything is in context. Still, there are certain rules for writing in the various media. Here are a few.

*Radio.* Because radio ads are relatively fleeting and short, you know you can't say too much. You just don't have the time to build a case, such as we saw in our Parker Pen ad, for example. Also, you have added problems with audience attention. As a background medium (talk show radio excluded), radio gets in and out of the audience's consciousness. Thus, what you write needs to reflect your concern for such a problem.

When it comes to words, however, radio presents an immense and often invigorating challenge. Here you have a medium unlike any other because it's not seen. It's heard. But, as Shakespeare realized centuries ago, what's not seen can produce extraordinary impact on an audience. In Shakespeare's plays murders were often committed off stage, relying on the audience's imagination to conjure up the most painful and horrible scenes. In advertising, however, you want to be positive and nice, so murders are generally taboo. But you can still spark the audience's imagination, igniting it and making it lively in its response. For example, the following ad called "Stretching the Imagination" written by famed writer and comedian Stan Freberg sparks the imagination while extolling the virtues of radio advertising.

*Stretching the Imagination*

| | |
|---|---|
| Man: | Radio? Why should I advertise on *radio*? There's nothing to look at...no pictures. |
| Freberg: | Listen, you can do things on radio...you couldn't *possibly* do on TV. |
| Man: | That'll be the day. |

| | |
|---|---|
| Freberg: | Alright, watch this. (Echo) Okay, people, when I give you the cue, I want the 700-foot mountain of whipped cream to be shoved into Lake Michigan, which has been drained and filled with hot chocolate. Then the Royal Canadian Air Force will appear overhead, towing a 10-ton maraschino cherry, which will be dropped into the whipped cream to the cheering of 25,000 extras. Alright, cue the mountain! |
| Sound: | (Great breaking of mountain into giant splash) |
| Freberg: | Cue the air force! |
| Sound: | (Drone of many planes) |
| Freberg: | Cue the maraschino cherry! |
| Sound: | (long whistle into huge splattt!) |
| Freberg: | Okayyy, 25,000 cheering extras! |
| Sound: | (Great crowd cheering which suddenly cuts off sharply.) |
| Freberg: | Now, you want to try that on television? |
| Man: | We-e-ell... |
| Freberg: | You see, radio's a very special medium, because it stretches the imagination. |
| Man: | But doesn't *television* stretch the imagination? |
| Freberg: | Up to 27 inches, yes. |

Often referred to as "the theater of the mind," radio can spark the listener's imagination. And since you want your audience to remember you, an active and involved imagination can yield positive results in the memory department. Once the listener has allowed the ad inside through the listener's active imagination, then remembering what you've said becomes easier.

At the same time, the basic goals we've discussed right along don't go away simply because radio is unique among media. Those goals such as closing the distance or unifying theme, idea, and content remain steadfast. It's just that the methods for achieving them change because of radio's uniqueness. For instance, with radio you have the wide-open availability of sound effects to help crystallize or reinforce the meaning of what you say. You also have the added benefits of voice and music.

Overall, in considering what to say on radio you should bear in mind that you can't say too much. You should keep what you say simple and easily understandable. Radio is not the medium for complex messages. Also, since radio is fleeting you should repeat key points. Moreover, because radio is an intrusive medium, you should pay close attention to what you say in the first few seconds of your ad, while keeping an open mind to doing the unusual so as to involve the listener. The first few seconds are where the success or failure of your ad takes place.

Finally, with radio you should give consideration to creating story lines for your theme. Often story lines involve two or more characters in a problem situation resolved by the product. For instance, Stan Freberg's radio spot contains a story line involving two characters. In the spot, it's the power of radio to tap the imagination (the theme), which becomes the solution to the problem confronted by the prospective advertiser (the Man in the Freberg spot).

*Television.*   As with radio, television is a fleeting medium. Ads on TV are here and gone. Again, this means you can't say much. And what you do say must fit tightly with your governing theme and idea. Because television has the added advantage of sight, and because most ads are viewed in the context of various programming involving human drama (soaps, sitcoms, game shows, sports events, news), then one of the things you'll notice about TV advertising is how often it relies on a story line to convey the theme and idea.

Figure 8–7 contains a public service ad from The Advertising Council. Notice how it relies on a story line to make its main point, the theme. And notice how all of what's said and shown in the ad revolves around that theme.

In somewhat typical fashion, the writer builds a story by dropping the viewer into the middle of an action. The ad begins with a young woman seated alone in a car. Her problem is clear. Her drunk boyfriend is about to drive, and she's afraid. Thus we have the first third of the ad. Then the voiceover announcer breaks in with some sage advice and a terrifying warning brought to life by the visuals of what could happen if the young woman (and the viewer) refused to take a stand. Finally, the ad closes with the young woman taking a stand. And the keys. The familiar visual of glasses about to crash together and the copy line, "Friends don't let friends drive drunk," close the ad. A ten second version of the close can also be seen in Figure 8–7.

This technique of building a scene or action prior to announcing the "pitch" is a popular one in television commercials. It has been termed a blind lead-in, and it stimulates viewer involvement without an immediate prospect of a sales pitch. Meanwhile, the human element, complete with personal dialogue, breathes drama into the action.

With TV advertising, the human element is critical. Ads should be personalized, which means that what you say should revolve around people, their problems, joys, heartbreaks, and daily lives. The key is that your product acts as the hero, solving the problem, bringing happiness or joy, easing the heartbreak, and making daily life easier and

# THE ADVERTISING COUNCIL, INC.
# DRUNK DRIVING PREVENTION CAMPAIGN

Public Service Announcements for U.S. Department of Transportation
National Highway Traffic Safety Administration

"KEVIN" :30 (CNTD-1430)                    Also available in :20 (CNTD-1120) & :15 (CNTD-1315)

   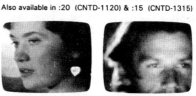

GIRL: (VO) After dating the guy forever, you'd think | I could tell him anything. | Why is this so hard? I'm really scared. | ANNCR: (VO) It takes a lot of guts to tell someone he's too drunk to drive, but you can do it.

Just say it. | Because, if you don't... | | (SFX: CRASH)

...there may be nothing left to say. | GIRL: Kevin, | I'm going to drive. | ANNCR: (VO) Take the keys, call a cab, take a stand. Friends don't let friends drive drunk.

"CRASHING GLASSES REV. 1990" :30 (CNTD-0430)           Also available in :10 (CNTD-0110)

ANNCR: (VO) When friends don't stop friends from drinking and driving...(SFX: CAR SKIDDING AND CRASHING) friends die from drinking and driving...(SFX: CAR SKIDDING AND CRASHING) friends die from drinking and...(SFX: CAR SKIDDING) Friends don't let friends drive drunk. (SFX: LIQUID FALLING INTO GLASS)

Please discontinue use: January 1, 1993.

Volunteer Agency: Wells Rich Greene, Inc.
Volunteer Campaign Director: Richard S. Helstein, General Foods, USA

1191

**FIGURE 8–7   Advertisement reprinted courtesy of The Advertising Council.**

more fulfilling. What you say, then, depends on your story line and the people who move it along. Always, however, that story line should be directed to the product as it fills a need or solves a problem.

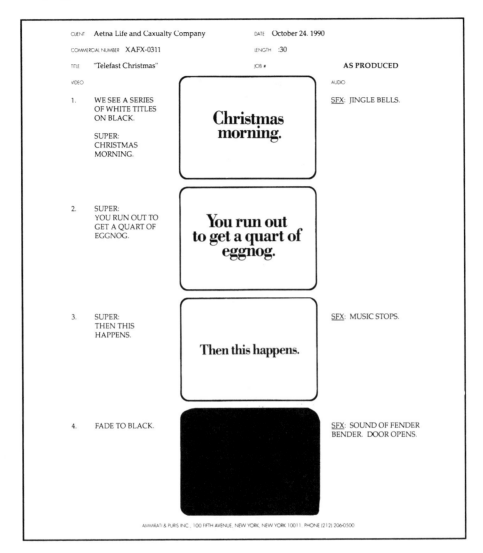

**FIGURE 8–8** Advertisement reprinted courtesy of Aetna Life & Casualty.

At the same time, since advertising creative ideas often strive for differences, then you may be inclined to do the opposite of what's normally shown in a medium. For example, since television programming typically presents human life drama and most TV ads do the same, you may consider doing what Aetna Life and Casualty Company has done in the ad in Figure 8–8.

Notice that you don't see people in this ad. In fact, you don't see much of anything except for typescript superimposed on the screen. But you do hear things such as "Jingle Bells" contrasted with the sound of an

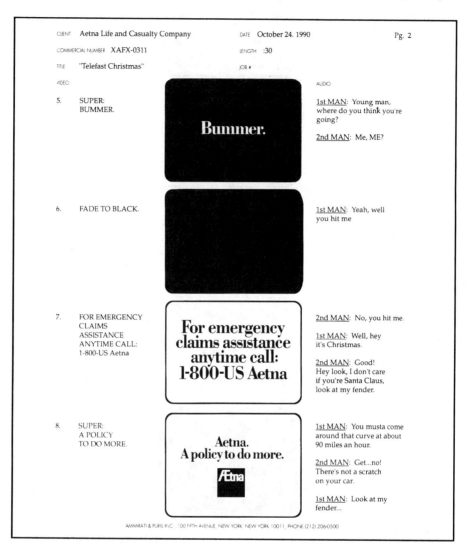

**FIGURE 8–8    Advertisement reprinted courtesy of Aetna Life & Casualty (*continued*).**

accident and the argument between the two men. However, notice how the argument never really gets nasty. Instead, it's in keeping with the Christmas spirit. In many ways, this Aetna commercial should remind you of a radio ad. Yet it's an ad for television, but one that pays close attention to the dynamics of the medium to create an arresting creative idea.

*Words Read, Not Heard.*    Unlike radio and television, what you say in print advertising, primarily newspapers, magazines, and direct mail, can be more detailed. The reader can digest your message at leisure and in varying lengths of time. In fact, the message can be reviewed. Magazines, for instance, tend to stick around, getting looked at often and at different times. Newspapers, though more bound to time constraints than magazines, tend to stick around also, though they're often obsolete the very next day. Still, this is different from being obsolete the very next minute as with radio and television.

Recall our discussion in the previous chapter when we mentioned how magazines are targeted more personally than newspapers, though newspapers are read more closely for timely and perhaps local information. Both facts, however, shape what you should say in your ads. For example, assuming the magazine is one with a highly targeted focus such as we might see with *Sports Illustrated* or *Cosmopolitan*, your ad copy will speak directly to a specific person with an interest in sports or concerns of young women. Appropriately, then, what you say may hitchhike on that interest, assuming of course that your theme and idea display the same relevance to reader interest.

Despite the fact that newspapers and magazines are often clumped together under the rubric of print advertising, they're distinctly different in several important respects. For instance, notice how ads in your local newspaper are often action-oriented. Oftentimes placed by local retailers who realize that people go to their newspapers for "newsy" information, local retail and service ads prompt reader action. They urge the reader to visit and buy now, not later. Retail ads are more bold in this respect than typical consumer goods ads. Their overriding purpose urges audience action, so what you say will often play to this purpose.

Naturally, the words we read in advertising don't stop with newspapers and magazines. Direct mail, outdoor posters and billboards, brochures, collateral materials, and specialty items contain words as well. But even here the basic principles stay intact, though each specific medium suggests its own individualized allowances for what you can say. For instance, with direct mail the main problem is getting the audience to open it. With a cluttered mailbox and an antipathy toward direct mail, there is considerable reluctance to open what one has been sent. So what you say begins with the envelope or enclosure. And since that envelope or enclosure carries the bulk of responsibility for whether the direct mail piece will get opened or not, what you say should be narrowly focused on achieving that end. As with retail newspaper advertising, a call to action and bold promises are important here.

Once the envelope or enclosure is opened, you can count on someone at least skimming what's inside. In the first place, in going inside your mail piece your reader showed an interest, however fleeting it may have been. No doubt prodded by the urge or promise on the envelope or enclosure, the audience now wants relevant and pointed information. Naturally that information should support your theme, and since maintaining the audience's close attention is necessary, that information should cater to benefits.

Remember that you do have time with direct mail. You can build a story or spend considerable time closing the distance between your product and the reader. Again, this would mean extending your hand to the reader and proving that you care.

With outdoor advertising, particularly billboards, what you say must again take into consideration the environment in which the audience comes in contact with your message. With direct mail, for instance, the environment was somewhat relaxed, personalized, and conducive to reading. With outdoor billboards that's not the case. Here you're dealing with an audience confronting a very busy visual field, usually from a moving vehicle. As with radio, outdoor advertising tends to be intrusive. Other things dominate the audience's mind. Driving. Listening to the radio. Daydreaming. In short, a host of distractions pulling the audience away from your billboard or poster.

Given these environmental factors for outdoor ads, what you say in your copy should be brief and to the point. Not only that, it should be clever, perhaps using word plays such as double meanings, rhymes, or alliteration. In stretching the limits of the language in these respects, you counteract the many influences pulling your viewer away from your message.

As with direct mail, brochures and reports are meant to be read. What you say in them, though, can cover a large range of information, depending on the length and primary objectives of the piece. Once again, however, keeping yourself in tune with closing the distance and hooking into your governing theme and idea continue to be important considerations. Equally so, graphic breaks or highlights such as bullets, screens, or bold and italic type to keep reader interest become important to longer pieces. Even in direct mail this is the case, as you'll notice in the mail you receive, which may have underlinings, scribblings in the margins, or other special "touches" that make the piece more personal and readable. Our Parker pen ad, which contained a relatively long copy story, had the scribblings of famous men in the margins.

Because words truly don't exist on their own and only in the context of a host of variables, it's important for you to weigh the characteristics and importance of those variables. They exert influence on what you can say, if for no other reason than that they suggest how much or little you can say. With media, your determinations of what to say are shaped by the individual medium's limitations and allowances.

Even more than media, however, your determinations of what to say are shaped by your strategy and governing theme, and idea. Once realized, the strategy, theme and idea give you a copy center, a hub around which your ad content should revolve. During our discussion we've seen several ways of presenting that content, such as warming up the audience at the beginning, relating back to the idea, supporting the benefit, and circling back to the idea at the close. However you organize and present your ad content, though, if you keep your mind fixed on the strategy, theme, and idea, you know you can't go too far wrong. And you know your copy will be tight and controlled.

As you go through your daily life, scan the various ads you see or hear. Notice how they reflect the limitations and allowances of their respective media. For instance, notice the urge to action in the newspaper ad, the story development and personalized content in the direct mail letter, and the brevity and playfulness in the billboard. Yes, these are standard rules, but as you know, rules in advertising are made to be broken. Importantly, though, you should know the rules you break.

## ✍ WRAP-UP ✍

We've covered a great deal of ground in this chapter, but because of its allegiance to strategy considerations, it's important ground. A copywriter writes with a part of the mind fixed on strategy. A copywriter writes, not for the self, but for another. And a copywriter writes knowing that the other is always the most important consideration when it comes to deciding what to write.

Despite the bulk of information in this chapter, there should be some choice kernels of insight that you take and tuck away into the safe of your writer's mind. For example, a large part of your copywriting job is to pull things together into a meaningful and clearly understood whole. This means you should be wary when you find your copy drifting from the theme, the promise of your ad. It also means you should be sensitive to matching the copy with the theme and idea, indeed, with the entire strategy. It should all fit together like hand in glove.

Beyond formal strategy considerations as expressed in your creative plan, you should remember that your main job is to sell. In deciding what to say, the goal of selling should be foremost in your mind. That's fine, of course, but the question is, How do you sell?

Conceive of selling as audience on one hand and you on the other. The audience may be far off or not so far off. Your job is to bring the audience and your product together on a common ground. Often, that common ground depends on the relevance of the promise you make to the audience. We've referred to it as your *theme* or *benefit*.

Unfortunately, there are many times when the audience is suspicious, when it casts into doubt the sincerity or believability of your promise. That's why your ad content should try to support that promise, support often found in product features, tests, comparisons, guarantees, and the like. Moreover, what you say should express your concern and understanding for the audience's problem. It should help shorten the distance and bring the audience closer to you. Being positive and nice are important here. And even when your creative idea isn't so positive and nice, your copy content should be.

There's probably no greater truth to selling than a realization that someone will accept your pitch if it's genuine, personal, and in that person's best interest. That's why your ad content should be true, personal, and relevant to the audience, meaning it's in the audience's best interest.

Naturally, media considerations also shape what you should say in your ad. Sometimes you can say a lot, as in direct mail or magazine. Sometimes you can't, as in radio or billboard. This means you may have to make accommodations or compromises in your copy in order to align it with the media. At the same time, and always in the back of your mind, you should at least consider the possibility of breaking standard media rules. This keeps you open to creative possibilities.

More than anything else, however, what you should gain from this chapter involves a sense of oneness and tightness about your ad content. The ad content doesn't drift. It doesn't scatter its shot. Instead, it's tightly focused. It's coiled around your theme and idea. It's bound to your audience and the shortening of the distance between you and that audience. All of what you say should work inward to the ad's core. In this way, your ad will be unified and understood.

## ✍ THINGS TO DO ✍

1.    Find two ads, one that instantly links the theme and idea together, even though the idea may be unusual. For example, I recently saw a Tropicana Orange Juice ad showing a man trying to push a straw through an orange. He succeeds. That's unusual since straws typically can't puncture oranges. Yet it's also strategically right since the ad's theme is that Tropicana Orange Juice is pure orange juice. Regarding the other ad you find, try to make it one where the theme and idea seem miles apart.

2.    Sell somebody something. It can be anything sold to anyone. Sell someone on going out with you. Sell someone a product. An idea. A

service. Keep track of how you managed to sell what you sold. What did you say or do to sell it? Why did that work?

3.　Imagine yourself talking to three distinctly different types of people. Different from yourself, that is. Different ages. Different backgrounds. Your goal is to get them to like and trust you. What do you say? How do you say it? How, in short, did you reach common ground?

4.　Imagine the following ads in different media. How would you convey the theme and idea? How would your copy be different, if at all? Saint Mary-of-the-Woods. Timberland. Royal Viking. Imagine, though, that you're trying to keep the same basic themes and ideas already expressed in the ads as you've seen or read them.

5.　Pick a product. Any product. Map out a strategy, complete with a target audience and media selection. Then write a one-page narrative about one or more of the product features and how those features lead to the benefit. Try to shape the narrative into ad copy, complete with a governing theme and idea.

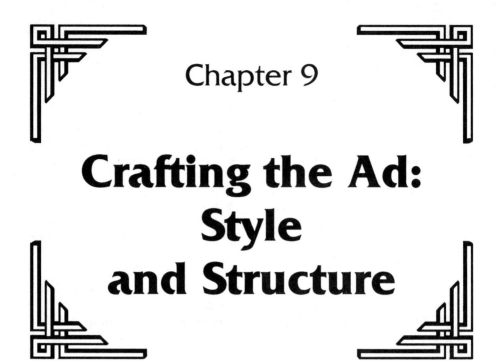

# Chapter 9

# Crafting the Ad: Style and Structure

Ad *content* is what you say. Ad *style* is how you say it. Yet despite this distinct difference between content and style, the same strategic principles and guidelines govern both. Keeping your mind focused on the creative plan, for instance. Or relating everything to theme and idea as well. The main difference, however, is that with ad style there are some new principles and guidelines to keep in mind. In many ways they act as tools on your writing belt, reminding you of our earlier chapters when we discussed words and their arrangements. In fact, a great deal of our discussion in this chapter will be reminiscent of those earlier chapters. We have, after all, logged significant time wrestling over matters of style. Recall, for instance, our discussion of the Cover Girl Luminesse Lipstick ad copy or the importance of how words sound.

Still, much of what we'll discuss in this chapter relates directly to the tools on your writing belt and how to use them to improve your writing skills. Though that improvement centers on advertising copywriting skills, the fact of the matter is that many of the suggestions relate as well to various types of writing. There's great writing and awful writing, with plenty of room in between for degrees of difference. And whether we talk about ad copy, poetry, fiction, news editorial, letters, or a host of other forms of writing, what makes some writing great and some writing awful often crosses over from genre to genre.

On the other hand, the various genres do contain distinct differences, ad copywriting included. Because ad copy must sell, it's bound to certain principles and guidelines not relevant to other forms of writing. For example, if you're writing news then your personal voice shouldn't be heard. Your goal is to be totally objective. Then again, if you're writing poetry you may want your personal voice heard. In fact, you may want your poetry to be your voice exclusively.

With ad copywriting, however, you're in between these two extremes, at least much of the time. You don't want your voice, your style, to drown out what you say. But then again, you don't want your voice or style to be so sterile or dry that your copy reads like dust. When it's all said and done, you do want your copy to have some juice. More so, to be an advertising copywriter stylistically means finding the right voice or style for your copy. And often that voice or style, as juicy as it may be, isn't yours at all. It's someone else's.

To be an ad copywriter you must be an impressionist. You must be willing to lose yourself in favor of others. When you write you're really not you; you're someone else. In ad copy your job stylistically is to capture the voice and style of your audience. The same usually isn't true when it comes to writing in genres such as news or poetry.

Obviously this makes the copywriter's job extremely difficult. Think about it. As a copywriter, one minute you're writing copy for someone reveling in the prospect of an upcoming marriage. Meanwhile you just broke up with your boyfriend or girlfriend. Another minute you're writing copy for individuals more concerned about their children than themselves, and you might not even have children. And before your day is done, you're writing copy for someone fighting against the prospect of entering a nursing home, while you have trouble believing you'll ever get old.

Knowing you must capture the voice and style of another places considerable pressure on you as a copywriter. No longer is it good enough to build a believable case for the legitimacy of your promise. No longer can well-organized copy content do the entire selling job. Now you must craft what you say according to the person on the receiving end of your ad.

At the same time, deciding how to write what you want to say requires considerations of key concerns such as your creative idea, theme, strategy, and media. As we've discussed right along, these concerns act as contexts for your ad. They exert influence on the crafting of the ad. As a result, you must consider them before and during your writing.

## ✍ THE AD'S GESTALT ✍

Let's start our chapter with an ad's gestalt, its wholeness or oneness. The ad's totality. Its unity.

In Chapter 3 we discussed how viewers sweep together elements from a visual field into a unified whole. There is this human tendency to create wholeness and unity in what we see. The same holds true with what we read or hear. Yes, all the things we see, read, or hear contain numerous and often diverse elements. But we tend to group them together, to construct a clear and unified meaning out of those elements. How we respond to ads is no different. Whether we're seeing or listening, we tend to scan the elements, all the while trying to pull them together into a whole.

Think of pulling an ad's elements together as the car you once had that always pulled to the left or right. You could wrestle with the steering wheel, but if you didn't, the natural tendency was for the vehicle to pull one way or the other. With ads our natural tendency is to keep their various and diverse elements aligned according to the main meaning. If the elements are so diverse and resist this tendency too strongly, then we know the ad needs repair. We may even set it aside rather than go through the struggle to make it meaningful in a unified way.

This relationship with an ad begins as soon as we come in contact with it. In essence, we step inside and test the steering. We want to know if the ad is aligned and in working order. And during this beginning part of the relationship, it's the creative idea that bears responsibility for making sure we'll get the ad out on the open road.

## The Creative Idea

The creative idea grows from the soil of the theme. You know what you want to say, the theme, but you're just not sure how to say it. It's at this point that you've arrived at the stage of idea generation, that period of time when you enter the great unknown, the mysterious, elusive, and infinite space of your imagination. With the theme fertile in your mind you brainstorm for ideas, planting the seeds of many possibilities along the way.

When your "big idea" starts to grow, you make certain it's aligned with your strategy, particularly the problem to be solved, objective, key benefit, and tone. These parts of your strategy evolve to your theme, the main message you want remembered, the *what* of your ad. But at this new stage, and while keeping the importance of tone front and center in your mind, you begin to craft your idea, the *how* of your ad.

As it relates to your audience, the idea should complete two primary tasks. One is to grab audience attention. The other is to orient the audience to the ad's theme. But as it relates to you, the writer, the idea should complete one primary task. It should give your copy direction in respect to both content and, as we'll discuss here, style.

To see how this works let's recall two of the ads we've discussed along the way. In Figure 9–1 and Figure 9–2 you'll see, respectively, the Parker pen and potato ads again. Notice how their creative ideas set the stage for the copy style.

The creative idea for the Parker pen ad (Figure 9–1) is nothing extraordinary, really. It's simple and direct, using the bold product photo to frame in the headline and copy. But still, the creative idea reflects a dignified and somewhat formal tone. Recall, for instance, our discussion in Chapter 6 of how the ad visually creates balance, thus dignity.

There's no game-playing here with this ad. And though there's a touch of wit in the copy, it's very much understated. In fact, all of the copy is fairly serious, even a bit stuffy at times. This doesn't mean it's impersonal, and it is "nice" right from the start. But it's not overly friendly. Indeed, it's a bit distant for the most part. Nice. Positive. But not too friendly, perhaps because this particular audience may take offense at an ad coming on too strong with gratuitous backslapping and glad-handing.

In this Parker pen ad the creative idea predisposes the reader for the ad copy to follow. The idea is a formal visual and headline presentation of product and promise avoiding gimmickry and novelty for the most part. The copy is the same, though it's written with flair. In effect, the writer has dressed the copy in coat and tails.

In the potato ad (Figure 9–2), we see a slightly different approach and tone to the creative idea. Here, uniqueness and surprise result from the visual showing the potato being painted green. The tone is more playful, more off-beat, and more casual than the tone in the Parker pen ad. As you read the copy you'll find that it follows suit. It's more down to earth. More down home. More casual. And more earthy as a result. It avoids the classy, upscale language we read in the Parker pen ad.

Of course, as both of these ads demonstrate, the creative idea and the copy that follows should reflect the brand image and character. Fountain pens are more uppity than potatoes. They're more aloof than potatoes. They're more suave and debonair than potatoes. More literary. More refined. After all, potatoes are potatoes. Cut and garnish them as we may, in the end they're still potatoes. But a Parker Premier fountain pen? It's not exactly something you keep in your bookbag and drag out to take notes with while you're wolfing down some Mickey D fries and burgers.

All of these concerns center on the matter of style. Style begins with the idea, which should reflect the match between product and audience. It should be consistent with the brand image or character. Overall, it should provide the core for the ad's gestalt. Everything following, copy and visuals included, should bend to that core. Only in this way will your ad be unified and convey a clear and distinct message to the audience.

**FIGURE 9-1** Copyright Parker Pen USA Ltd. Advertisement reprinted with permission of Parker Pen USA Ltd., Janesville, WI.

FIGURE 9-2   Advertisement reprinted courtesy of The Potato Board.

Think back to many of the examples you've seen in this book, advertising or otherwise. As you think them through, notice how they were consistent in style and how the creative idea behind them launched that consistency. Even in a poem such as "Jabberwocky," the style word to word, line to line, and stanza to stanza was consistent. But it was the idea behind the poem headlined with the title "Jabberwocky" and the promise of onomatopoetic words to create scene and action that oriented us to the poem's style. The same holds true with our ads. In our Schlitz ad, for instance, the creative idea of a manly man living "gusto" on a sailing ship opened the door for the vigorous ad copy to follow. And recall our Stan Freberg radio spot in contrast to our drunk-driving television ad. The ad ideas were at stylistic extremes to one another, reflecting extremes in tones and personalities. As such, those extremes led to the copy style in both ads.

In many ways the copy style refers to tonal and stylistic consistency, dependent in large measure on the creative idea. In fact, without reading or listening to any of the copy, your audience should get the right feeling and message immediately from the idea, usually expressed in the headline and visual. To resurrect an analogy from the beginning of the chapter, based on your idea and now entering your copy, your audience knows there will be no pulling to the left or right if the ad is taken out of the driveway and onto the open road. There should be no prospect of wrestling with the steering wheel.

Conceive of this as well by way of the analogy we've used throughout key points in the book. The audience doesn't want anything to do with your wild curveball far from the plate. No doubt about it. Once the audience commits to the creative idea, audience members assume that in riding with the ad or standing up at the plate, there will be no problems, no inconsistencies or unpleasant surprises to divert them from their goal, which is to arrive at a relevant and clear meaning. Your copy should not disappoint them.

## ✍ BENDING TO THE CORE ✍

Once the idea is in place, you know its tone. It can be whimsical, witty, lighthearted, and imaginative such as in our Stan Freberg radio spot. Or it can be serious, straightforward, foreboding, and stark as in our drunk-driving ad. This paves the way for all of the ad's elements.

Our reference to *bending to the core* here refers to style, but obviously it carries over to content as well. Everything bends to the ad's core, including the creative idea. Everything. Stylistically, this means that how you say something should reflect a similar tone to the creative idea. That's all well and good, but the question is, How do you do that?

### Choosing the Right Word

Mark Twain once said that the difference between the right word and the almost right word was the difference between lightning and a lightning bug. Of course, we've made that distinction often in previous chapters. Recall, for instance, our discussion of the word "wrought" from the Parker pen ad. In fact, recall our discussions of how words contain genders, age, and tone.

In bending your copy style to the core, the creative idea, you should consider the first step, that of the individual word. Since your creative idea reflects a certain tone and your goal is to be consistent throughout the entire ad, then your choices of individual words should reflect the same tone. In addition, that tone should reflect the common ground between your product and audience. Again, the word "wrought" reflects the serious crafting of the Parker fountain pen. But it also reflects the serious concerns of the audience, particularly in terms of what a fine fountain pen can mean to the audience's writing and image.

In effect, your choices of individual words contribute a great deal to the consistency, the gestalt, of your entire ad. All of your strategic considerations—theme, idea, tone, product, audience, and even media—influence those choices of words. As a process, you pore over your copy, wrestling with how to say this or that, until words take shape and sense in your mind. Then you send them through a filtering process, a kind of test for their appropriateness and consistency with all you've considered. Those that pass the test stay. Those that don't, go.

Think, for example, of the word *Fahrvergnügen*. I haven't the foggiest idea what that word means, at least in respect to a surface meaning, the kind you get from a dictionary. But does it really matter? The word sounds great. It especially sounds great if you're thinking about cars. Stereotypically, we attach engineering and mechanical expertise to the Germans, particularly in their cars. The German word *Fahrvergnügen* suggests that expertise. You don't have to know what it means by way of dictionary definition. All you have to know is what it means as you take it inside yourself and ascribe meaning to it through associations accrued over the years.

This, of course, echoes back to our earlier chapters and how words *mean*. Let's apply some of the learning from those chapters in light of some recent considerations you make in choosing the right word.

In Chapter 4 you read copy from a Y & R Steinway piano ad. Here's the copy again, this time shown within the context of the entire ad in Figure 9–3.

How would you describe the Steinway ad's tone? Would you describe it as artistic, elegant, cultured, and refined? Those words are reflected in the ad's presentation, aren't they? They may not be stated, but they are reflected. Notice, for instance, the artistic presentation of the visual (use of proportion here in having the visual occupy more than one-half of the ad) through the contrast of lights and darks. Notice, too, the choice of typefaces for the headline, not to mention the precise choice of words in the body copy, which lend to the governing and singular tone.

STEINWAY
*The Instrument of the Immortals*

There has been but one supreme piano in the history of music. In the days
of Liszt and Wagner, of Rubinstein and Berlioz, the pre-eminence of the
Steinway was as unquestioned as it is today. It stood then, as it stands now,
the chosen instrument of the masters—the inevitable preference
wherever great music is understood and esteemed.

STEINWAY & SONS, Steinway Hall, 107-109 E. 14th St., New York
*Subway Express Stations at the Door*

**FIGURE 9–3   Advertisement reprinted courtesy of Steinway & Sons.**

How would you describe the ad's theme? Is it that Steinway
assures you of the highest quality available? It seems a logical reading
between the lines and images of the ad. And what of support? Does history play an important role in substantiating what turns out to be a
vaunting claim of superiority? No doubt it does.

With this single-minded approach to the ad, the writer knew that
the choices of individual words required consistency with the theme,
the idea as expressed in the visual and headline, the tone, and the
overall strategy behind the ad, audience included. That's why you read

words such as *supreme, pre-eminence, inevitable,* and *esteemed.* Recall our discussion of such words when we first read the Steinway copy in Chapter 4.

The writing for this ad reflects careful consideration for the right word, not the almost right word. In some ways, the tone of the individual words parallels the tone in our Parker pen ad copy or even the Nuveen & Company investment firm copy meant for those in higher education. The reason for the similarity should be clear. The reading audiences are similar. Though no doubt different in certain respects, each of the audiences lives a lifestyle consistent with the words in the various pieces of ad copy. Those audiences are literate and educated. They read. They write. They're in responsible positions. Overall, they're upscale.

With this in mind, and matching the individual words as contributors to an ad's gestalt, can you re-create the audiences for the following copy lines? And can you re-create at least an initial opening impression of how these copy lines reflect their ads' tones, themes, ideas, and strategies? All but one of the copy lines have appeared throughout this text. The words in italics represent key words for helping you answer the questions.

Something *ineffable* exists between an artist and his instrument.

You go around looking like a *dork*...

If somebody you know drives a Nissan Hardbody 4 × 4, you might as well disregard all their *bogus* reasons for not showing up to class.

So grab for all the *gusto* you can.

The first copy line is from another Steinway piano ad, one you haven't seen before. Notice the choice of the word *ineffable.* Do you know what ineffable means? And does it really matter if you don't? After all, it sounds great in the context of an ad for Steinway pianos. It matches the audience for that ad. It matches the tone and idea for that ad.

At the same time, you wouldn't use the word "dork" to talk to the audience for Steinway pianos. But you might be inclined to use it when talking to a younger audience, one more irreverent and playful. Perhaps the same audience that would understand the word "bogus." *Bogus* means fake or artificial. But how would the copy line from that Nissan ad sound with the words *fake* or *artificial*? Perhaps not so bad if the ad were meant for someone older. As it stands, though, the ad is meant for college students.

And would the word "gusto" mean the same thing to the reader of the Steinway ad as it would to the reader of the Schlitz ad?

Even as you consider these words in the contexts of their ad gestalts, you know that the word "ineffable" would be part of an ad reflecting a tone of elegance and refinement. You know that the word "dork" would be part of an ad reflecting the tone of youthfulness and perhaps irreverence.

Surely, all of the italicized words in these copy lines say something more than their individualized and surface meanings. They reach beyond those meanings to the audiences, the various strategic considerations leading to the ads, and the creative ideas controlling those ads.

Since a great deal of what you write and how you write it depends on closing the distance to the common ground between your product and your audience, the words you choose should be consistent with the product and audience. They should speak as the product would speak. If the product talked, how would it talk? Would Steinway pianos talk the same way as Reeboks? Would Schlitz beer talk the same way as Cover Girl Luminesse Lipstick? And since you're targeting your copy to a specific individual, how would that individual talk? Does a college professor or dean talk the same way as a college student? Does a classical pianist talk the same way as someone on the assembly line at General Motors?

No value judgments here when it comes to ad copy. Just a realization and understanding that the words you choose should reflect the single-minded effort, the gestalt of your ad. And they should link the product with the audience. To do that, just as we do it in real life, you should speak the language of the audience. You should prove that your product stands on common ground with your audience.

Remember, it's your idea and copy that are the ultimate reflections of how your product relates to the audience. When the audience reads or hears your copy it's really reading or hearing your product. As a copywriter, you're simply a medium, a voice box for your product. And your job is to join it with the audience. In making careful selections of individual words, those that talk both the audience's and product's language, you make the movement to the common ground that much easier.

No doubt, given the many ads you've seen and read thus far, you've come across instances where certain individual words trumpeted their own importance in uniting the product with the audience. Perhaps, though, you didn't pull them together in any one ad to see how they were consistent with the tone and overall strategy of the ad. Let's do that now by highlighting some of the key words from two ads you've seen. Notice how these words suggest selective decision-making by the writers, decision-making bent toward the ads' gestalts.

> For Royal Viking: elegance, little touches, worthy, remarkable, unhurried, prepare, fine delicacies, appear magically, spacious, strollable, gracious, inspired, choose.

> For Saint Mary-of-the-Woods: tubular, mondo-cool, zods, airheads, space cadets, bummer, grody, max, fer sure.

Right away, you get a sense that the writers were writing for very different audiences here. There can be no mistake about it, and that certainty hinges on the selection of individual words. Remember, every word selected suggests words not selected. And it's this kind of aesthetic and strategic decision making that often separates good writers from bad.

*Action Verbs and Present Tense.* Of all the parts of speech, the verb is your most important. With vast potential for creating meaning and breathing life into your ad copy, the verb stimulates movement in your audience's mind, particularly, of course, if the verb is an action verb and not one of the quiet or helping verbs such as "is." For example, recall the writer's use of the verb "grab" in the Schlitz ad. As the audience you're invited to "grab for all the gusto you can." You're not invited to reach for the gusto or hold it or achieve it. Instead, you're invited to "grab" it. Very much a vigorous action.

If you think of some powerful headlines or copy lines controlling many of the ads you meet each day, you'll recognize the importance of the action verb. Consider, for instance, the headline "Reach Out and Touch Someone," for AT&T. Two action verbs. Both endear AT&T Long Distance to the audience. Both coordinate the meaning as a benefit to the audience. And both act as invitations for the audience. In fact, both rely on multiple, reverberating meanings to give the message high impact. "Touch," for example, can mean tactile touch, but can also mean to touch someone emotionally.

When it comes to your choice of verbs, choose them according to their consistency with the ad's tone as it relates to the theme, idea, product, and audience. In fact, this should be the way you choose any word in your copy. But with verbs you need to be more selective since they're the part of speech that most involve your audience. And one sure stylistic way to involve your audience includes stimulating their minds to action in the construction of meaning.

Again, if you examine the AT&T headline, action verbs stimulate the audience's mind. But they stimulate the mind to positive and endearing emotions. Verbs have that power. Still another reason for the power in those two AT&T verbs exists in their tense. The actions of *reaching* and *touching* take place in the here and now. They're immediate. They don't ask the reader to retreat in time. Instead, they ask the reader to concentrate on the present. This brings the meaning of the verbs and the message overall closer to the audience. With the swiftness of a moment, the audience's mind sweeps the benefit of AT&T Long Distance directly into the present.

As you review much of the copy we've discussed throughout the book, notice how often action verbs, or action verb forms such as participles and gerunds, take center stage in the movement toward meaning. And notice how the choices of verbs and verb forms suggest the writers' tight and unwavering commitment to the ad's gestalt. Here, then, are some familiar copy lines to review. Pay attention to their verbs and verb forms, highlighted in italics.

> The ruthenium tip *is sculptured* under a microscope... (Parker fountain pen)
>
> The roomy passenger compartment of a Volvo *is surrounded* by six steel pillars. (Volvo)
>
> Drinking and Driving *can kill* a friendship. (Drunk Driving)
>
> "We *engineered* these shoes so you *could dance* on a very different surface." (Timberland)
>
> "They keep *going* and *going* and *going*..." (Eveready® Batteries)
>
> "Really, Sister, this whole recruitment brochure just kinda *freaks* me out." (Saint Mary-of-the-Woods)

Certainly we've picked our spots here, and as you look at the verbs notice that the spots aren't always so great. For example, if you were to rewrite the Volvo line to make it more active, would you be inclined to write, "Six steel pillars surround the Volvo's roomy passenger compartment"? In this rewritten version of the line, we've placed the emphasis on the surrounding of the compartment rather than on the compartment itself in the original version. We've avoided the quiet "is" in the first version. And we've made the surrounding more immediate, more in the present than in the first version.

Still, the verbs in these copy lines move the sentences along in the mind. They qualify the nouns, bringing them to life and defining their meaning. In the Timberland copy line, for instance, the verb *engineered* suggests the high technology of the boat shoe. In the Eveready® Energizer® line, the verb form, going, suggests the long-lasting nature of the battery. Verbs own this power. They lift your writing beyond the staid and ordinary. They energize your writing so that when it's read or heard, the audience becomes involved.

## Choosing the Right Word Arrangements

As we know, words don't stand alone, although they do have individual degrees of power in contributing to meaning. Always, however, they're in context with something else. Often that context is other words. In Chapter 2 we discussed the importance of words surrounding words as an important context for you to consider when writing. In Chapter 5 we spent considerable time discussing the importance of how words are arranged around other words. Recall, for instance, the emphasis given to sequencing and the roles of sentences, paragraphs, and parts of speech. In Chapter 6 we began to apply this kind of stylistic approach to ads by charting the sentences in the first five paragraphs of our Parker pen ad copy.

Using those three chapters as a base, but including relevant material from others as well, let's look at some word arrangements within ad copy. Two car ads are shown in Figure 9–4 and Figure 9–5. You've seen one before, the classic ad for Volkswagen. The other you haven't seen.

**FIGURE 9–4** Advertisement copyrighted by Volkswagen of America, Inc. Advertisement reprinted with permission of Volkswagen of America, Inc.

## Think small.

Our little car isn't so much of a novelty any more.

A couple of dozen college kids don't try to squeeze inside it.

The guy at the gas station doesn't ask where the gas goes.

Nobody even stares at our shape.

In fact, some people who drive our little flivver don't even think 32 miles to the gallon is going any great guns.

Or using five pints of oil instead of five quarts.

Or never needing anti-freeze.

Or racking up 40,000 miles on a set of tires.

That's because once you get used to some of our economies, you don't even think about them any more.

Except when you squeeze into a small parking spot. Or renew your small insurance. Or pay a small repair bill. Or trade in your old VW for a new one.

Think it over.

WE DRESSED IN SILENCE.

AND DROVE.

WHEN WE WALKED IN,

SHE SAID SOMETHING TO THE PIANO PLAYER.

NEXT THING, I HEAR THIS SONG WE USED TO LOVE.

SHE TAKES MY HAND. WE DANCE. AND SOMETHING

THAT WAS THERE BEFORE, WAS BACK. ONLY STRONGER.

## MERCURY SABLE

THE NEW, REMARKABLY SOPHISTICATED SABLE.

ITS BODY HAS BEEN TOTALLY RESTYLED.

ITS INTERIOR SO THOROUGHLY REDESIGNED

EVEN THE CONTROLS ARE EASIER TO READ AND REACH.

IT HAS STANDARD DRIVER AND OPTIONAL PASSENGER AIR BAGS.*

IT RIDES SMOOTHER. QUIETER.

AND MAKES DRIVING MORE OF A PLEASURE.

THE CAR THAT STARTED IT ALL

DOES IT AGAIN. / 800 446-8888

LINCOLN-MERCURY DIVISION
*Supplemental Restraint System.
Always wear your safety belts.

**FIGURE 9–5**  Advertisement reprinted courtesy of the Ford Motor Co., Lincoln-Mercury Division.

It's for the new Mercury Sable. Let's look at the ads for how their word arrangements contribute to the dominant gestalt.

Obviously, these are two very different car ads. They should be. They're for a very different audience. Each promises different benefits. Each reflects different strategies. For example, the "bug," as Volkswagen was known, positioned itself as a less expensive car. And less expense went beyond the selling price. But the Mercury Sable positions itself as a luxury car. With the Sable, expense proves to be unimportant. Other selling points rule the ad's roost.

As you read over the Volkswagen ad notice how the sentences and paragraphs are small. There are eleven paragraphs containing approximately 140 words. That's roughly a dozen words per paragraph. Not many, to be sure. Beyond that, however, notice how the sentences are arranged. You have the initial copy line stating that the car "isn't so much of a novelty any more." This is a standard word arrangement. Subject + verb + object, with a few modifiers tossed in for emphasis. But in the next two sentences notice the balanced arrangements. The two sentences sound similar to one another. They have the same basic structure. In keeping with the first sentence, they rely on negatives ("don't" and "doesn't") to help create the balance. Then, the fourth sentence offers a variation on that basic sentence structure.

By the time we get to the fifth sentence, though, there's a shift in the arrangement. The sentence is longer than the previous sentences, for instance. And it begins to highlight the ad's tone of whimsy, fun, and lightheartedness. The word "flivver" is used. Not exactly a word for the Mercury Sable. And the colloquial expression "any great guns" is also used, no doubt consistent with the ad's tone.

When we get to the sixth, seventh, and eighth sentences, we're back to a balanced structure. All of the sentences begin with "Or," extend for approximately the same length, and sound similar in our minds as we read. But when we get to the ninth sentence, the balanced structure disappears again, this time replaced with a longer sentence. Then, with the start of the long paragraph and the tenth sentence, we're gradually led back to the same balancing technique used at the copy's beginning and again at its middle. The final copy line invites thought from the audience, while at the same time circling back to a key word in the headline, "Think."

Overall, this arranging of words by the writer blends with the ad's product, its audience, idea, and governing strategy. The product is an economical car. A fun, peppy kind of playful car. Words such as "flivver" add to that playfulness. The audience for the ad wants economy. It also wants the peppiness, verve, and playfulness that the car offers. That's why the arranging of words into fragment sentences, short paragraphs, and balanced constructions suggests appropriateness to the writer. The audience knows what a Volkswagen is, and the writer knows how to communicate with that audience.

Notice the creative idea, the small car taking up small space and urging the reader to "Think small." In keeping with the idea, the writer chooses fragments and small paragraphs. To tighten this allegiance to the idea even more, complete with the idea's tone, the writer embeds the word "small" three times toward the end of the copy. The word "little" is used twice at the beginning of the copy. By the time the audience finishes with the ad, there can be no mistaking what you'll get with a Volkswagen.

Now, though, take another look at the Mercury Sable ad and copy. The visual is distinctly different from the Volkswagen visual. Here, the silhouetted effects create an elegance and refinement similar to our Steinway piano ad. The layout itself creates the drama of that elegance and refinement. And the copy doesn't drift from the governing idea and tone. Instead, it blends with both.

Remember, we don't buy things. We buy what things can do for us, even on very abstract levels. With our Sable ad, the car should complement our need for recapturing feelings, especially romantic ones. Not sexy ones, necessarily. But elegantly romantic ones. Sexy and romantic can be different, remember.

The first half of the copy tells a story, a narrative. Action verbs move the narrative along so that we go from the dressing room to a club or restaurant. But notice how the writer arranges the words.

The first sentence is a simple one. Subject + verb + prepositional phrase as modifier describing how the couple dressed. The second sentence is a short fragment. The third sentence is longer than the first, still containing the standard structure of subject + verb but also including an introductory phrase as a modifier. The fourth sentence is shorter than the third, but longer than the others. It also repeats the third sentence's use of an introductory phrase.

With the fifth sentence we're guided back to the basic structure without any embellishments. The sixth sentence contains two words, "We dance." The seventh sentence goes back to being longer, while at the same time changing the basic structure. Now, the subject, "Something," is detached from the verb, "was back." Finally, the closing sentence is a fragment emphasizing the renewed feeling from times past. And do you think it's a mistake that the renewed feeling is expressed in the present tense? Certainly not. Instead, the present tense, "takes" and "dance," accentuates this renewed feeling, making it immediate and more intense.

Of course, the copy goes on from there, telling the story of the changes in the Mercury Sable. But it's this first half of the copy that closes the distance between product and audience. It's this first half of the copy that sets the stage for the product story and establishes the brand image and character. It also reinforces the ad's tone, blending in with the striking visual quality of the creative idea.

## Repetition and Variation

As you think about the Volkswagen and Mercury Sable ads, it should be clear that they accomplish the same things but in very different ways. They both lead the readers to a gestalt of meaning. The words don't digress from the visuals. They don't change the tones of the ad. They don't undermine the themes or creative ideas. Instead, they reinforce and complement the themes and ideas, adding their individual charm to each ad's totality, its unity and gestalt.

At the same time, think about how the writers varied their word arrangements. Not too much variation, mind you. That would produce chaos. But enough variation to make the reading pleasant and in keeping with the ad's gestalt. On the other hand, think about how the writers repeated word arrangements. Again, not too much. That would lead to monotony and boredom. But enough repetition to blend nicely with the variations.

It's this combination of repetition and variation that often distinguishes good writing from bad. Too much of one or the other produces negative effects. But a balance of both contributes to positive effects. Of course, it's often impossible to keep them completely balanced. And, in fact, you may want to have one or the other dominate depending on the product, audience, idea, and tone. For example, if your ad is zesty, peppy, and snappy, and if the product follows suit, then your word arrangements may lean toward shorter sentences and more variation than repetition. But if you're after a smooth, languishing effect, then your sentences may lean toward more repetition than variation.

As we've seen in the Volkswagen and Sable ads, repetition and variation include word arrangements as they relate to the basic structure of subject + verb. But they also relate to sentence or paragraph length. Not too much of one or the other is the safe rule. At the same time, as a copywriter you're an artist, so you must make artistic decisions. The kind that play a large role in determining your style. Naturally, many of those decisions are grounded in all of your strategic considerations. But still, many of the decisions take root in your artistic soul. This means you must apply a great deal of what we've been discussing for more than 200 pages.

As we did with the Parker pen ad in Chapter 6, let's chart the copy for the Volkswagen and Sable ads. Since we discussed only the first half of the Sable ad copy, we'll keep our charting to those word arrangements. Each line representing a sentence or fragment is noted by a slash. And paragraphs are indicated by the indented left-hand margin.

The Volkswagen ad's copy would look like this.

_____.
_____.
_____.
_____.
_____.
_____.
_____.
_____.
_____.
_____.
_____._____.
_____. _____.
_____.

The first half of the Mercury Sable copy would look like this.

_____. _____. _____.
_____. _____.
_____. _____. _____.

As suggested in Chapter 6, a good practice for you to follow is to sound out your copy. This doesn't necessarily mean reading it aloud, though that's certainly advised as well. What it does mean is humming out the lengths of your sentences. If the humming drones on without variations, then you should probably rework the copy. At the other extreme, you should probably rework the copy if the humming sounds choppy or staccato.

Another way to conceptualize your word arrangements is by charting the words and parts of speech within individual sentences. As with sentence lengths, here too you're looking for a balance of repetition and variation. For example, in the first half of the Sable copy the individual sentences, apart from how they compare in length with other sentences, contain their own repetitions and variations. In the first sentence, for instance, we have a standard subject + verb + object arrangement. But in the second complete sentence, "When we walked in, she said something to the piano player," the arrangement changes. The next sentence, "Next thing, I hear this song we used to love," contains a similar arrangement. But the following sentence, "She takes my hand," changes again, this time back to the basic structure of the first sentence.

In like fashion to how we charted the sentence lengths as they compared with each other, let's chart the internal structures of each individual sentence, especially as the structures are crafted around the core of the English sentence, subject + verb.

*We dressed in silence.* = Subject + verb + prepositional phrase modifying "dressed" or, S + V + _____.

*And drove.* = Conjunction + verb or, _____ + V.

*When we walked in, she said something to the piano player.* = Introductory clause + subject + verb + object + prepositional phrase modifying "said" or, _____ + S + V + _____.

*Next thing, I hear this song we used to love.* = Introductory phrase + subject + verb + object + subordinate clause or, _____ + S + V + _____.

*She takes my hand.* = Subject + verb + object or, S + V _____.

*We dance.* = Subject + verb or, S + V.

*And something that was there before, was back.* = Conjunction + subject + subordinate clause + verb or, _____ + S + _____ + V.

*Only stronger.* = Adverbs modifying "was back" or, _____.

When just the charting is viewed, the copy looks like this.

S + V + _____.

_____ + V.

_____ + S + V + _____.

_____ + S + V + _____.

S + V + _____.

S + V.

_____ + S + _____ + V.

_____.

As you view this charting of the sentences, notice how the writer varied the internal structures so that three of the eight sentences begin with subjects + verbs. Then, two sentences begin with conjunctions, and three sentences begin with introductory phrases or clauses. Notice, too, how the writer branched some sentences to the left and some to the right. And finally, notice how the writer even included one sentence where a phrase is embedded between the basic subject + verb structure.

The point of this, of course, is to show you how writers use variation, both within paragraphs and within sentences. By adding modifiers or subordinate clauses, you can branch left or right within sentences and avoid the monotony of too much repetition of the basic structure of subject + verb. At the same time, you don't want too much variation, so to maintain or repeat the basic structure of subject + verb is also important.

Choosing the right words and then arranging them in the right order within sentences in paragraphs involves multiple layers of your thinking. On one hand you're asked to be deliberate and strategic in making your choices. You know that those choices should revolve around your product, theme, creative idea, and tone. Even more so, they should revolve around your audience. They should reflect that audience, a specific person reacting to your ad. The choices should sound like the audience sounds when it talks. That way you close the distance and create the common ground. And the choices should bend to the ad's core, its essence, or what we've termed as its gestalt.

This kind of decision making on your part calls for careful deliberation of your strategic considerations. But there's another type of decision making you should practice, and that's keeping yourself stylistically flexible, open and even playful when you write. Given the constraints of your strategic thinking, this can be a very difficult practice. It's necessary, however. And it's necessary because ad copy tends to clip along, to make haste, and to convey a positive and friendly sense of vigor and verve. Ad copy often has amplitude and range, both of which lend themselves to easy reading or listening. Well, if you're tense or tight, then your copy won't have a positive and friendly sense of vigor and verve.

What this boils down to is this. Over time you should internalize what we've discussed to this point and to follow. You should practice the methods one at a time when the worth of your ad copy isn't on the line. In practicing, you'll internalize the methods. Soon they'll become an inseparable part of your writing arsenal so that when you sit down to write, they'll be ready, willing, and able to reveal themselves when you lower the pen to paper or strike the first letter on your keyboard.

Transitions

In Chapter 3, which focuses on visual literacy, we discussed the importance of sequencing or how an artist moves the eye from line to line, shape to shape, or image to image. The same principle applies to writing. There you are with a jumble of copy points, and one of the daunting challenges facing you is how to move the audience's mind from point to point. There are several ways to do that, and each involves building a bridge between the points. A bridge the audience can easily walk over to get from one point to another.

In looking back to our Parker pen ad copy, the writer devoted the first half of the copy to establishing the common ground between product and audience. The writer told the reader how the Parker fountain pen would inspire contemplation and ease the writing process. But to get from that audience-centered part of the copy to the product-centered part required a transition. The writer wrote, "Thank the nib for that. And the extremes we go to making it."

Notice how the two sentences sequence the reader's thought. From the reader's self-involvement developed in the copy's first part, the writer moves the reader to the pen's nib, which controls the second part. Even more so, the writer moves the reader to the extremes that Parker goes to in making the nib. And this support for the quality of the nib becomes the controlling focus of the copy's second part.

With transitions, repetition of key words can be helpful. With the Parker pen copy, the word "nib" is introduced in that first transitional sentence. Since we read or hear word to word and line to line, the introduction of the word "nib" has pointed our minds in a new direction, bridging the prior copy focus with the focus to come.

Of course, you could always rely on the less organized and convincing ways for creating transitions, but often they take on the spectre of cliches. For example, phrases such as "And there's more" certainly sequence the audience's mind into the next copy line or point. But there's also something a bit cheap about such transitions, especially when contrasted with transitions based on the ad's inherent content and organization. Some writing theorists, for instance, believe that if your transitions are based specifically on the copy points to come, then your writing has passed one test for organization. But if the transitions are not based on those points to come, then you've faked the organization, at least to an extent.

Whichever way you choose to create transitions, the point is that they should exist. And ideally, they should exist as bridges linking what's just been said with what's to come. To thank the nib, for instance, looks back to all of the benefits elaborated in the copy's first part. But it also looks forward to the nib's story in the copy's second part. Combining key words or concepts from one part to another provides you with ready access in building effective transitional bridges.

## ✍ AD STRUCTURE ✍

To this point we've worked through some specific elements of ad style, namely individual words, sentences, and paragraphs. But as we know, these specific elements should contribute to and blend with the whole. To that end, let's discuss one of the most common and pervasive ad structures, the circle.

### Creating Circular Unity

As a shape the circle implies unity. Each of us has a family circle and a circle of friends. The very way we refer to these people suggests togetherness and wholeness. Besides, traditionally the circle has been considered the symbolic shape of unity. This is why it's so important to have it available as a stylistic tool for your writing belt. As a tried and true ad structure, the circle yokes the various elements of your ad together. It tightens and focuses your ads, corraling everything to the ad's center, its core. In the end this leads to a more concise, clear, and unmistakable meaning for your audience.

Looked at more largely now than we did with words, sentences, and paragraphs, the circular structure of ads means that stylistically they end where they begin. And even during the course of the circle's arcs, the various elements, such as copy points and support, don't stray from the circle's dominant line. One of the most recent ads we've looked at serves as a classic example of this type of circular structure: the Volkswagen ad.

If you recall, the ad's visual shouts smallness. A small car contrasted with a large white space. Then the headline, "Think Small," repeats that theme. Together, headline and visual comprise the creative idea. But it's up to the copy to keep things tight within the circular line of that theme and idea. That's why the word "little" is mentioned twice in the copy's beginning, and the word "small" is mentioned three times at the copy's close. And a last copy line, "Think it over," completes this circular shape by referring back to the totality of the ad idea. At the same time, that final copy line urges an action on the part of the audience. Yes, it's a subtle action, but it does involve the audience doing something.

As you read through ads, notice how often the ends of copy achieve two goals. First, they circle back to the main idea that has been woven throughout the copy. Second, they call for action on the part of the audience. Here, for example, are some beginnings and ends of ads that you've seen or read throughout this book.

For Perdue Chickens:
Headline: My Chickens Eat Better Than You Do.
First copy line: The problem with you is that you're allowed to eat whatever you want.
Last copy lines: If you want to start eating as good as my chickens, take a tip from me. Eat my chickens.

For Nissan Pathfinder:
Headline: There Are No City Limits.
First copy lines: They've got traffic in Trenton. Potholes in Pasadena. And noise in New Orleans.
Last copy lines: Which means now, driving will be fun in Philadelphia. Comfortable in Columbus. And smooth in Smyrna.

For Cover Girl Luminesse Lipstick:
Headline: Capture the Spirit.
First copy line: Nothing else captures the spirit of satin like Luminesse Lipstick.
Last copy line: Capture it.

Because of this common copy structure we could continue on indefinitely with ads that form the circular shape. It's pervasive in advertising, whether in print or broadcast, though broadcast ads, more than print ads, tend to rely on a narrative structure.

Crafting the Narrative

It's the story line that separates narrative ads from non-narrative ads. For example, our Volkswagen ad doesn't contain a narrative per se, mainly because there is no passage of time. As readers we don't gain a sense of people moving about within the context of time.

With our Sable car ad, however, the brief narrative at the beginning conveys this sense of time passing. Recall that the writer described two people dressing, then driving, arriving at a club, and finally dancing. Though the narrative contained descriptive sentences to heighten the emotional effect, overall there was a passage of time when actions occurred. This tends to be the standard in radio and television ads, but that doesn't mean print advertising avoids the narrative structure. To the contrary, and as you've seen with our Sable car and Parker pen ads, it's very possible and often advisable to build a narrative structure into your print copy. Take, for example, The Nature Company ad in Figure 9–6. You read part of the copy at the close of Chapter 5 under "Things to Do."

Despite the fact that The Nature Company ad is for print media, a narrative dominates the copy, meaning the writer tells a story. In a large sense the story relates to the innermost thoughts and desires of the audience. To achieve that, the writer had to project himself into the audience. We sense that's what happened with copy lines such as "Should you have married that ski instructor?" or "You'll be birding with Sven, having his children. Or you'll be walking with Gwenne in that secret meadow by the creek." Beyond the writer's imaginative powers at work, we also have a breezy, conversational story.

The story begins with reference to the dreams of the reader (recall our other ads, which start from the point of view of the audience). But in the second paragraph, we're introduced to the clock. Then in the third paragraph we're back to the audience. And in the fourth paragraph we're back to the clock. Meanwhile, by the time we've finished the copy we've gained a keyhole look into the dreams of a real person, that person's lifestyle, and the relevance of the potato-powered clock to that individual life. Notice, by the way, how the writer changes the sentence rhythms and very much talks the language of an audience who might be interested in such a product. After all, words such as *birding, bentjes, kennebecs,* and *karma* aren't meant for everyone.

Since a narrative usually requires the passage of time and characters confronting various situations during that time, then you need to consider the context of situations. They provide you with a framework for determining what your characters should say. For example, let's go back to our drunk-driving ad to see how this works. It's shown again in Figure 9–7.

BY  L. BAKER  RUNYAN

# Is your life
## complete without
## a potato-powered clock?

This is a clock for people who work indoors

but whose hearts are, well, elsewhere. Should you have married that ski instructor instead? Been a forest ranger? Will you some-day have that little cabin out there where men are men, women are women, so on and so forth? Yeah, maybe.

*"Grocer, two of your most accurate tubers, please."*

meadow by the creek. Stuff like that. A master-ful balance of digital watch technology (and isn't <u>that</u> still amazing) and two russets, white roses, bentjes, or kennebecs, this clock will give you honest time. Real

But while you're hanging around waiting to see how it all shakes out, wouldn't this clock be a nice way to count the minutes?

At every glance, you'll be hiking, biking, breathing clean air, eating sandwiches smashed in the bottom of your pack. You'll be birding with Sven, having his children. Or you'll be walking with Gwenne in that secret

*You need not be present to shop. Our catalog, 1-800-227-1114.*

time. Tater time. It tells month and date, too. It even runs on soda pop (if that ruins the karma for you, forget we said it).

# THE NATURE
# COMPANY

And one more thing. That ski instructor? A bum. You just forgot. $16.95.
Thank you.

---

FIGURE 9–6    Advertisement reprinted courtesy of The Nature Company.

# THE ADVERTISING COUNCIL, INC.
# DRUNK DRIVING PREVENTION CAMPAIGN
Public Service Announcements for U.S. Department of Transportation
National Highway Traffic Safety Administration

"KEVIN" :30 (CNTD-1430)                    Also available in :20 (CNTD-1120) & :15 (CNTD-1315)

   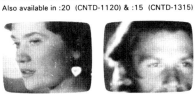

GIRL: (VO) After dating the guy forever, you'd think | I could tell him anything. | Why is this so hard? I'm really scared. | ANNCR: (VO) It takes a lot of guts to tell someone he's too drunk to drive, but you can do it.

Just say it. | Because, if you don't... | | (SFX: CRASH)

...there may be nothing left to say. | GIRL: Kevin, | I'm going to drive. | ANNCR: (VO) Take the keys, call a cab, take a stand. Friends don't let friends drive drunk.

"CRASHING GLASSES REV. 1990" :30 (CNTD-0430)          Also available in :10 (CNTD-0110)

ANNCR: (VO) When friends don't stop friends from drinking and driving...(SFX: CAR SKIDDING AND CRASHING) friends die from drinking and driving...(SFX: CAR SKIDDING AND CRASHING) friends die from drinking and...(SFX: CAR SKIDDING) Friends don't let friends drive drunk. (SFX: LIQUID FALLING INTO GLASS)

Please discontinue use: January 1, 1993.

Volunteer Agency: Wells Rich Greene, Inc.
Volunteer Campaign Director: Richard S. Helstein, General Foods, USA

1191

**FIGURE 9–7    Advertisement reprinted courtesy of The Advertising Council.**

Given the theme for the commercial, the obvious choice of characters and a situation includes young people and a car. But notice how the writer builds tension within the characters and situation. Right away, for instance, the viewer can feel the tension and pressure of the young woman. The development of her problem situation occupies approximately one-third of the entire ad. Notice, too, that the two characters obviously care for one another, having dated for a long time. Yes, there's the tension of the problem, but at the same time there are also emotional bonds clashing with the problem.

During the ad's next third, the nightmarish horror of what could happen if the boyfriend drives slams the ad's point home and seques into the ad's final third, a step out of the horror and into a more hopeful reality. Here, the young woman solves the problem, and all is well, presumably with the two characters safe and sound.

As copywriter for an ad such as this, your job is to create the governing structure and make certain that what's said and shown relate to your strategic considerations. Since the ad moves through time, you also need to consider the ways to sequence the actions. Clearly, the writer of this ad structured it around thirds (remember proportion and not dividing an ad in half). The first third reveals the problem. The second third reveals what will happen if the young woman does nothing about the problem. And the final third reveals the pleasant result when she takes it upon herself to solve the problem.

If you look at or listen to television or radio ads, you'll find that this narrative method of introducing a problem and then resolving it—usually in a positive way—is common. For instance, recall the Aetna Life and Casualty Company TV ad in our previous chapter and how the problem of a car accident interrupted a Christmas morning (immediately we're riveted because of the nature of the problem). Yet before the spot ended, everything turned out fine. And why? Because of Aetna, that's why.

We've referred to this kind of problem introduction earlier as the blind lead-in, a method where you stimulate viewer or listener interest prior to introducing your product or selling message. And once you introduce your product or selling message, it proves to be the problem solution. In the following radio ad for AT&T Long Distance, you can witness this technique in practice.

| | |
|---|---|
| Cathianne: | Hello. |
| Danny: | Oh, hi. You probably still remember me, Edward introduced us at the seminar... |
| Cathianne: | Oh, the guy with the nice beard. |
| Danny: | I don't know whether it's nice... |
| Cathianne: | It's a gorgeous beard. |
| Danny: | Well, thank you, uh, listen, I'm gonna, uh, be in the city next Tuesday and I was, y'know, wondering if we could sorta, y'know, get together for lunch. |
| Cathianne: | How 'bout dinner? |

| | |
|---|---|
| Danny: | Dinner? Dinner! Dinner's a better idea. You could pick your favorite restaurant and... |
| Cathianne: | How 'bout my place? I'm my favorite cook. |
| Danny: | Uh, your place. Right. Sure. That's great to me. |
| Cathianne: | Me too. It'll be fun. |
| Danny: | Yeah...listen, I'll bring the wine. |
| Cathianne: | Perfect. I'll drink it. |
| Both: | (laugh) |
| Danny: | Well, OK, then, I guess it's a date. I'll see you Tuesday. |
| Cathianne: | Tuesday. Great. |
| Danny: | Actually, I just, uh, called to see how you were and y'know, Tuesday sounds fine! |
| (Sound effects): | (phone hangs up) |
| Danny: | (yelling) Tuesday.... Ahhhh.... She's gonna see me Tuesday. |
| Singers: | Reach out, reach out and touch someone. |

As you read through the radio ad, notice how the product never gets mentioned until the close. Instead, brimming with charm and niceness the real-life situation controls the entire ad. But, at the ad's beginning a problem exists, even though it pales in comparison to the major problem in the drunk-driving ad. In this AT&T ad, the problem involves the young man's insecurity in contacting the young woman. His hemming and hawing reflect that insecurity. And as the conversation between the two continues, gradually his insecurity wanes until the very close, when the endearing and warm copy line lilts into the listener's ear.

This doesn't mean that your broadcast narrative must contain a problem. True, this is often the case, just as it's the case that the product enters to solve the problem. But even if you don't pose a problem, your product should be the hero of the situation, such as in this version of an AT&T Long Distance ad in Figure 9–8.

Here, the familiarity of actor Cliff Robertson dominates the ad. As narrator and spokesman, he projects a warm, personal appeal on behalf of AT&T. At the same time, he also projects a seasoned and reassuring persona to the viewer as he highlights the benefits of using AT&T Long Distance. Moving about in an easy manner, and thus taking the viewer with him, he conveys the information necessary for someone to choose AT&T as a reasonable and reassuring selection to meet their long-distance telephone needs. With AT&T,

# AT&T Communications/Residence

TITLE: "NOTE IN A BOTTLE"
COMMERCIAL NUMBER: AXLL 3558
LENGTH: :30 sec.

ROBERTSON: There are lots of ways

to communicate over long distances.

But with some, you may not be able to reach

everywhere you want anytime you want...

And a faraway message may feel far away.

But you can always count on AT&T.

The only long distance service that lets you call from anywhere

to anywhere with operators standing by.

And with AT&T, your calls will sound as close as next door.

So why settle for anything less?

AT&T. The more you hear the better we sound.

SINGERS: Reach out and touch someone.

**FIGURE 9–8    Advertisement reprinted courtesy of AT&T Long Distance**

you can reach out and touch someone, precisely the benefit of long-distance telephoning.

With each of the ads we've looked at in this chapter, and throughout the book for that matter, the concern for style steps up front and center whenever you pay attention to what the ads say.

What you say is most important, of course, but how you say it can add luster to the message.

With ad structure, the concern for how you say or show the message means seeing your ad in various parts leading inevitably to a whole. The result should be that your audience pulls the parts together into that whole, the ad's gestalt, its core, its promise. In a way you're crafting a seamless web where everything fits tightly and pointedly together. Yes, you can craft your ad around thirds or fifths, but when it's finished, it should look and read and sound like one thing.

At the same time, notice how the various print and broadcast ads rely to a large extent on a similar structure. In the print ads most of the visual field tends to be dominated by either picture or copy, but not both. One rules. In recalling Chapter 3, this is the principle of proportion. And with broadcast as well, proportion becomes important. Notice, for instance, how the St. Mary-of-the-Woods and AT&T Long Distance radio ads rely on a narrative, basically a give-and-take between two people, one that establishes the problem. Then the ads introduce the advertiser, ultimately circling back to the creative idea at the close. This is the same as what we've discussed in reference to print. The familiar circle of ad structure.

### ✍ WRAP-UP ✍

Naturally, the best way to learn about ad style is to study ads and then write them. If you recall from Chapter 2, that's exactly what writers do. They study their craft as it's practiced by others. Then they write. This means they pay attention to how things get done, how certain effects get achieved, and how they and other writers move their audiences. Much of this attention concerns style. It concerns reading, viewing, and listening for structures and techniques. It concerns leaving your daily self and becoming another, either your audience or the self you call the writer.

As we near the book's end, this chapter should provide you with tools to use when you sit down to craft your ad. But as the diversity of ads shows, a host of tools are available. To use them involves paying attention and learning. Learning how others do it. Learning how you as a prospective audience and a watchful and inquisitive writer react when you're face-to-face with an ad. Only by this kind of allegiance to the art and craft of writing will you feel yourself improving day-to-day and assignment-to-assignment. No one said it would be easy. But then again, the best things in life aren't.

As we close here, let me speak from the heart. I've told you that I'm not that good a writer. I'm okay, but not great. But I'm learning, and I'm probably at least twice as old as many of you. If I thought I were great I wouldn't bother learning any more. I could delude myself. Many do. But I wouldn't get any better, would I? I believe the same holds true for you. If you're really intent on being a writer, any kind of writer, then that's enough. The fire of intent will move you to action, to reading, seeing, behaving, and, of course, writing. The rest, such as getting better, will come. For some it will come years from now. For a few it's here, maybe. And for most, it will come over a lifetime. The writing God demands that kind of devotion.

For the writer, nothing gets in the way. Nothing, that is, except death. Sure, there are tugs and pulls all the time. Even washing dishes has its own immense charm when measured against the prospect of a blank and intimidating page. But if you're a writer in heart and soul, then you'll be inescapably drawn back to that page. And drawn back regularly.

Call it a curse. Call it a blessing. Call it whatever you will. The fact of the matter is that a writer writes, and having written, writes some more.

A writer reads, changing glasses from time to time.
A writer sees, smells, tastes, feels, and hears.
A writer revels in words. Nothing can be finer than that.
A writer communicates, if even with the self.

And with ad copy, a writer knows what turns on all sorts of people. An advertising copywriter knows the strategy of communication and persuasion. An ad copywriter knows what it means to sell. An ad copywriter knows what it means to live in the world of words. An ad copywriter knows what it means to live in the world of many others. An ad copywriter writes. Again. And again. And again.

Throughout these pages we've spent all our time thinking about and discussing writing. We've intentionally avoided going anywhere else with our words. Take from this book what you consider important and useful. Then hang it on your writing belt. After you do, go out and find more tools. Hang *them* on your belt. Practice using them. Practice over and over until you see your writing swing getting smoother and smoother. And finally, take a look at all you've written and find reward enough in that, tempered, of course, with the desire to improve. Even if it takes you a lifetime.

## ✍ THINGS TO DO ✍

1. Take the following copy lines and talk about them to no one in particular or to anyone you choose. Talk about them in the context of all we've discussed. In fact, see how long you can talk about them, making sense as you go. The sense should relate to what you've learned from

your reading of this book. In short, read between the lines, and read as far as you can.

Royal Viking: Surrounding each vessel are the most spacious, most strollable decks.

Aetna: Christmas morning. You run out to get a quart of eggnog. Then this happens. Bummer.

Timberland: The storm-blackened foredeck of a boat that's bucking like a rodeo bull.

The Nature Company: Real time. Tater time. It tells month and date, too. It even runs on soda pop (if that ruins the karma for you, forget we said it).

The Potato Board: Then again, carrots are orange, squash is yellow, and cauliflower is white. And you consider those vegetables, don't you?

Parker Pen: Buy the Parker Premier and even if you never write anything magnificent, at least you will never write anything but magnificently.

Saint Mary-of-the-Woods: When you come to Saint Mary-of-the-Woods you'll be enriched, fulfilled, enlightened, but Sister Marguerite, you will not be blown away.

2.    The final thing for you to do? Hmmm, let me see. What could it be? Tough choice. Oh, yeah, I've got it. Go write. Then when you're done, write some more. But don't keep writing the same thing or the same way over and over. Play with the writing. And get better.

# Suggested Readings and Assorted Tips

The following list of readings and tips is by no means all-inclusive. However, these readings and tips should give you some background for this text and should also help you hone your writing skills and lifestyle.

## ✍ FOR THE READER IN YOU ✍

If you would like to know more about reading and reader-response theory, take a look at the following. These books are seminal works. They're also thought-provoking, but beware, they can be thick with theory.

Fish, Stanley. *Is There A Text in This Class? The Authority of Interpretive Communities.* Cambridge, Mass.: Harvard University Press, 1980.

Ingarden, Roman. *The Cognition of the Literary Work of Art.* Trans., Ruthann Crowley and Kenneth R. Olsen. Evanston, Ill.: Northwestern University Press, 1973.

Iser, Wolfgang. *The Act of Reading: A Theory of Aesthetic Response.* Baltimore, Md.: The Johns Hopkins University Press, 1978.

Nystrand, Martin. *The Structure of Written Communication: Studies in Reciprocity Between Writers and Readers.* Orlando, Fla.: Academic Press, Inc., 1986.

Rosenblatt, Louise M. *The Reader, The Text, The Poem: The Transactional Theory of The Literary Work.* Carbondale, Ill.: Southern Illinois Press, 1978.

Slatoff, Walter J. *With Respect to Readers: Dimensions of Literary Response.* Ithaca, N.Y.: Cornell University Press, 1970.

## ✍ FOR THE OBSERVER IN YOU ✍

To get up to minimum speed in design principles, take a look at the following:

Bevlin, Marjorie E. *Design Through Discovery: An Introduction to Art and Design.* 5th ed. New York: Holt, Rinehart and Winston, Inc., 1989.

Curtiss, Deborah. *An Introduction to Visual Literacy: A Guide to the Visual Arts and Communication.* Englewood Cliffs, N.J.: Prentice Hall, 1987.

Dondis, Donis A. *A Primer of Visual Literacy.* Cambridge, Mass.: MIT Press, 1973.

Lauer, David A. *Design Basics.* 2nd ed. New York: Holt, Rinehart and Winston Inc., 1979.

Nelson, Roy Paul. *The Design of Advertising.* Dubuque, Iowa: Wm. C. Brown Company Publishers, editions beginning with 1981.

If you care to swim around in the deep waters of aesthetic or visual theory, take a look at the following:

Arnheim, Rudolf. *Visual Thinking.* Berkeley, Calif.: University of California Press, 1969.

————. *The Power of the Center: A Study of Composition in the Visual Arts.* Berkeley, Calif.: University of California Press, 1982.

Beardsley, Monroe C. *Aesthetics: Problems in the Philosophy of Criticism.* New York: Harcourt, Brace & World, Inc., 1958.

Berenson, Bernard. *Seeing and Knowing.* New York: The Macmillan Company, 1953.

Chiari, Joseph. *Art and Knowledge.* New York: Gordian Press, 1977.

Gombrich, E. H. *Art and Illusion: A Study in the Psychology of Pictorial Representation.* Princeton, N.J.: Princeton University Press, 1960.

————. *The Image and the Eye: Further Studies in the Psychology of Pictorial Representation.* Ithaca, N.Y.: Cornell University Press, 1982.

## ✍ FOR THE WRITER IN YOU ✍

If you want to read about writing theory, innovative ways to solve your writing problems, or models of writing processes and practices, try these. Often they'll help you cope better with your difficulties.

Barzun, Jacques. *Simple and Direct: A Rhetoric for Writers.* New York: Harper & Row, Publishers, 1975.

Boles, Paul Darcy. *Storycrafting.* Cincinnati, Ohio: Writer's Digest Books, 1984.

Bunge, Nancy L., ed. *Finding the Words: Conversations with Writers Who Teach.* Athens, Ohio: Swallow Press, 1985.

Egri, Lajos. *The Art of Creative Writing.* New York: The Citadel Press, 1965.

Elbow, Peter. *Writing Without Teachers*. London: Oxford University Press, 1973.

———. *Writing With Power: Techniques for Mastering the Writing Process*. New York: Oxford University Press, 1981.

Franklin, Jon. *Writing for Story: Craft Secrets of Dramatic Nonfiction*. New York: Atheneum Press, 1986.

Kaye, Sanford. *Writing Under Pressure: The Quick-Writing Process*. New York: Oxford University Press, 1989.

Kessler, Lauren and Duncan McDonald. *When Words Collide: A Journalist's Guide to Grammar and Style*. Belmont, Calif.: Wadsworth Publishing Company, 1984.

Lanham, Richard A. *Style: An Anti-Textbook*. New Haven, Conn.: Yale University Press, 1974.

Gregg, Lee W. and Erwin R. Steinberg, eds. *Cognitive Processes in Writing*. Hillsdale, N.J.: Lawrence Erlbaum Associates, Publishers, 1980.

Nystrand, Martin, ed. *What Writers Know: The Language, Process and Structure of Written Discourse*. New York: Academic Press, 1982.

Rose, Michael, ed. *When a Writer Can't Write: Research on Writer's Block and Other Writing Problems*. New York: Guilford Press, 1986.

Rubenstein, S. Leonard. *Writing: A Habit of Mind*. Dubuque, Iowa: Wm. C. Brown Publishers, 1972.

Zinsser, William. *On Writing Well: An Informal Guide to Writing Nonfiction*. New York: Harper & Row Publishers, 1980.

## ✍ FOR THE AD STRATEGIST AND COPYWRITER IN YOU ✍

Your school library probably has a separate section on advertising. Check it out and see what's there. Meanwhile, think about taking a look at these books found in your library, on your professors' shelves, in various bookstores, or from the publishers themselves.

Albright, Jim. *Creating the Advertising Message*. Mountain View, Calif.: Mayfield Publishing Company, 1992.

Barry, Ann Marie. *The Advertising Portfolio: Creating an Effective Presentation of Your Work*. Lincolnwood, Ill.: NTC Business Books, 1990.

Bendinger, Bruce. *The Copy Workshop Workbook*. Chicago: The Copy Workshop, 1988.

Burton, Philip Ward. *Advertising Copywriting*. 6th ed. Lincolnwood, Ill.: NTC Business Books, 1990.

Della Femina, Jerry. *From Those Wonderful Folks Who Gave You Pearl Harbor: Front-Line Dispatches from the Advertising War*. Englewood Cliffs, N.J.: Simon & Schuster, 1970.

Jewler, A. Jerome. *Creative Strategy in Advertising*. 4th ed. Belmont, Calif.: Wadsworth Publishing Company, 1992.

Haberstroh, Jack and Paul D. Wright, eds. *Copywriting Assignments from America's Best Copywriters*. Englewood Cliffs, N.J.: Simon & Schuster, 1989.

Hafer, W. Keith and Gordon E. White. *Advertising Writing: Putting Creative Strategy to Work.* 3rd ed. St. Paul, Minn.: West Publishing Company, 1989.

Malickson, David L. and John W. Nason. *Advertising: How to Write the Kind That Works.* New York: Charles Scribner's Sons, 1982.

Moriarty, Sandra E. *Creative Advertising: Theory and Practice.* Englewood Cliffs, N.J.: Prentice Hall, 1991.

NTC Business Books. *The Art of Writing Advertising: Conversations with Masters of the Craft.* Lincolnwood, Ill.: NTC Business Books, 1987.

Ogilvy, David. *Oglivy on Advertising.* London: Pan Books, 1983.

Paetro, Maxine. *How to Put Your Book Together and Get a Job in Advertising.* Chicago, Ill.: The Copy Workshop, 1990.

Roman, Kenneth and Jane Maas. *The New How to Advertise.* New York: St. Martin's Press, 1992.

Schultz, Don E. *The Essentials of Advertising Strategy.* Lincolnwood, Ill.: NTC Business Books, 1986.

Young, James Webb. *A Technique for Producing Ideas.* Lincolnwood, Ill.: NTC Business Books, 1986.

## ✍ TIPS ✍

Beyond culling through the suggested readings, there are many more things you can do if you're serious about writing. Here are some suggestions.

1. Subscribe to some publications such as *Advertising Age, AdWeek,* and *Writer's Digest.*

2. Enjoy the solitude of bookstores and libraries. Enjoy the social gatherings of those with similar interests, maybe in writing clubs, pubs, or workshops.

3. Take as many writing courses as you can in college. Don't be afraid of fiction, poetry, or scriptwriting courses, either. Also, take choice courses in the arts, humanities, and business programs.

4. Intern. But try to make sure it's not just grunt work you'll be doing.

5. Write in different genres and for different markets and publications. For example, write for your campus literary magazine, newspaper, or department publications.

6. Keep a copy of Strunk and White's *The Elements of Style* on hand. Maybe even memorize the juicy parts. Ditto for a good dictionary,

thesaurus, and even handbooks on antonyms and synonyms, underground dictionaries, and slang.

7.   Read any book that's "hot." For example, take a look at the books written by Al Ries and Jack Trout.

8.   Contact the Creative Education Foundation, Inc., Buffalo, N.Y. 14222 for a list of programs and readings. Ditto for various advertising organizations, writer's groups and workshops, and your local media. Then follow-up where you see such programs or readings helping you.

# Index

# S

# T